FROZEN FOODS

BIOGRAPHY OF
AN INDUSTRY

FROZEN FOODS

BIOGRAPHY OF

AN INDUSTRY

By E.W. Williams

Publisher of

Quick Frozen Foods

CAHNERS BOOK DIVISION
CAHNERS PUBLISHING COMPANY
BOSTON, MASS. 02116

Library of Congress Catalog Card Number: 74-111762
Copyright © 1963 by E. W. Williams Publications, Inc.
New material copyright © 1968 by E. W. Williams Publications, Inc.,
Division of Cahners Publishing Company, Inc.
New material copyright © 1970 by E. W. Williams
Printed in the United States of America
Halliday Lithograph Corporation, Hanover, Massachusetts, U.S.A.

Introduction

THIRTY YEARS—three decades, roll by with amazing speed. In this History of the Frozen Foods Industry they span a depression, a war, the lean and growing years . . . from infancy to almost, perhaps not quite, maturity. Those who were in at the beginning and this goes back to 1930, become fewer and fewer. The industry's great upward surge came after World War II.

In this Biography of an Industry I have tried to cover as much material as was possible within the limitations of space. This is a story of many people and firms—of ideas, courage and errors, of leadership and pioneering. Above all, it is a story of amazing growth which I have been privileged to experience. Frozen foods is fundamentally an American industry, indigenous to this country and spurred by American ingenuity. These first thirty years can only be the end of the first chapter.

Contents

1

The Prewar Years

One day in 1935 I saw an exhibition of the properties of dry ice, then just being introduced. The demonstrator produced a goldfish in a bowl, took the fish out, froze it quickly in dry ice and then placed it back in the bowl. The fish dropped to the bottom, but after a while its tail began to wiggle and shortly thereafter it swam about just as lively as before. This, explained the demonstrator, was *suspended animation,* a phrase which intrigued me. Not long after that I saw an early Birds Eye exhibit at a food show and I was attracted by the fact that "strawberries could be eaten in December" and that you didn't have to shell peas or wash spinach any more.

Here, I thought, was an industry with a future. Here was a budding business that ought to have a magazine of its own, a publication which could help it grow and which, if properly and aggressively run, should show a profit to its owner. I was already a publisher, having taken my first plunge by becoming owner of the *Butchers' Advocate,* a meat trade weekly, in November, 1934.

It was still too early to start a trade publication. There were only twenty or thirty packers, few distributors and those mostly institutional. Production amounted to a few million pounds. But we did run a column each week in the *Butchers' Advocate* entitled "Quick Frozen Foods" and thus acquired the name the magazine now bears.

I bought and ate all the frozen foods I could lay my hands on: vegetables, fruits, meats, poultry and seafoods. Stores handling Birds Eye, then the only important line, were visited, managers interviewed. Information was culled from every quarter and by early 1938 the plans were drawn for the first issue of QUICK FROZEN FOODS. Little did I realize then that the goldfish demonstration was to set me on a path which would absorb all my interests for the next thirty years!

Although freezing of "cold pack" strawberries and fruits took place in the northwest as early as 1908, it might be said that the quick freezing industry as we know it today had its official birth on July 31, 1923, when the first freezing company was formed by Clarence Birdseye with a $20,000 subscription of stock, used to establish the first fish freezing plant in New York.

A short time before, Mr. Birdseye, with whom I later became very friendly and who remained an editorial advisor of QFF up to the time of his death, had returned from Labrador where he discovered that quick frozen fish were far better than cold storage fish. He was convinced he had unlocked one of nature's secrets. Mr. Birdseye was in Labrador from 1912-1915 where he started his first freezing experiments. He said: "When I went to Labrador I knew nothing of the virtues of quick freezing, I couldn't in fact have told a refrigerator compressor from a condenser. But that first winter I saw natives catching fish in fifty below zero weather, which froze stiff almost as soon as they were taken out of the water. Months later, when they were thawed out, some of these fish were still alive." He conducted other experiments with birds, game and even cabbage. More than ten years of intensive study and many dis- appointments followed. Clarence Birdseye did not invent the freezing process, nor was he the first man to freeze foods commercially. He once said: "My contribution was to take Eskimo knowledge and the scientists' theories and adapt them to quantity production."

Actually, in 1876, frozen meat, using ice and salt, was shipped from the U.S. to England. H. A. Baker, Sr., was slow freezing berries in barrels in Puyallup, Wash., as early as 1912. Commercial freezing began at the Ray-Maling plant in Hillsboro, Ore., in 1929, later owned by General Foods. The first commercial freezer used in this country was the Ottoson brine freezer. In 1921 Paul W. Peterson developed an indirect freezer— one in which the refrigerant and the product did not come into direct contact. In 1923 Gordon F. Taylor built a direct contact freezer for whole fish. Thus, several years before the introduction of the first multiple plate freezer, fish fillets were produced. Clarence Birdseye formed a company in 1924 with the issuance of $60,000 of preferred stock. There were now several stockholders including Wetmore Hodges, Bassett Jones, I. L. Rice and others. The new plant was established in Gloucester under the name of General Seafoods Corp. Joe Guinane was then the industry's first production manager.

The First Million Lbs.

Incidentally, Henry Ford was attracted to the idea and, sensing its future, made some financial overtures, though nothing came of them. About this time Clarence Birdseye—first began to work on his multiple freezer. In 1928 about one million pounds of fruits and vegetables were frozen.

During the early months of 1929 another expanding company was look- ing around for growth projects. This was the Postum Co. (now General Foods Corp.). Goldman, Sachs, an investment house brought the two together, and right before the stock market crash, Postum bought out Birdseye's company for $22 million—$20 million for the patents and $2 million for other assets. A tremendous sum in those days, as it is now! Mr. Birdseye's name was to be the trademark—as two separate words. He received just under $1 million. But already the country was sliding into a depression which was to last for several years and consequently it was not until 1935 when frozen foods were again brought before the public on a large scale. *A new industry was finally on its way!*

The First Day—Springfield

After building up a back-log of frozen foods for six months, the General Foods Corp. of Boston was ready for D-Day. Under Coe Suydam, on a March day in 1930, Birds Eye packaged products suddenly appeared for the first time in many stores in Springfield, Mass. Two vegetables were offered, peas and spinach; three fruits, raspberries, loganberries and cherries; and a selection of meats and fish. One salesman recalls: "It took about five minutes to fast-talk a reluctant housewife into buying a package of peas at 35¢." The main selling theme was "quick frozen vs. cold storage." Quick freezing, salesmen said, did not disrupt food cells, did not form ice crystals. Therefore, the flavor and juices did not drain off when the product thawed. By 1933 there were only 516 frozen food retail outlets in the U.S.

About that time the mecca for all frozen food information was the general headquarters of Birds Eye at 250 Park Avenue. These offices hummed with activity, all under the direction of Edward T. Gibson, who, but a few years later, played so vital a role in helping to save an industry almost threatened with extinction when the war broke out. A. E. Stevens, then vice president of the organization, gave me considerable encouragement and advice in those early years; he was responsible for the first sales and introduction of frozen foods throughout the country. Others who gave the young magazine a willing hand were Donald Barr, who died prematurely, the late Howard Lochrie, George Mentley, Al Huff, Joe Guinane, Bill Mundy, Coe Suydam, Harry Trimm, Ralph Garside and others. Another early contributor and guide was Edward J. White, a Californian by birth, but then a New York broker. Ed has since retired after a varied and distinguished career.

First Issue Appears

With the aid of three men who were on the staff of the *Butchers' Advocate,* I got up the first dummy which was presented to prospective advertisers, such as there then were. Stories were lined up, people interviewed. I will never forget the first editor. He was capable but had one weakness—the bottle. I remember seeing him on occasion with his head buried in his arms, crouched over the desk as if engrossed deep in thought. Upon later inspection it was found that he had bored a hole in his desk, through which he inserted a straw which, in turn, led into a bottle in the top drawer. A change of editors was soon found necessary.

At last the first issue, dated August, 1938, appeared. It contained 64 pages and its front cover was a beautiful picture of various vegetables. The cover format has remained practically the same ever since and up to this writing, QFF has never skipped an issue. Many features inaugurated in the first number have appeared regularly in the past twenty-five years. One was the *"Frozen Foods Forum,"* another the editorial page.

In this issue the first *wholesale market prices* ever published appeared, and they have been enlarged upon and printed monthly ever since. We also published the first public cold storage holdings; I might add that on July 1, 1938 there were 125 million pounds of fruits and 31 million pounds of vegetables in storage.

Our first editorial was about supermarkets and frozen foods. "Due to the fact that most supers are on a self service basis," it proclaimed, "cabinets should be placed near those departments which maintain clerks." We constantly urged that cabinet manufacturers develop *self-service cabinets* and the first ones appeared not long thereafter. Other articles in that first issue told about freezing berries in the northwest, transportation, about processing ducks, and there was a picture story about a Birds Eye market. We had a technical page entitled "From the Professor's Notebook" which discussed everything from the bacterial count in frozen hamburgers to the gas storage of eggs. In the west, Cedergreen and Ray-Maling were mentioned.

Advertisers came in, looking for recognition in this new industry. But progress was slow, issues thereafter were harder to fill and the magazine built up slowly. It grew along with the industry.

My hardest job was not to sell the magazine, *but the industry*. There were a surprising number of people who were not at all convinced that frozen foods were here to stay. "A passing fad," said some. "Too expensive to handle," said others. Some of these people are prominent in the industry today; I won't remind them of their early predictions. We all worked hard and for the next five years our principal job was to convince prospective advertisers that frozen foods were *not* a wild dream. For several years the industry floundered and indeed it was not until the war that quick freezing got its first real boost, but more of that later.

Only 10% Retail

In those days New York, Washington and Philadelphia were the strongholds of retail frozen foods. About 60% of the business was in bulk, still done with bakeries, preservers and ice cream manufacturers. The institutional trade accounted for another 30%, leaving 10% to retail.

Second to Birds Eye in importance in those days was Honor Brand, a label started by Waterman & Co., New York distributors. Honor Brand was later sold to Stokely-Van Camp.

I must here mention a packer who then had great influence on the industry—the late Charles Seabrook. He was a third generation farmer who, in southern New Jersey had introduced scientific farming in an area where it had hitherto been unknown. Seabrook's first frozen food venture took place in 1931 in lima beans. For many years thereafter, Seabrook

Clarence Birdseye, dressed in a suit of sealskin, poses on the Labrador coast.

The room in Labrador where Clarence Birdseye began his first experiments in quick freezing, about 1912.

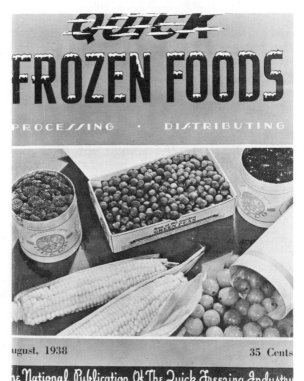

An historic occasion: the appearance of the first issue of QUICK FRO-ZEN FOODS, August, 1938. The cover, with its symbolism of "The Horn of Plenty," heralded the appearance of a publication that would provide the catalyst for the growth and maturity of an, industry.

Farms packed for Birds Eye. I first met Charles and Courtney Seabrook around 1939 and they were always helpful in opening up their extensive facilities to QFF. Jack Seabrook later came into the firm, but more recently other unforeseen developments took place and Seabrook is now owned by Seeman Bros. An early associate, too, was Mary Drumm who was probably the first woman broken in the industry.

While speaking of the distaff side, I cannot ignore other lady brokers, Velma Lee, Alice Sexton, Mary Cobb and Mildred Hagen, some are still active.

Now other brands began to become prominent; Bodle, Little America, Hershey, Cedergreen, Dulany Fairmont, etc.

But in 1939 something happened which was to turn the trend toward retail packages. For the first time, *one-third* of the strawberry pack went into consumer sizes and the foundation was laid for the acceptance of this popular berry. Strawberries were then quoted at 9¢ cost, peas at 10½¢ a pound. Now, the frozen strawberry, hitherto a bulk item for preservers, bakers and ice cream makers was to become an important retail leader— a position it was to occupy for years to come until it met with competition from new frozen desserts.

QFF Urges Trade Standards

As QFF grew and became an integral part of the frozen foods industry, in the early days following 1938, it built a vociferous and forceful editorial foundation around which the industry could—and did rally. There were plenty of things to fight for. Editorials appeared monthly, urging trade standards which were later established by the USDA. QFF later started a campaign for self-service cabinets; we urged the chains to handle frozen foods. As early as 1938 we combatted the then current argument that the retailer's profit on fresh produce was good and frozen foods were needed since cabinet costs were high, with the counter-argument that frozen produce *eliminated waste.* Many of these arguments, so powerfully advanced by QFF at that time, were later proven right, as events took their course. And QFF was then, and continued to be for many years, the *only* publication to act as a powerful voice for the industry. I might add here that QFF from the very beginning, continually urged the maintenance of high quality standards in all frozen products, and it still does so today.

During our first year a total of 268 million pounds of fruits, poultry, meats and seafoods were packed—as against some 9 billion pounds today! In 1940 frozen food sales totaled about $150 million—in 1963 well over $3 billion—and in 1968 close to $7 billion!

We early started a campaign to promote institutional frozen foods, especially in restaurants. About this time we had one energetic reporter who would visit first class restaurants and after eating the meal demand to see the proprietor. "Were those frozen peas I tasted?" he would ask. "We never use them," the proprietor would invariably reply. "Well, you should," our reporter answered and then tried to convince the restaurant owner why frozen foods were better. This reporter did a lot of good, but he became so enthusiastic in spreading the frozen foods gospel by eating in expensive restaurants, all at the magazine's expense, that we had to let him go.

Early Western Packers

I am indebted to Dr. "Dutch" Diehl and Robert G. Ketron for much of the information regarding early frozen food activities on the west coast. Diehl got his first background in frozen foods studying fruits under Dr. John Magness in Wenatchee, Wash. He worked on cold packing in 1923 and recalls in the year the freezing of 1000 barrels of cold pack berries at the Spokane Cold Storage warehouse. Later, with the USDA, "Dutch helped establish the first government frozen food laboratory at the Port of Seattle, after which he became chief of the Commodity Processing Division of the USDA and helped in the establishment of many regional laboratories, especially in Albany, Calif. As the managing director of TARS, a group of large refrigerated warehouses, Dr. Diehl did much to improve handling standards; he also became chairman of the All Industry FF Coordinating Committee which worked with regulatory officials on the AFDOUS code.

Some of the early scientists who worked on freezing on the west coast were Durward Fisher, Dr. Chas. Magoon, Dr. Taylor, Harold Locklin, Dr. C. D. Schwartze, J. A. Berry, Walter Clore, Horace Campbell, Dr. Karl Meyer, Chas. Townsend, Dr. Fred Blanck, Dr. Skinner, Dr. Harold Loeffler, now president of the Glacier Packing Co., Dr. John Nielsen, Dr. M. J. Copley and many others of equal importance, some of whom I may have inadvertently omitted.

At an early exhibit of frozen food packages during a National Canners' convention in Chicago in 1938, early brand names were shown by J. Frank Dotson, a pioneer broker of the northwest. His firm, Food Associates, started in 1936. Some of the first western brands were Hershey's, Frostkraft, Cedergreen, Bodle, Agen, Bird Valley, Blue Poppy, Console, Delnor, Dew, Dewkist, Flav-R-Pac, Fresh Frozen, Frigifood, Frost Queen, Froz-N-Prime, Kol-Pak, Mountain View, Naturipe, Pictsweet, Penguin, San Juan, Sierra Snow, Smith, Sparklets, Springbrook, Sterling, Twin Peaks, Valamont, York, Polar and some others. (Taken from QFF's first Directory.)

Some of the pioneering western packers included the old Drayer Fruit Co. in Oregon, Baker, Kelley & McLoughlin, Ralph Bodle, Mark Ewald, Bert Maling of Ray-Maling Co., Ed Burns, Sect. of the Northwest FF Ass'n., L. L. Brotherton, Bozeman Canning, Bill McCaffray Sr., Natl. Fruit Canning, Ben Hershey, Clyde Farquhar, Norman Cedergreen, Jim Agen, Art Symons, Art Chappel, B. F. Logan, Ed Watson, R. T. Shannon, John N. Seaman, R. Arneson—all these and some others, represented the "first wave" of western frozen foods men who left their indelible mark upon the industry. Others, such as George Roberton, Mario Ielmini, Gib Lamb, Arne Lervick, etc. emerged as the "post-war group" who greatly expanded the west coast industry.

Some early price quotations (around 1937-38) may be of interest. They were all institutional. For instance, 6/4 lb. beans at 20¢; 12/2 lb. broccoli at 21¢; 12/3 lb. peas at 18½¢; 12/2 lb. cauliflower at 24¢ and 12/3 lb. spinach at 17½¢. *Not much different today, with the exception of spinach, which is lower!*

Early Cabinets

Few retailers could be persuaded to buy frozen food cabinets. To get distribution, Birds Eye had the American Radiator Co. manufacture boxes which were then placed on a monthly payment or similar basis. Cabinets were of the closed type; some early manufacturers also included Hill, Sherman, Hussmann, McCray, Tyler, Oreole, Frigidaire, Schaefer, Grand Rapids, Sherer, Kelvinator, Carrier, Bastion-Blessing and others. What the modern highway was to the automobile, we maintained, the cabinet would be to frozen foods. At first lithographed placards were placed in the back of cabinets but later, when packages themselves took on more elaborate designs and as frozen foods became more popular, this was no longer necessary. The Hopp Press first introduced marking equipment especially designed for use with frozen products.

QFF early recognized the important role which home freezers were to play in the development of the industry. The more freezer space that could be installed in the home, we reasoned, the more frozen foods would be sold.

Early Developments in California

It was not until 1937 when the frozen vegetable industry started up in California; most of the companies then were small and still pioneering. But World War II gave the state's industry a big boost: by 1943 one-third of all frozen vegetables in the U.S. were going to the war effort. Most of the early packers were located in the San Francisco Bay area and later in the central valleys. Frostkraft Packing was one of the first, operated by Chas. J. Collins. L. F. Noonan started in 1937. California Consumers Corp. put up its Los Angeles plant in 1937 and expanded to Pasadena and E. D. Sims and Douglas Jardine were early officials. The Central Coast Area's first vegetable plant was built in 1938 at Santa Cruz by Stokely-Van Camp.

Another early pioneer was Peter Knudsen who opened in Mountain View. John Inglis started freezing in Lodi in 1942 as a means of supplying his Stockton bakery. Inglis has since become one of the biggest processors in the state. Ed Console added a small freezer line to his Watsonville Canning plant in 1942 and he, too, has since become one of the state's most important factors. In the Santa Barbara area, the Brendlin-Rice Co. started during the war; they are still in business. Other California pioneers include James O. Dempsey, Mel K. Spiegl, Mario Ielmini, H. Loeffler, Cleugh, Paul Case, Edward J. White, Ed Huddleson, A. L. Ruso, James Lawless, the Castroville artichoke packers, Ken Eberts, Sterling Doughty, Howard Lemon, Manteca Foods, Marshburn, Dick Driscoll, Herb Buxton, Bolfing, Hartman, Oxnard, Ventura, Pringle, Bridgeford, Pacific Grape, Frank Oliver, Atterbury, Western FF and some others. Eventually, Watsonville became the frozen food capital of California, but more on this later.

Locker Plants

During the industry's early days locker plants probably accounted for more frozen food business than did commercial freezing. There were 3000 plants in 1938 and new ones were opened at the rate of *50 a month*. During the war they were to mushroom, but with the advent of the supermarket and the availability of packaged frozen foods at every corner store after the war, the locker plant industry contracted until today, lockers are found mainly in rural areas. But for several years QUICK FROZEN FOODS ran a section on lockers though it was later dropped. Without locker plants QFF could not have existed during the first few years.

At the end of the first year, QFF had 4,853 subscribers. "During the first six months," we proudly announced, "QUICK FROZEN FOODS averaged 56 pages per issue and carried more advertising pages than have ever been run before by any medium covering frozen foods." Indeed, there was no other.

I paid many visits to the Midwest in those days. Several men were outstanding. Two were Charlie Petersen of E. A. Aaron, H. Shedd, a distributor and W. L. Pavlovski or "Pav" as he was familiarly known. These men and others made frozen foods in that area. Let me say here before going further, that I hope no one will take offense if I omit names. I will try to mention as many as I can but I am sure that my readers will understand the difficulty in writing about every one of the thousands who were active in the industry and who were mentioned in QUICK FROZEN FOODS.

QFF Organizes First Meetings

As the industry grew, the urge to get together, to form associations became evident. Here QFF took a leading part. The first was in Chicago on Dec. 13, 1939, at the Hotel Auditorium. I called this meeting which was attended by some 50 frozen foodsters, and then explained the purpose of the gathering, after which Al Sprague took the chair. He was elected first president and the new organization was known as the Chicago Frozen Foods Association. The only cost then was $1 for the luncheon; there were no dues. Since then, this group has grown to several hundred and has become a powerful influence in the Midwest.

About the same time, QFF helped to form a group in New York which later became the Eastern Frosted Foods Association. Our first meeting was held at the Lincoln Hotel and John Antun, who still operates his own brokerage firm in New York, was elected first president, a post he was to hold for seven years thereafter. Among the early founders were, the late Fritz Brahm and Frank Cogan. We met regularly once a month. After a while the idea of serving frozen foods at each meal struck me. I got packers to send their latest products which our membership, composed of many buyers, could sample. We then got a reduction from the hotel by supplying the food, which saving went into the association's treasury. A menu was printed which gave the packer credit. It is one of the few deals I ever heard of which made *everyone happy;* supplier, hotel and member. The practice later became popular with other groups throughout the country and the Eastern Frosted Foods Association has used it for many years with its smorgasbord.

Contributors Cited

I must here give credit to some important contributors of articles which, at the time, helped to inform an information-hungry industry. They were: H. D. Brown, Ohio State University, "Dutch" Diehl, G. A. Fitzgerald, Gardner Poole, W. J. Finnegan, Clarence and Miriam Birdseye, Harry Carlton, University of Tennessee, and many others.

About this time Stokely-Van Camp took over Honor Brand from Waterman & Co. in New York. Ed White became first president of Honor Brand and moved to Oakland. I could never understand why Stokely did not then lend its well-known name to the brand; I think it would have advanced much faster.

Now, with the prospect of the 1939 World's Fair in New York and in San Francisco, QFF plugged hard to get a frozen food exhibit before the public. Birds Eye did have an exhibit and I think there was one on the coast also.

In May, 1939, we opened the first "Cold Storage Warehouse Section" as well as the first "Brokers" division.

Meanwhile, in New England frozen foods began to grow. Such firms as Batchelder, Snyder, Albert Richards and Rival Foods began to promote frozen products to both store and institution. There, prices were better maintained in that area and credit losses were less. Business went along on a more even keel.

We devoted much space to encouraging the development of new and better seed varieties. Much work was done in those years by geneticists such as Gorden Morrison of Ferry, Morse, Dr. Floyd Winter of Associated Seed Growers and Northrup King. Their work did much to lay the cornerstone for frozen vegetable freezing.

The First Orange Juice

About this time we carried the first data on frozen whole orange juice, then packed by California Consumers Corp. But before this, both Borden and National Dairies had made attempts to sell frozen orange juice in small paper containers to be delivered by milkmen on their morning routes. The attempt failed. Frozen juice was marked in fair quantities but with indifferent success until 1945 when concentrate was perfected.

In June, 1940, QFF speculated on the future of this important product. The trade then knew that even whole juice was much better than canned juice but wasn't quite right. Some suggested that orange juice be frozen in a ball or in a square or packed in a carton or container. Slow defrosting was a drawback. Others suggested that orange juice be available in a fast defrosting form, something like a tea ball to be dropped in a glass or defrosted beforehand. I predicted that orange juice would be on breakfast tables more frequently if it were easier to make. What a blessing orange juice would be in an improved form, everyone thought! (But more on this later.)

Early Prepared Foods

As early as 1939 pre-cooked items were coming on the market. We announced that Birds Eye had introduced a new chicken fricasse; also a criss-cross steak. Others were bringing out brick soups, cooked and frozen creamed chicken, beef stew and roast turkey with dressing. But the real impact of prepared foods was to strike some four years later, and this is a story all of its own.

I must digress here as I recall an item in 1938. It was about frozen artichoke hearts and their possibilities. Yet this product really became known only about 5 or 6 years ago. There's *nothing new under the sun.*

Every month we used to print the most attractive consumer ads because they were rather sparse then. Birds Eye did most of the advertising in those days and for several years thereafter and, as has often been said, held an umbrella over the head of the industry. Most ads then were a lot more descriptive than they are now because they *had* to sell frozen foods—not price. One on asparagus read: "It's October. The fresh asparagus season closed months ago. Yet today we offer you quick frozen asparagus, actually field fresher than the king you get in the middle of the season. Here's why—asparagus changes fast after cutting. The sugars turn quickly to starch. Stringy fibers develop. Even in season, your average asparagus may take up to three days to reach your table. By that time it's but a dry, droopy copy of the green shoots the farmer cuts in the field." Price 29¢ for a 12-oz. box. I have never read a more descriptive ad since—we *really sold* in those days!

The First Carry-Over

And now this budding industry was faced with its first hurdle—*a carryover.* In July, 1939, over 130 million pounds of fruits and vegetables were reported in freezers, a large amount then. The Chicago *Tribune* carried an ominous story which predicted dire results if the problem was not solved. QUICK FROZEN FOODS sprang immediately to the industry's defense. We wrote the *Tribune* that "the situation is not serious" and pointed out that quality frozen foods were still at a premium. "The blight of inferior merchandise, while unfortunate," we said, "is nevertheless a growing pain of a young and vigorous industry." The answer was printed in the Chicago *Tribune*. Eight years later the *Wall Street Journal* was to publish a similar article with much more serious consequences!

In January, 1940, Birds Eye announced what was then a revolutionary new policy which was to mark a milestone and change the future course of distribution. Up to that time BE had been helpful to the industry as a whole during the formative stage of frozen foods distribution. It prevented haywire expansion, enabled quality maintenance. But such a rigid policy could not be maintained against increasing competition. Now George Mentley, the new national sales manager, caused a complete reversal. Mentley had joined the Birds Eye organization as a salesman in 1934 and this genial, hard worker was to hold a dominant position in the industry for the next two decades. The control of retail prices was relinquished and the policy of renting cabinets abandoned in favor of outright purchases by retailers. This policy led to more cabinet placement in chains, more national distribution and price competition.

In February 1940 we defined the attitude of big chains toward frozen foods as "lukewarm." Chain units in higher class communities, we pointed out, did not hesitate to install frozen foods but the main obstacle seemed to be "something to play with" in the form of a price special. Later on the chains found *more than enough to play with*.

About this time Donald Tressler, who had been with Birds Eye and later with the New York State Agricultural Station in Geneva, N.Y., was rapidly gaining recognition as a technical authority. He wrote several articles for QFF dealing with various aspects of freezing and packing. In Feb. 1940, QFF ran its first Packaging Issue in which is described various packages then on the market and the type of equipment being used.

Doubted FF Health Values

But I remember that there was considerable ignorance about the health factor of frozen foods. One packer had obtained statements from physicians as to the wholesomeness of his products. QFF strongly advocated that the industry get more legitimate medical endorsements. Shortly thereafter the American Medical Association included frozen fruits and vegetables in its list of accepted foods. But the cry was kept up for many years until, finally, the National Association of Frozen Food Packers recently put through its extensive and valuable nutritional program.

I recall a rather humorous incident which resulted in a tilt with Longchamps restaurants in N.Y. QFF took bitter exception to a card then attached to their menus which read "No frozen food deception here. Your doctor will tell you frozen foods can't give you all the fresh food vitamins." We wrote Longchamps and pointed out the findings of technical authorities in the industry on the vitamin content of frozen foods as being fully equivalent to that of fresh products. This excellent restaurant chain never again spoke disparagingly of frozen products.

The Northwest was still the center of production activity at that time. R. D. Bodle, whose founder had died the year before, was branching out into other labels. A new packer of importance was starting, a company which met a tragic end several years later—Samuel A. Moffett. Established in Seattle, its trade mark became Polar Brand. Moffett was to build up one of the most extensive distribution systems in the industry, only to be caught in the inventory squeeze which took place seven years later and which resulted in the firm's bankruptcy and eventually Moffett's death.

About Promoters

By the end of 1940 the industry was growing in all directions. In the field of distribution the leading activity was now centered in house-to-house delivery systems which were springing up all over the country. One was outstanding—Bob White. I shall never forget its promoter, Arthur Jones. He franchised many operations, some of which still bear the name. His theory was that every day thirty million bottles of milk were delivered to homes in America via the house-to-house route. So why not frozen foods, he reasoned? He furnished the name to licensees and the trade mark, a bobwhite, along with a whistle which emitted a sound resembling that which comes from the throat of a bobwhite. At the whistle, housewives were supposed to rush out and place their orders. Jones was one of the first promoters in the industry and I think he did a lot to get frozen foods known at that time. Since then, there have been many promoters of various types passing across the frozen foods scene. Some were good and some bad, and some exerted a lasting influence on the industry. I have become convinced that at certain stages of any industry's growth, *a good promoter* is essential.

In 1940 an industry census showed that there were 2641 wage earners in frozen foods with annual wages of $1.5 million. In contrast, it is now reported that investment in the industry is over nine billion dollars and we estimate that there are over 500,000 workers. In March 1941, QFF reported that there were between 12,000 and 15,000 cabinets in retail stores; today there are over 400,000 stores with cabinets.

Early Transport Problems

At this time QFF was vitally interested in transportation of frozen foods. It was then generally thought that 20° was satisfactory but we hammered away for zero temperatures and eventually lower temperatures came about. We began to urge railroads to develop better facilities. The only refrigerant employed was salt and ice. The general attitude of many railroad men was that three cars of fresh produce would bring them considerably *more revenue* than one car of frozen. I think the reverse is true now. A milestone was reached in 1939 when Brown Packing Co. of Philadelphia shipped a load of frozen strawberries from the south in a car utilizing dry ice. Another important development was the first insulated canvas frozen food containers for L.C.L. shipments, made by Meese, Inc., now Containers Co. Yet another important contributor to transportation progress was Major Church, the originator of the Church container, used in express shipments for many years.

No history of frozen food would be complete without mention of M. T. Zarotschenzeff, then known as "Mr. Z." He was the inventor of the Z freezing process, used mostly for poultry, he travelled widely and he gave us regular reports of the progress of freezing in other countries.

As far back as 1929, Edwin T. Gibson, president of Birds Eye, and about whom more will be said as this history progresses, wrote in QFF about the future of frozen meats. Meats were then an important part of the Birds Eye line. Mr. Gibson pointed out that retailers purchasing frozen meats would know their costs on each item and he predicted that "we shall live to see the day when a large portion of meat is quick frozen and distributed as such." But we will have more to say about meat later on.

We thought a milestone had been reached when, in 1940, Macy's N.Y. store installed frozen foods. This was Birds Eye's second line, "Coldseal," since abandoned. Department stores all over the country were beginning to install frozen foods. So were chains. One of the first was Albers Supermarkets who reported increased sales of 40% during the first year.

One of the first packing plants I visited was that of John H. Dulany & Son, in Fruitland, Md., and I was privileged to meet and to make a friend of one of the first gentlemen of the industry. Ralph Dulany was then packing for Birds Eye but soon went all out on his own brand and expanded his operation to include modern plants at Exmore, Md., and Bridgeville, Del. Dulany has since been sold to Green Giant, then to United Foods. The firm had begun freezing strawberries in retail packages in 1933, and in 1940 brought out a complete retail line under the Dulany label. Over the years the company has worked almost exclusively with distributors. Ralph Dulany, one of the few Phi Beta Kappas in the industry, has been president of both the National Canners and National Frozen Food Packers Associations.

Freezing Starts in England

In the early '30's, the fish firm of Smethursts, was producing frozen foods by means of cold air blown through a tunnel. But it was left to Unilever to show the first real interest and as far back as 1933 they had discussed samples of Birds Eye frozen foods from the U.S. Chivers & Sons, large preserve firm, was actually the first to freeze, with equipment acquired from Frosted Foods Corp., a subsidiary of General Foods. In 1938 Frosted Foods Ltd. was incorporated to run the Birds Eye business in the U.K. Whereas the initial market testing of Birds Eye foods in the U.S. took place in 1930, the first English introduction of frozen products was launched in 1938 at a press party in London. In April, 1941, Unilever, Ltd., first discussed the idea of buying Frosted Foods, Ltd., in which General Foods then had an important interest. After further somewhat involved negotiations, in 1943 Birds Eye was finally launched as a Unilever brand. Unilever hoped to see Birds Eye companies in operation all over the world, as well as in England. Earlier, arrangements had been made in Canada for the Hudson's Bay Company to market frozen foods.

The manager of this company was the late G. W. Muddiman who later went to the U.K. and became very active in the initial stages of Birds Eye's development there.

The outbreak of war however, brought frozen food developments to a virtual standstill. I quote from *"Birds Eye In England, The Early Years,"* by W. J. Reader. "For several years after the end of the Second World War, drabness hung in the air of England and the mood of the people was grey, irritable and pessimistic, though practically nobody was out of work, wages were high. . . . The rationing of food lasted from 1940 to 1954, and it had some curious side-effects. It engendered a new attitude toward the buying of food. There were no brands, and as to quality, you took what was in the shop that week and that was the end of it. The English eating week remained stubbornly built around the Sunday joint and two vegetables, which reappeared later in various forms until it was finished. These are some of the things which Birds Eye had to take into account in the early post-war years. On the bright side there was people's deep desire to be rid of dreariness. On the other hand, people were known to be suspicious of new-fangled ideas and frozen foods would be expensive."

It was into this market that Unilever plunged with Birds Eye rights for the world, outside of the U.S. and Switzerland. Up to now all processing had been done through Chivers. At this point, however, I should mention that Smedley's, a large English canner, had also started to freeze before the war and took it up again in 1945. Recently, Smedley was sold to the Imperial Tobacco Co.

The First Profit

By 1945 Birds Eye, despite conflicts with the Ministry of Food, which supervised rationing, first froze institutional peas. Yarmouth, in southern England, was chosen as the site for the first Birds Eye factory and this plant has now grown to be the largest in Europe. In January, 1946, the late George Muddiman became chairman and remained in that post for ten years. Another early developer was K. M. Scamell, who made frequent trips to the U. S.

I might say that from this time on, not only Birds Eye but others who became prominent in the frozen foods industry in Britain, were fortunate to have the American experience as a precedent—not only to *do* things, but more particularly how *not* to. They benefitted by the pioneering mistakes made in the U.S. In 1948, J. P. Van den Bergh, Unilever director, reported that the total pack was 12 million lbs. By 1949 Birds Eye had 900 shops. In that year $25,000 was appropriated for advertising. It was not until 1951 that the company made its first real profit of around $300,000 on a volume of about $3 million. There were now 4600 stores. By 1953 advertising rose to $200,000; G. T. Gear was appointed a director.

Meanwhile, other operations started. In Holland, Unilever also owns Iglo; in Australia and New Zealand there were early operations and

C. Birdseye

E. T. Gibson

C. Seabrook

H. C. Diehl

G. Mentley

R. Dulany

The "inventor" of frozen foods went all out to promote his wares to a sometimes skeptical market. In this scene from the early 1930's, a Boston hotel was the location of an exhibit of Birds Eye Frosted Foods. The sign on the display case says: "See a demonstration of quick frosting by Mr. Clarence Birdseye, inventor of the famous quick freezing process . . . Meet Mrs. Clarence Birdseye." Mr. Birdseye stands behind the cabinet answering the questions of a prospective purchaser, who is identified as Sir Wilfred Grenfell.

today there are Unilever plants in Germany and Austria. Western Europe is the Unilever domain and here Birds Eye will undoubtedly grow through the operation of its own factories. The more recent developments of frozen foods abroad will be related later in this History.

QFF Runs First Convention

At that time most frozen food packers, brokers and distributors made the annual Canners' convention their headquarters and meeting place for whatever business was transacted. There was casual talk about the formation of an association. I wrote in 1939: "Such a move is still premature by about two years but an association must be formed eventually." The war hastened its coming.

In late 1940 many felt that the time had come for the industry to hold its own convention, to rally all those interested in frozen foods under one banner. I arranged the industry's first exhibit and meeting during the 1941 Canner's Convention. Up to now, most packers, distributors and brokers transacted their business during this show. I obtained the mezzanine of the Auditorium Hotel (now a college) on Michigan Ave. in Chicago, next door to the Congress Hotel. The show was called the First Annual National Quick Frozen Foods Exhibit & Conference and it was held on January 21-24th, 1941. I was surprised, however, when *over 1,000 visited our show,* including packers, distributors, equipment people, brokers, retailers, lockermen, etc. There were 21 exhibitors including Swift, Armour, Honor Brand, Weber Showcase, Sutherland Paper, Snider Packing, Meese, Deepfreeze, Cedergreen, Booth, Little America, Sherman and many others. Our luncheon served over 200 guests and my chairman at the head table was Al Sprague. Speakers included Paul Williams, head of the U.S. Bureau of Standards; Howard Shedd, then president of the Chicago Frozen Foods Association; Donald Barr of Birds Eye; R. P. Fletcher, Jr., president of Booth Fisheries, Harry Carlton of the University of Tennessee; John Antun, president, of the Eastern Frosted Foods Association; V. R. Greene, Charles Triggs, Ed White, then president of Honor Brand. Credit was given to QUICK FROZEN FOODS for sponsoring the show.

I must point out here that QFF started early and continue down through the years to caution the industry about *quality.* Over twenty years ago we wrote: "Now that the industry is on the threshold of the greatest expansion it must especially watch out for any letdown in quality and it must guard against uneconomical over-production." These two admonitions still hold good today.

Meanwhile, the industry still lacked promotions. Birds Eye was doing by far the most. It brought out a movie entitled "Imprisoned Freshness" which showed the freezing process from the field to the kitchen. I have seen many frozen food movies since but I don't think any have ever equalled this one for clarity and effectiveness.

Fairmont early began to build a reputation for whole frozen strawberries, originally distributed mainly in New York and Chicago. Today whole berries are more popular.

In those days window packages were quite popular and were used on vegetables as well as on seafoods and poultry. Cellophane was the universal wrap. But now a new innovation appeared in poultry selling—a predetermined weight on the package. One firm advertised that it was "raising chickens to fit the box."

2

The War Years

The entire Middlewest was taking to frozen foods rapidly and so, in October 1941, I decided to open a permanent office in Chicago. I moved my family there for a six months' stay while getting the new branch started at 612 North Michigan Ave. This office has continued ever since, operated by two men and a secretary and its present location is at 5 So. Wabash Ave.

On Sunday, December 7th, I was in the office writing an article about our 2nd frozen food convention which was to take place in January, 1942, when the radio blared forth the news about Pearl Harbor. The whole industry was electrified. What would our entrance into the war presage? Would it mean the end of all our plans and hopes? Was the industry, still in the luxury class, doomed? Would the vital equipment—freezing and processing machinery, cabinets, trucks, rail transportation—now be curtailed?

Our December 1941 issued carried the following on the masthead: "Our state of national emergency, the duration of which is unpredictable. This industry from now on gladly and willingly dedicates more and more of its efforts toward the supreme task of winning the war. And no less does this magazine. No task, no sacrifice will be considered too great toward this end. Private ambitions, personal differences must all be relinquished in the face of our great goal—*Victory!*"

We then embarked on a campaign—"Frozen Foods will help win the war." In our industry all efforts were concentrated on supplying the demand for food. The "plowing under" days were gone. The Army and Navy were buying more frozen foods, especially boned, quick frozen meats. On the second day after Pearl Harbor, Chicago meat packers boned, quick froze and shipped over a million pounds of beef to the Pacific.

At the same time we published statements from leaders of the industry. Ed Gibson, then president of Birds Eye, said: "Civilian life must go on in order to take care of war time production. Food has always played an extremely important part in any war and it seems certain that frozen food production will play an important part in the government plans for the present war." From the Northwest, the late R. T. Shannon, or "Trav" as he was known, then with R. D. Bodle, wrote that he did not expect production of frozen foods would be seriously curtailed on the Pacific Coast. But this area relied a great deal on Japanese labor and farming. The Japanese were permitted to make shipments, but payments to them were held in a blocked account.

At this time too, eviscerated poultry was growing at high speed. The Army had determined that the use of this product was more economical and easier to handle in the mess and in the field than fresh poultry. QFF lost no time in promoting frozen poultry not only to the armed forces but to the industry itself.

The Industry Is Threatened

Many packers now became worried about the shortage of labor and equipment necessary to expand production. Everything went under allocation by the War Production Board. Some endeavors went by the wayside. The house-to-house selling idea which had been booming had to be abandoned. Many prepared foods went out of the picture. But the locker plant industry boomed on the principle that locally raised foods could now be processed, frozen and consumed without recourse to high priority transportation. Locker plants grew ten-fold in number and received early priorities on materials and this expansion was to last until after the war.

Despite the fact that President Roosevelt had declared that America would not go to war, many people became increasingly concerned over the conflict in Europe. The repercussions were felt in our own industry. In England, where frozen foods had just started, the industry was nipped in the bud.

Many in the U.S. thought that frozen foods, with their no-waste advantage, should have a huge appeal to army camps and large concentrations of men. QFF ventured to predict what effect the conflict would have: "Battleships and many lighter war craft have large freezer compartments where frozen foods may be kept during long cruises," we said. A. E. Stevens, then vice president of Birds Eye, suggested that quick frozen foods would become very valuable in the war effort because waste would be practically eliminated at the source of production, resulting in economies of transportation and warehousing, and also that the use of frozen foods would lessen the drain of valuable metal, ordinarily used in food packaging, since frozen food packaging consisted of board and papers. This theme was to be used not long thereafter and it was to prove the salvation of the industry.

As I look back over the past 25 years and go through the pages of QFF, I am amazed at the large number of people and firms who appear, reappear or pass from the scene. But many stayed. It is especially remarkable how few who really got a foothold in the industry ever say die, no matter how tough the going becomes. Whether it be the allure of expansion and profits to come, or the thrill that goes into pioneering a new industry that holds them, must remain the secret of every member of the trade. When the war broke out in Europe we wrote: "When this struggle is over we can be sure that we will have gained considerable more knowledge to write down in the book of frozen food experience."

Non-Essential?

But the commercial industry, so laboriously built up during the past seven years faced a dire crisis. It was seriously threatened with curtailment as "non-essential." And so was the life of our magazine. Packers now made a concentrated effort to show the government why frozen foods were essential. The second frozen food convention, which I had planned before the beginning of the Japanese war, was destined to take place one month after its outbreak. We therefore changed the program considerably to emphasize the advantages of quick freezing in wartime. Incidentally, we published our third Packers' Directory about this time; it had 250 names.

I must say here that the industry owes a debt of gratitude which it can never repay to Ed Gibson of General Foods for his energy and ability during this time of crisis. His efforts to convince the then hectic and harrassed officials in Washington of the industry's value in the war effort bore almost immediate fruit. This industry, which had once been regarded as a "silk stocking" one, was now to be looked upon as a means of conserving the nation's food resources. Others of course helped too, and they will be mentioned as we go on. The writer and QFF also played an important role during this period.

Soon everyone in the industry knew that tin would be severely curtailed and that canners would be expected to set aside important quantities for the Armed Forces and for lend-lease. The government took over 45% of the canned asparagus pack, over 22% of the lima bean pack and 38% of the pea pack. How will this affect frozen foods?—everyone was asking. In February 1942 I wrote: "This may well be the making of our industry. Shortages which may become apparent in domestic distribution of fruits and vegetables can be supplied by quick frozen foods. The industry may make greater strides in *the next two or three years* than it has made in the entire time since its inception."

In short—tin went to war; frozen foods stayed at home!

The industry's packaging versatility became important. It did not have to rely on one material such as tin; it could use board, bags, parchment, cellophane, wax paper, round containers, etc.

Birth of the Association

In January 1942, when the war was only a month old, the National Association of Frozen Food Packers was born. Edwin T. Gibson who became its first president, called a meeting of packers in Chicago. The purpose was to lay plans for closer cooperation with the Federal government in making available information on the resources of the industry.

Ralph Dulany and John N. Seaman, then of Bozeman, were named vice presidents. The job of temporary secretary was given to A. E. Stevens. The first board of directors included Roy Ingalls, Roy Hagen, A. F. Wentworth, B. L. Seabrook, B. C. Olney and the late M. T. Fannaly. E. M. Burns, who up to that time had been secretary of the Northwest Frozen Foods Association, became the first paid secretary and he departed immediately for Washington.

We Introduce New Ass'n.

The first public presentation of the newly formed Association's officers took place at the luncheon of our Convention, sponsored by QFF. This second convention, held at the La Salle Hotel in Chicago, was attended by over 1400 people. It had 35 exhibitors. Other guests who attended this four-day meeting were Woody Meyers of the War Production Board and H. C. Diehl of the U.S.D.A. He told the convention that Germany was freezing a billion pounds of perishables a year. Several west coast packers who attended expressed concern that the government would not assist Japanese in whose hands much of the produce production was centered in Oregon and Washington. At that time Japanese farmers produced over 80% of certain vegetables and strawberries. Donald Barr told the convention that there were then 25,000 stores selling frozen foods. Clarence Birdseye was another visitor.

Auto Dealers Enter

An interesting sidelight was the fact that we had more than 50 automobile dealers in attendance. Bewildered by the sudden turn of events that left the nation's 44,000 auto outlets with empty showrooms, many dealers were anxious for information about the frozen foods industry and how they could get into distribution. Several important distributors today and at least one packer I know, came from these ranks.

We now began to publish information which would be of interest to those in charge of vital materials for industry. One such chart which proved very useful and persuasive (see photo), showed the materials which go into the packaging and shipping of 50 million pounds of food-stuffs, the number of railroad cars required to transport this amount and the shipping weights. On all counts frozen foods *used less vital equipment*. We also pointed out that 20 million pounds of vegetables would require about 2600 tons of steel in addition to tin requirements, while this amount of steel would be enough to erect several badly needed cold storage warehouses, as well as frozen food and locker plants, equipped to hold 20 million pounds of frozen foods. This might be something to remember for a future war!

From Plenty to Shortage

And other arguments appeared in QFF. One was that there were then only three methods of food preservation: canning, freezing and dehydrating. Canning and dehydrating went to war, so freezing was about the only method left. We showed that it was impossible to preserve flesh foods such as poultry, fish and meats adequately without freezing, as well as many fruits and vegetables. All these facts were brought out strongly before authorities in Washington. Allotments of steel for low temperature storage, for home freezers and store cabinets were also a necessity and eventually priority was given to this type of equipment from a precious store of rationed material.

In the few months after Pearl Harbor the frozen food market turned from one of plenty to one of shortages. Distributors stocked up quickly. Fish freezing production declined because of submarine activity off both our coasts which prevented fishermen from venturing forth. Strawberries were selling around 15¢, cherries around 10¢ a pound, peas at $1.30 a dozen, lima beans at 21¢, spinach at 12½¢ and asparagus at 18¢. But these prices were to rise.

In 1942 we were anxious to keep advertisers, many of whom had little or nothing to sell. I remember running an ad at that time which read: "Wilkie lost the election but he keeps before the American public! Why?— because he is preparing now for 1944 when the next election takes place. Then he won't be forgotten. You, as a producer or manufacturer may be 'out of the running' now, but it is an unwise policy to go out of the picture. Keep your name before your trade; prepare for 'after,' now."

Meanwhile chains were getting more interested in frozen foods. We reported that the Jewel Food Stores in Chicago was the first in the Midwest to go all out on frozen foods and they installed cabinets in each of their 150 stores. The fact that they purchased these cabinets outright was a big event in those days. Another chain which began to sell frozen foods was King Kullen in the New York metropolitan area.

Casualties were now appearing weekly on the canned goods list, items which could no longer be put up in tin. Some were corn, spinach, soups, apricots, carrots, coffee. Time proved that the frozen foods industry was actually "tailor made" for the war effort.

About this time several frozen food men took official positions in Washington. One was A. E. Stevens who remained as Administrator of the Fruit & Vegetable Section of the OPA. Another was R. P. Juhnichen who took up duties as a consultant to the Frozen Food Section of the War Production Board. Carl Kolb, who was later to play an important role in buying for the armed forces, took up a post as frozen food consultant for the Quartermaster Corps. I went often to Washington and was in on many conferences and later was an OPA deputy for a while.

Shades of the OPA

The government had clamped price restrictions on all industries and under the Office of Price Administration, more complications began to arise. In early 1942 the whole pricing structure was in a snarl. The industry could not price its merchandise because of lack of instructions from Washington. Several conferences were held between packers and OPA officials. QFF complained that "gross inequities had appeared" and we urged that present ceilings be applied to last year's pack and new ceilings to the new pack. It was a very complicated situation to figure out, further confused by the numerous lawyers who permeated every bureau and buried everything under the most unintelligible legal phraseology. QUICK FROZEN FOODS assumed the task of translating the numerous orders affecting the industry coming from Washington into understandable language. We now devoted a good deal of space to pricing, in which everyone was interested and the magazine was widely referred to *as a necessity* in order to find out what was going on. This greatly increased QFF's circulation. But we did not neglect frozen foods on the home front and many articles appeared about merchandising, packaging, freezing and processing techniques, etc.

The need for greater speed in packaging and filling machinery was growing and one of our aims was to encourage the development of machinery which would bring down the cost of packaging.

In March of 1942 an effort was made to get subsidies to take care of increased costs of farm products and labor, but the effort failed. At this time Larry Martin made his first appearance on the scene in the role of head of the Frozen Food Section of the OPA. Several months later he was elected secretary of the National Association, a position which he held until his retirement. At that time Harold Humphrey of Birds Eye and Ed Huddleson of Stokely took active parts in Washington meetings. Ed Booker of Winter Garden attended many, as did Fritz Brahm. These men and others devoted their own time to the meetings and some travelled considerable distances. The work required monumental patience and diplomacy. We urged a priority on frozen food cabinets so that more frozen foods could be handled in retail stores.

QFF's War Coverage

In looking over the issues of QFF that appeared during that period, I think that anyone would be impressed by the adequate coverage we gave and the information we disseminated.

At that time I started the first frozen foods News Letter ever published in the industry and this appeared regularly until about 1955 when we had a subscription of over 2000.

As the draft continued, labor became a greater problem than ever. Many packers reported spoilages and the inability to harvest crops. In the fish industry many boats became mine-sweepers. Poultry production was heavy since poultry was not under ceilings. Eventually the Association was able to obtain price ceilings which were satisfactory.

In those days QFF was frequently quoted in the press. It was then we published a release, widely used, about frozen meats. "The blood stained butcher block will someday be a thing of the past" was the phrase we used. We said that quick frozen meats would take meat merchandising out of the cracker barrel stage and place it on a par with packaged goods.

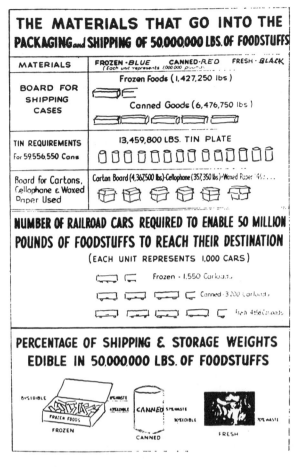

THE MATERIALS THAT GO INTO THE PACKAGING and SHIPPING OF 50,000,000 LBS. OF FOODSTUFFS

MATERIALS	FROZEN - *BLUE* CANNED - RED FRESH - *BLACK*
	(Each unit represents 1,000,000 pounds)
BOARD FOR SHIPPING CASES	Frozen Foods (1,427,250 lbs)
	Canned Goods (6,476,750 lbs)
TIN REQUIREMENTS For 59,556,550 Cans	13,459,800 LBS. TIN PLATE
Board for Cartons, Cellophane & Waxed Paper Used	Carton Board (4,367,500 lbs)-Cellophane (357,350 lbs)-Waxed Paper 46:...

NUMBER OF RAILROAD CARS REQUIRED TO ENABLE 50 MILLION POUNDS OF FOODSTUFFS TO REACH THEIR DESTINATION

(EACH UNIT REPRESENTS 1,000 CARS)

Frozen - 1,550 Carloads

Canned - 3,200 Carloads

Fresh 4,560 Carloads

PERCENTAGE OF SHIPPING & STORAGE WEIGHTS EDIBLE IN 50,000,000 LBS. OF FOODSTUFFS

FROZEN

CANNED

FRESH

Charts like this one appeared on QFF during the war years and illustrated the advantages of frozen foods over fresh and canned foods in times of emergency.

E. J. White

E. E. Huddleson

Events later showed that in this prediction we were considerably ahead of reality.

Ten and 12 ounce packages were becoming more popular and many of them were replacing the 16 ounce size. Many ideas came to the fore at that time. One was an idea for the post war quick freezing of foods in the stratosphere. Ralph Grayson, an engineer, thought that low temperatures prevailing high above the earth could be harnessed to freeze foods and transport them at the same time. There would be plenty of planes around after the war, he reasoned.

First "Set Aside"

In September 1942 the armed forces asked that frozen food packers set aside a minimum of 35 to 60 million pounds of vegetables of the coming 1943 pack. This was the highest amount ever demanded and the industry immediately complied. Shortly thereafter the War Production Board allocated 2,000 tons of metal to the industry where it was very welcome.

Meanwhile, our circulation rose steadily. In October 1942 it was up to 8000 of which 80% was on a paid basis. In that month, I had a new editor, Miss Galena Hopkins, who was to remain with me seven years. She became well known to many in the industry and did an outstanding job. She left QFF to go to England where she married and now resides.

Prepared frozen foods were little known then, although in 1942 Birds Eye introduced baked beans. Corned beef hash was also on the market. In one issue we speculated as to what the post-war frozen food cabinet would look like. A picture appeared in QFF of an open display case, not very different from those now in use.

70 Million Lbs. for the Army

Toward the end of 1942 an important conference was held in Washington attended by freezers, canners, dehydrators and preservers. Carl Kolb was made Chief Procurement Officer of the U.S. Quartermaster Corps. He announced that the aim of his department was to procure at least 70 million pounds of frozen foods in 1943 for the armed forces. I spent several days in Washington for this particular meeting, much time of which was occupied with boiling down lengthy and complicated government releases into understandable form. The late Ted Waterman, formerly of Honor Brand, was also then in the Food Branch of the OPA and he had much to do with rationing. When food rationing first came out many feared it would hurt retailing but the facts were that eventually frozen foods were in more demand than ever before.

The late Ross-Duggan, an Englishman of marked military bearing, joined QFF in Chicago. He covered the whole midwest for several years up to his retirement and became very well known in that section of the country.

Dehydrated Foods

At that time we speculated considerably as to what the market would be for dehydrated foods after the war. In 1943 I started a Dehydration Section in the magazine, and continued it until 1946. In 1943 over $800 million worth of dehydrated foods were sold. And here is where I made my first and only venture into book publishing: I got Lawrence K. Harper, president of the National Dehydrators Association, to write a book on dehydrated foods and we published it. We sold several thousand copies. To those interested, the book is entitled *Dehydration—Its Post-War Future*. At that time the proponents of dehydrated foods felt that after the war these foods would be popular with consumers because of the lower cost. This actually happened in the case of soups, soft drink powders, certain forms of potatoes, seasonings and dry milk. However, when the war ended, many ex-service people who had lived on a diet of dehydrated products for some time wouldn't touch them with a ten-foot pole. I think now, as I did then, that dehydration is strictly an emergency or economy method. But freeze-drying may be something a little different.

Free Advertising

Would coupon rationing spur or retard the industry? As it turned out, rationing by points was the first free mass advertising that frozen foods received in the home market. Each store had to put up posters showing the point values of various foods, thus frozen fruits and vegetables immediately appeared in a prominent position on the official OPA store posters which had to be bulletined in approximately 600,000 food stores throughout the country, regardless of whether or not they sold frozen foods. Newspapers all over the country pictured frozen foods along with canned goods. In this way frozen foods were brought forcefully to the attention of people who had never considered them before. At the same time, other companies such as Honor Brand and Dulany advertised "Get more for your ration coupons" and the public responded. Meanwhile the Washington conferences continued.

Huddleson

An active worker for the industry in those days was the late Ed Huddleson of the Santa Cruz Packing Co., later sold to Stokely, of whose board Huddleson became a member. This tall, lanky Tennessean represented the spirit of the west when he first met with eastern frozen food packers during the war crisis. Later, his guidance of Honor Brand proved a valuable contribution to Stokely. Huddleson played an important role in the development of frozen foods, both during and after the war, and he was a president of the NAFFP.

First Chain Label

And now the industry was to see the first chain label, a trend which was to become so vitally important ten years later. Penn Fruit Co. had decided to switch from national brands to its own "Green Valley" label. It brought out a complete line of fruits and vegetables under that name, and all its stores were equipped with self-service units. About this time, too, covers were removed from cabinets and this helped the merchandising of frozen foods greatly.

Our New Policy

During the first four years QFF improved considerably and circulation increased, but the size of the magazine did not change very much. We just about broke even. However, in mid-1943 QUICK FROZEN FOODS began to grow at a fast pace. New advertisers, sensing that frozen foods were here to stay, rushed into the book. The magazine, by that time, was carrying three complete sections: freezing, dehydrated foods and locker plants. We published the following ad of our own: *"What makes a good trade paper? It has always been the policy of QFF to offer its readers the best—regardless of expense. Every issue of QFF is as complete as it is possible to make it. But this is not enough. Articles describing new processing and packaging methods, new techniques and ideas in marketing and distribution, are equally essential. Yet, a good trade paper has still something else, a third dimension you might call it. It's that something that reflects the pulse of the industry—that indescribable factor that makes the difference between the good and the indifferent trade publication. Perhaps that's why* QUICK FROZEN FOODS *today is considered the 'bible' of the frozen foods industry."*

At that time I laid down policy to which we have adhered strictly through the years: that each issue carry articles of sufficient diversification so that there will always be *something for everyone.* We carried articles for packers, distributors, brokers, warehousemen, production men, etc. The industry was and still is so interrelated that each branch is interested in the other, and *all* come under the common denominator of quick freezing.

First Prepared Food Ad

Another reason prepared frozen foods began to appear at this time was that they were *not rationed.* I think one of the first ads we ever ran on precooked frozen foods was in December 1943. This was for a firm known as The Old Newfields Co., Boston, who advertised a series of entree dishes which included seafoods a la queen, flaked shrimp, lobster and fish in a milk sauce, clam chowder and similar New England dishes. To my recollection, they were the first to use the phrase "heat and eat." But still more cooked foods came on the market: welsh rarebit, chop suey and French fried potatoes. One of the pioneers was the Bridgeford Packing Co. in San Diego, who put out corned beef hash, baked beans and applesauce. By the end of 1943 about eight million pounds of prepared foods had been frozen. But the avalanche was yet to come!

New items were appearing on the market. One was frozen dog food, produced by Hill Packing Co., which incidentally, was recently sold for

$10 million. Due to the wartime shortage of standard items, many people were encouraged to experiment in new products. Some of these were frozen clams, codfish cakes, pork and beans, pork and cabbage, meat balls in tomato sauce, chile con carne, corned beef hash, various patties, and chicken a la king.

As early as 1943 we wrote "the market for some frozen soups should be a very attractive one." Actually, it took more than ten years to fulfill this prediction.

Paper Shortage

Everything was under OPA ceilings. They were fair enough to enable the industry to operate profitably, although costs were high. At that time paper for printing QFF was harder and harder to get. But it's an ill wind that blows no good. Consumer magazines like the *Saturday Evening Post* and the *New Yorker* were harder hit than we were, and they had to ration advertising because of lack of paper, and their salesmen were left with no space to sell. As a result we obtained the services of one of the *New Yorker's* best advertising men, Robert Feyl, who worked for us until the war's end and then returned to the *New Yorker*.

We now had a Washington correspondent, three on the West Coast and one in Chicago.

On the locker end, S. P. Warrington was then connected with the Farm Credit Administration in Washington and was in charge of the locker plan program. All those who had applications to build plants had to come to him. He was responsible for the erection of many plants.

It was at this point that I sold the *Butchers' Advocate,* which was a weekly. QUICK FROZEN FOODS was growing and needed all my attention, and I never found it possible to do a good job working on two different magazines at the same time. I preferred to have one that was outstanding, and one to which I could devote all my efforts.

Home Freezers Boom

General Foods, at this time, acquired Snider Packing Co. and shortly thereafter Cady Olney was made new general manager of Birds Eye, a post which he held for several years.

During the war home freezers were in great demand. One company bought up all the old ice cream cabinets it could find, rebuilt them, and sold them at a huge profit. I remember that one small ad in the N.Y. *Times* in 1943 brought 5,000 inquiries for home freezers. They sold for prices ranging from $500 to $2,000!

By the end of 1943, packers had no trouble in selling their products. Strawberry sales were practically nonexistent. Cherries had almost disappeared from the market. Lima beans were short, with the government taking up most of the pack. Fruits and berries were used widely in preserves which went to the armed forces.

We now had good reason to become worried about the cabinet shortage. At the beginning of 1944 there were only about 30,000 low temperature cabinets in the field but it was estimated that 300 million pounds of frozen foods would have to pass through these boxes, many of which were used for ice cream, poultry and meats as well. QFF sponsored meetings to discuss the situation and to plan for the post-war cabinet. In 1944 the Eastern Frosted Foods Association in New York held such a luncheon which was addressed by D. K. Tressler, Ted Waterman of the WPB, Van R. Greene, refrigeration authorities and the late Miss Mary Pennington, internationally known refrigeration engineer and the only woman in that profession. John Antun was then president of the group. Another such meeting was held in Chicago and it was attended by several hundred people, including W. L. Pavlovski, then manager of the Beatrice Creameries, N. S. Morse of Jewel Food Stores, and many cabinet manufacturers such as C. V. Hill, Hussmann, Frigidaire, Kelvinator, General Electric, Tyler, McCray and others. I think that, as a result of these meetings, many manufacturers were spurred to design post-war cabinets and they were particularly made *conscious of the demand.*

The Northwest Group

At that time we also started a supermarket survey to determine the type of equipment most desired by operators and the approximate amount of space going into frozen foods. The result was that 95% wanted self-service cabinets and the average amount of "cold space" in stores was about 380 cu. ft.

In the Northwest the association was active too. The Northwest Frozen Foods group, in January, 1944, met and elected Norman Cedergreen president. Some who were active at the time were Jim Agen, Fred Becker, R. T. Shannon, Ray Maling, Sam Moffett and others.

The magazine continued to grow. It now averaged 80 to 84 pages regularly. For the first time we sold our front cover to Shellmar, and this valuable space has been occupied ever since. In April, 1944, *Clarence Birdseye* joined QFF's technical advisory board, on which he remained until his death a few years ago. He had one of the most ingenious and inventive minds I have ever seen and his expert technical help and guidance proved very valuable to all who needed it.

Rationing Ends

About this time rationing was taken off frozen foods altogether and this gave the domestic market a tremendous boost. In April, 1944, we wrote: "After the initial rush of precooked foods, there now is a big lull. But many men who had, up to now, regarded frozen foods as a passing fad were changing their minds. One was a large marketing co-op and another a canner of considerable importance. Both have since become important factors in freezing.

FROZEN FOODS COST LESS POINTS
THAN CANNED GOODS!

QUICK FROZEN FOODS has prepared the below chart on the basis of more portions per point. Official government point values are, (as published on Page 14), based on total gross weight. Actually, when excess liquid has been drained off, frozen foods are shown to cost less points than canned foods. Buyers are only interested in the net amount of food obtained and present point values bring out the economy of frozen foods most strikingly

When point count was a greater concern than price, frozen foods showed up well, as this chart from the February, 1943, QFF indicates.

HOW FAMILY OF FOUR WITH 192 POINTS SAVES WITH FROZEN FOODS	
2 Packages Beans	...10 points each 20 points
4 Packages Peas	...10 points each 40 points
2 Packages Spinach	...10 points each 20 points
4 Packages Mixed Veg.	... 6 points each 24 points
4 Packages Brussel Sprouts	... 6 points each 24 points
4 Packages Cut Corn	... 7 points each 28 points
4 Packages Cut Green Beans	... 7 points each 28 points
1 Package Squash	... 8 points each 8 points
25 FROZEN PACKAGES or 25 MEALS, COST 192 PTS.	

SAME FAMILY SPENDS 192 PTS. FOR CANNED	
3 cans Peas No. 2	... 16 points each 48 points
2 cans Spinach No. 2½	...17 points each 34 points
2 cans Green Limas	...16 points each 32 points
2 cans Cut Corn	...... 16 points each 32 points
2 cans Wax or Green Beans	...14 points each 28 points
1 can Mixed Veg.	...14 points each 14 points
1 can Peaches, 12 oz.	...14 points each 8 points
13 CANS or 13 MEALS, COST	192 PTS.

POINT VALUES FOR CONTAINERS SERVING FOUR PERSONS		
Product	Pts. for Canned	Pts. for Frozen
Peas	16	10
Beans, Green & Waxed	14	7
Lima Beans	16	10
Spinach	14	10
Asparagus	14	10
Cut Corn	8	7
Peaches	17	13
Strawberries	14	13

COMPARISONS ON A PER POUND BASIS			
Product	Official Pts. Required for Frozen Products	Official Pts. Required for Canned Foods	Points Actually Yielded for Canned on Drained Weight Basis
Cut Corn	13 per pound	11 per pound	16.3 per lb.
Peas	13 per pound	13 per pound	20.5 per lb.
Limas	13 per pound	13 per pound	17.7 per lb.
Beans, Green	13 per pound	11 per pound	18.3 per lb.
Peas & Carrots	8 per pound	11 per pound	17.2 per lb.
Spinach	13 per pound	11 per pound	14.7 per lb.

(For a basis of comparison it might be considered that a 16 ounce package of Strawberries or Peaches is equivalent to a No. 2½ Can of the same products on a drained weight basis.)

The original belt froster developed by Clarence Birdseye in Gloucester, Mass. Joseph Guinane assisted in the development of the 1926 model, which was designed for fish. The belt froster was the predecessor of the multiple plate freezer.

One of the earlier frozen food cabinets built specifically for this industry. This type of unit was termed a "coffin cabinet" because products were buried out of sight in its interior. The customer made her selections from a menu-like list, and then the clerk blindly dug up the desired items.

One of the original 10 stores in the United States to handle frozen foods was Davidson's, in Springfield, Mass. It is the only one of that group still in business today.

The year QFF was born, 1938, the men in this picture were among the most important in the frozen food world. They were The Birds Eye Marketing Team operating under the aegis of the Frosted Food Sales Corp., at 250 Park Ave., New York City. Left to right were: Richard Crooker, retail sales manager; Al Farnham, New York branch sales manager; Russ Brown, staff assistant; George Mentley, institutional sales manager; Ambrose E. Stevens, vice president for marketing; Don Ban, advertising manager and product manager; and Howard Lochrie, assistant advertising manager.

The Birds Eye production team in 1938 (left to right): William Mundry, staff assistant, personnel; Al Huff, manager of transportation; Al Brackett, manager of packaging; Karl Norton, production manager, fruits and vegetables; Joseph Guinane, production manager, fish, meat and poultry; Richard Poole, refrigeration engineer; and Rudy Rudnick, staff assistant.

The second national frozen foods convention sponsored by QFF was held in Chicago in January, 1942. It drew over 400 delegates from all segments of the industry, as well as Army and government representatives. This gathering was marked by the announcement of the birth of the National Association of Frozen Food Packers. At the head table were (left to right): W. Meyers, W. E. Guest, Dr. J. G. Woodroof, E. J. White, Roy M. Hagen, Edwin T. Gibson, 1st Lt. James M. Gwin, Albert Sprague, John J. Antun, H. C. Diehl, Donald Barr, Dr. App, Frank Glidden, L. B. Dodd, and T. H. Truslow. Also seated at the dais, but not shown in the picture, were Ralph Dulany and E. W. Williams.

At the January, 1940, Canners Convention in Chicago, QFF arranged a Frozen Food Luncheon. Seated at the head table were (left to right): Donald Barr, William Bowen, Pendleton Dudley, John J. Antun, J. D. Rankin and L. F. Noonan. The occasion previewed the first frozen food industry convention held the following year under QFF sponsorship.

The first frozen foods convention, sponsored in January, 1941, by QFF, brought more than 200 industry leaders together at a luncheon meeting where they could have their frozen food problems discussed by experts from all parts of the country.

In 1947, first annual convention of National Association of Frozen Food Packers, in San Francisco. Officers and directors elected at that meeting, seated (left to right): Lawrence S. Martin, secretary-treasurer; F. J. Becker, first vice president; C. Courtney Seabrook, president; Joseph Braden, second vice president. Standing (left to right): directors C. L. Snavely, Ted McAffray, Karl B. Norton, M. T. Fannally, G. O. Bailey, Rolland Jory and E. J. White. Not pictured are E. E. Huddleson, A. J. Rogers and Stanley Macklem.

"Post-War Cabinet" Forum was held in New York in 1944, to discuss the future frozen food cabinet. At the speaker's table were: John J. Antun, E. W. Williams, Ted C. Waterman, Mrs. Nancy K. Masterman, Peter Schladermundt and Hubert Hilder.

An early board of directors of the National Association of Frozen Food Packers, 1946. At head of table are E. E. Huddleson and Ralph Dulany.

E. W. Williams, QFF's publisher, third from left, converses with Clarence Birdseye at a 1947 industry meeting sponsored by the magazine. All the other people in the picture are editors or editorial consultants of QFF.

Expansion

There was new activity in California too. Sacramento Frozen Foods erected a new plant and Ed White became interested in the company. In Modesto another new plant was established by Pringle which later became California Frozen Foods. Santa Clara Frozen Foods was operating full blast and F. G. Lamb in Milton, Oregon, expanded its operations. So did the Bozeman Canning Co., later to become PictSweet.

Just about then, however, an important change came about. The Army decided to *reduce* its buying of frozen vegetables and this immediately made large quantities available to packers for the development of home markets. The news was welcome to most freezers and distributors who were looking at the long range picture. The reason for the reduction was the increasing movement of troops overseas and out of domestic camps where most frozen vegetables had been used. Nevertheless, from now on the market became "heavier." Some items were beginning to show up in excess quantities and this trend was to continue until its culmination in 1946. Baked beans were a drug on the market; 25 million pounds had been frozen, five times the amount of the previous year.

Peace was not far away.

West Coast Trips Begin

In June of 1944 I made the first of my comprehensive trips to the west coast. I have made 25 annual trips since. I started in Los Angeles and went up to Seattle, visiting almost every plant and reporting production prospects, improvements and news in subsequent issues of QUICK FROZEN FOODS. On this trip I observed that money interests were now beginning to regard the frozen foods industry as a distinctly *profitable post-war investment* with all kinds of firms—and banks—seemingly ready to back almost any kind of logical quick freezing venture. I reported that there were about eight new freezers in Southern California alone and that the moment the war was over, 20 to 30 new plants were in a position to start. The industry was indeed at the brink of a wild spree of expansion.

Fruits Impressive

In California I was impressed with the size and flavor of apricots which were as large as our eastern peaches. I remember the late Pete Knudsen taking me into his apricot orchards and showing me his crop. I never knew a man who was so proud of his apricots. I was excited about the future of California in freezing and wrote: "Here frozen foods are just beginning to hit their stride. Henceforth, a greater and greater portion of these products *must* come from this state, so abundant in lush valleys and in the necessary enthusiasm to produce these new frozen products." I also visited several dehydration plants, some of which were later to become important freezers, such as Spiegl Farms in Salinas, Chapman in Modesto and Simplot in Idaho.

High Strawberry Output

In California, E. F. Driscoll emerged for the first time as California's largest strawberry freezer. His output totalled more than a million pounds—he has since produced over 17 million! The firm is now known as Santa Fe-Driscoll.

I visited Watsonville in war time and there was no hotel space available. I finally put up in a gymnasium of the local YMCA which had been turned into a dormitory. One of the early freezers was the Watsonville Canning Co. under Ed Console. Fresh Frozen Fruits was operating, as was Frank Oliver, Western Frozen Foods, Ruso and Papac. Honor Brand was freezing at the Santa Cruz Packing Co. Richmond Chase in San Jose was an important Birds Eye freezer then.

The Apple Sauce Craze

I was there when the run on frozen cooked apple sauce started. This turned out to be like the famous tulip speculation in Holland three hundred years ago. Everyone was packing the product which was soon to pile up in such huge quantities that some of it was still around — eight years later! Personally, I never thought it a bad product; served immediately after defrosting it was cool and refreshing. But perhaps the timing was poor.

In Oakland I met Alvin Langfield who was then distributing under the name of Frozen Food Distributors. Langfield has since been through the thick and thin of this industry but through consistent effort and study of the best policies he has managed to stay on top and today is one of the country's leading distributors.

Industry at 'Brink of Expansion'

In the Northwest I saw Maling in Hillsboro which was a Birds Eye operation. Kelley, Farquhar was operating in Tacoma. I will never forget Art Chappel of R. D. Bodle who always went out of his way to make me most welcome, nor Ben Logan, his sales manager. I met Jim Agen and Sam Moffett. In Mt. Vernon, the Bozeman Canning Co., under the direction of L. L. Brotherton, was already packing around 12 million pounds and had developed the PictSweet label. Now, for the first time, many northwestern packers who had hitherto packed for others, were beginning to bring out their own labels. Active too then were Art Symonds of the Hershey Packing Co., one of the oldest firms in the northwest and a budding newcomer, Cedergreen Frozen Foods at Wenatchee. Norman Cedergreen, who has since become a good friend, was the biggest packer east of the mountains. He is today, once again, head of Cedergreen Frozen Foods and a leading broker as well.

After returning to the east I wrote: "The west coast today is a curious mixture of conservatism stemming from the older packers who have known rough going, mixed with a strong undercurrent of aggressiveness, enterprise and planning for the future as exemplified by the new buildings being erected. The packers today are *fully* awake to their opportunities and the increasing demands which will be made upon them. The whole West Coast stands on the brink of a great expansion."

In 1944 QFF, though a business magazine, came out for Dewey. He took a keen interest in frozen foods. I remember hearing him make a speech when he was Governor of New York at an agricultural college in which he boosted freezing. After the meeting I talked with him and he told me that he always had a home freezer and liked to experiment with new products.

First Concentrate Experiments

And now, in August 1944, QFF ran its first article about concentrated orange juice. It was written by Arthur L. Stahl of the Florida Agricultural Experimental Station. There have been many claims as to the originator of concentrating and certainly I would not venture into this delicate controversy. However, Mr. Stahl, in his article, told what was being done. Ways were eagerly being sought which would give more and wider distribution to Florida's then $139 million a year citrus crop. Everyone was looking for a means of preserving orange juice in a way that retained the appearance, taste and nutritional values of fresh juice. Stahl described a method which concentrated by freezing and centrifuging and which resulted in the best product to date. It was merely a method of concentration by freezing out the water. Actually, I think the idea of concentration may have been inspired by what had been happening for years in Europe and America where, in certain districts, small casks of fruit and wine were placed out of doors on nights when very low temperatures were expected, to draw off the liquor from the central core. The soluble portion of the wine would then be concentrated and a sweet liquor type of product was obtained.

At that time a pilot plant was being set up in Gainesville, Florida, in co-operation with the Florida Citrus Commission, for the purpose of producing orange juice. QFF said: "A widespread adoption of citrus juice concentration by freezing is predicted." But more about this later.

Distributors Waiting

In October 1944 it was interesting to note that the main thing bothering distributors was where to get a line of fruits and vegetables. Many distributors were registering their names with packers to get preferential treatment after the war was over. At that time we reported: "So far as QFF can estimate, there is a backlog of 200-300 good wholesalers waiting to handle frozen foods. Commercial freezers, perhaps, fail to realize the immense distributing potential that has been built up since war restrictions were placed upon the industry." Also at the time George Mentley of Birds Eye expressed the fear that, since retailers did not have to sell during the war when practically any item on the shelf "walked out of the store," the retail grocer might not be sufficiently alert to meet post-war competition.

We were then speculating on what made a complete line, and finally came to the conclusion that 14 vegetables and 7 fruits would represent a fairly complete assortment. Strawberries, by the end of 1944, were selling around 30¢ lb. because of the great demand from army camps and others. About this time QFF hit its first 100-page issue and from then on growth was at a more rapid pace.

In the packaging field such companies as Menasha, later to become Marathon Corp. and then a part of American Can, was doing an outstanding job. The company was the first to introduce high speed filling and packaging equipment to the industry.

In October 1944, QFF published its first authoritative article on frozen meats and their future. Many predictions we made then came true, but we did overlook one important development—the coming popularity of precooked, prepared and "upgraded" meats which have since become very successful.

Brokers Grow

Now our brokers became more active and our brokers' pages began to grow. Where we had only two columns in the beginning we now had five full pages devoted to leading frozen food brokers and these listings were frequently referred to by packers. The late Jim Fenwick in Portland was one of the first northwest brokers to advertise. Frank Dotson was another. I have always admired his grasp of the market and he was always helpful and friendly on my many coast trips. Bill Hasselman in Pittsburgh was another early advertiser. In New York, Ries, Munoz & Antun were one of the first, as were White, Davenport and Ashenfelter & Morrow. J. B. Ruth in Los Angeles and William Lindenberger were regular advertisers and in San Francisco D. B. Berelson, formerly importers, brokerage business. Clyde Le Baron, helped by his five sons, was yet another early broker. In the Midwest the late Ed Hayes, Sr., was a good friend whose marketing advice was of great help to us in those days. We originated a slogan for him: "Since frozen foods began," which he has used ever since. Another beginner was the active Henry Brock. Otto Cuyler in New York State was not only a broker then but a distributor and packer as well. C. W. Cornwell, now Moretta & Meredith, was active in Philadelphia.

First FF Store

In November 1944 we began to look ahead. In a published ad we stated: *"The blueprints have been drawn for a greater post-war* QUICK FROZEN FOODS. *As soon as the supply of printing paper becomes more plentiful we will put into effect some important plans which have been made for greater service to the industry."* We planned a complete market reporting section, a technical and engineering section, one on meats and poultry, cabinets and seafoods. We also laid plans to put out the first Directory of Packers which became a reality the following year. Other

D. K. Tressler   J. Guinane

Magazines, published since, have followed the sectional divisions which we laid down in those days.

Before the end of the war manufacturers of home freezers were eagerly awaiting the release of materials. "They are forming up at the waiting line," QFF wrote, "waiting for the pistol to go off." Owning a home freezer then was considered a privilege. It was much like owning a boat; you always wanted a larger one.

The first frozen food store was started in White Plains, called the Frostar Frozen Food Center. The late Carl Seabergh was president. This was followed by another in Chicago and then the frozen food store idea really began to roll. Several stores in the Washington, D.C. area were opened by Deep Freeze Distributors. Department stores, too, became interested in frozen foods. L. Bamberger in Newark began their own freezing and packaging. So did R. H. Macy. M. P. Hood Sons in Boston began to distribute a line. In Canada, B. C. Packers in Vancouver began to supply the Canadian market.

Toward the end of 1944 we estimated that the pack would be around 32-35 million pounds of strawberries, about 80 million pounds of peas and about 10-12 million pounds of broccoli. What a far cry from present figures!

At the time were were concerned with the confusing terminology being used by the industry. We suggested that "quick freezing" be accepted as the common denominator of the process upon which the industry rests rather than "sharp" or "fast" freezing. A commercial operator, we said should be called a "freezer" rather than a packer, or processor.

In early 1945 the leading associations then in the industry were the National Association of Frozen Food Packers, the Northwest Frozen Foods Association, the National Frozen Locker Association, the Frozen Food

Distributors Council of California, the Eastern Frosted Foods Association, the Chicago Frozen Foods Association, and the Western Frozen Foods Processors Association.

The first concentrate orange juice ad we ran was in December 1944 by Florida Frozen Fruits of Haines City, Florida. "Distributors wanted for frozen orange juice concentrate" the ad read. Charles Henderson was one of the partners; he was more recently connected with Mrs. Smith's Pies.

Growth Was Slow

In going over these issues covering the early years I am constantly impressed by the fact that our growth, and the industry's as well, *was slow, not fast.* It required hard work, year after year, with occasional setbacks every now and then. For many years QFF had to continue to sell prospective advertisers on the industry and its permanency.

I early realized that I had to know *two businesses*—that of being a publisher and being a frozen foods man as well. In this industry people want information and we had to be in a position to give it to them. Through the years QFF became a sort of "clearing house." We received many visitors each week; some were sent to us by others. They all wanted information on a number of diverse subjects ranging from products to food stores. I continually impressed upon our editors and advertising men the necessity of *learning the industry* so that we would know more about it than most of the people we talked to. If we didn't know the industry inside out, I figured, who would?

Several months before the Japanese surrender another vital meeting was held in Washington. The demand by the armed forces for leading frozen food items was ahead of the supply. Those who attended this meeting included George Hyslop, then Major Hyslop, B. C. Olney, Ed Huddleson, Ralph Dulany, Charles Seabrook, Ed White, A. B. Chappel, H. A. Carpenter, Ed Booker, F. J. Becker, Ted Skinner, A. J. Rogers, C. L. Snavely and others. The writer also attended the meeting.

Libby Starts

It was then that a large, new packer entered the field—Libby, McNeill & Libby. Under the direction of the late W. C. Mitchell, the company began to operate nationally. Almost from the beginning, it sold direct and through distributors and brokers. It probably had the smallest sales staff of any large packer—and still has. Our Chicago office was of some help to Libby in the matter of statistics and other information at this juncture.

I remember in 1945 making predictions about companies who would come into business. These included California Packing, Campbell, H. J. Heinz and Dole. Two right, two wrong! Campbell came in in a big way and so did Dole. But Del Monte still flirts on the edges, although Heinz does some limited freezing.

Standard Brands then operated several thousand wagon jobbing routes throughout the country and thereby had access to over 100,000 retailers.

Many times this company has been on the brink of going into the frozen foods business, but so far it hasn't taken the plunge.

Now all points were taken off frozen foods and the field was left wide open. This immediately encouraged the widespread production of all kinds of prepared and specialty foods. For instance a new operation was started in Oak Park, Ill., a joint freezing plant and retail store devoted entirely to the freezing of baked goods. This was called Frigid Dough Products Co., and it was quite successful. It probably was the first of the commercially baked goods operations which have since become so important in the industry. Among the first products packed were pies, muffins, chicken pies, cakes, rolls, angel food cake, clover leaf rolls, etc. I think this organization produced the first chicken pie that came out.

First Complete Meal

During this period the first commercial frozen cooked meal appeared on the market. This was a partially cooked platter, ready to heat and serve and developed by the W. L. Maxson Co. in New York. Each meal consisted of meat, vegetables, and potatoes frozen on an especially treated heat-resistant blue plate. The entire output was taken by the armed forces and a special oven was constructed for quick reheating.

There are now many Chinese frozen foods on the market but I will wager that few today can name the first packer of this nationality dish. It was the Breyer Ice Cream Co., under the name "Golden Pagoda." The line included frozen chow mein and chop suey with vegetables.

In May 1945 I wrote an article predicting the growth of the complete meal, then by no means perfected. I have never wavered from this belief and I still think that the meal will continue to grow for several years to come. Then, the few meals made were expensive; today a *far better* meal can be bought for 59¢ or less. Where can a consumer buy its equivalent in a restaurant? It is economical, saves dishes and cooking. It is the perfect answer to modern living. Of course, not every one wants a frozen meal but I believe there are *enough* Americans who will sacrifice home cooking for convenience. I also think there is room for a somewhat fancier meal in a slightly higher bracket.

What I consider to be an important turning point now came along—the introduction of a new packaging machine jointly developed by the Marathon Corp. and the Food Machinery Corp. For the first time a machine was now available which automatically set, opened, filled and closed a carton, and attained a speed of 80 12-ounce packages per minute. The machine was an immediate success and, with improvements, is still a leader today.

But the industry had its flops too. One was the North Wind Packing Co., in Washington, under the direction of Pat Conrad. Later, Associated Frozen Food Packers was to go in the same direction.

By this time QFF was running about 125 pages monthly and circulation had jumped to 9000. We had built up a good organization, including some

16 people. I made regular trips to all parts of the country and we had paid correspondents located in sixteen cities and covering 34 states.

Discouraged FF Stores

We received many inquiries about opening frozen food stores and I personally discouraged many young men whom I did not think qualified. To answer these inquiries we published a pamphlet entitled "I Want to Open a Frozen Food Store" which set forth the hazards and risks in such an enterprise as well as the glamour. We also published a handy, pocket-size book entitled "The Story of the Industry" which had wide distribution.

Those who did not live through this period, which prevailed until the end of the war, cannot conceive of the tremendous latent demand which had developed for frozen foods. Only a portion of what had been packed during the war trickled through to the consumer. Now, sensing a bonanza in frozen foods—and with the public's appetite whetted by samplings they had bought during the war—all were eager to get on the bandwagon. Orders piled up in 1945 for a crop not yet produced. Every indication pointed to a great increase in the number of packers and distributors as soon as equipment was released. Already, California had an anticipated pack of over 100 million pounds. With this background in mind, it is easier to understand the big post-war frozen food boom which ended in an inventory glut and price collapse.

3

Postwar Period – The War Is Over

With the cessation of hostilities came the relaxation of all restrictions except price ceilings. The War Production Board released vital materials. Bans on packaging and other materials were removed. The road was clear ahead.

Right after the war we issued our First Packers' Directory, a pocket-size book, purposely so made for men who travel. This issue listed 800 packers, as well as products and brand names, cross-listed three different ways.

By this time the avalanche of prepared frozen foods had started in earnest. Each issue of QFF carried scores of names of new packers of almost every conceivable item. Most of these names disappeared soon from the lists and were never heard from again. I remember going to New Orleans at the time. I have always considered this town as the birthplace of some of the more exotic dishes. A local restaurant, La Louisianne, began to market a line of precooked foods including some of their famous menu dishes. This was probably the first of a number of famous restaurants who used their name to promote their specialty dishes in frozen form. Those who followed suit were Maxim's of Paris, Luchow's and Chambord in New York.

We now began to worry about the quality of many frozen foods. In August, 1945, I wrote, "The quality of such items as peas is only fair; apricots and peaches, poor. Help is still scarce. Perhaps the wisest wartime policy adopted by any company was the one followed by Wrigley's Chewing Gum which, rather than lower its quality, took its name off the market until the firm could produce the same pre-war product. In these days quality, or lack of it, is often forgotten by the producer, distributor and retailer, but it is never forgotten by the consumer. A packer who doesn't watch quality can make money, fill orders and supply his trade. In fact he has nothing to lose but his *reputation.*"

I imagine the editorial was read, but everybody was busy filling orders and making money.

We Move to Wall Street

Our office was then located at 34th Street and Broadway where I had started. One day my assistant who knew we needed more space, came to me and said, "I've found just the place. It's at 82 Wall Street, and occupies the entire ground floor. And the entrance has bronze doors." I went down to see it and it was just what we needed and so, in 1945 we moved into those quarters. At first I was afraid that a Wall Street address might give the wrong impression, since the location still carried the stigma of the 1929 crash and depression, especially to people in the west. For a long time I carried the address "northwest corner of Water and Wall" on our letterheads. But in time we overcame our embarrassment about being associated with the financial district.

That summer I made my second trip to the West Coast and it was very revealing. I was impressed with the lush Wenatchee Valley which borders on the Columbia Basin. Today that area, which is near Lake Moses, has been irrigated and watered by the Grand Coulee Dam and offers tremendous opportunities for agriculture.

Enthusiasm Abounds

I was struck with the fast growth of cooperatives in the frozen food business, a trend which has continued ever since. Producer co-ops already were doing more than $5 billion worth of business and consumer co-ops an additional $2 billion. I think it would be interesting *now* to see the proportion of business done today in frozen foods by the producer co-ops.

With the end of the war, enthusiasm abounded on the West Coast. A strong retail trend in packing was evident in all products. At this time per capita consumption was 3.16 pounds. Everyone was aiming to increase it.

A new packer, whose product impressed me greatly, was Pacific Grape Products of Modesto, since gone out of business. The operation then was run by Stanley Tripplet and I think that many in the industry will agree that he produced the best frozen peaches and apricots ever seen up to that time. He used a vacuum pack can of the asparagus type and employed immersion freezing. The result was a firm, fresh appearing fruit that sold well.

But there were many new packers who did *not* know their business. Too many products were being packed for which there was no market. In an editorial QFF said: "The border line which exists between products that are canned and frozen often becomes very thin—the overstepping of which frequently spells disaster. Often packers are tempted to freeze what should rightfully be canned.

It is interesting to note that by 1945 there were 11 freezers of orange juice, all in or around the Los Angeles area. They were putting up *whole juice;* somehow the concentrate never got started in California. But in those days, orange juice was packed either in a can, bag, carton or even in glass jars. Many of these packers have since gone out of business: Consolidated Frozen Foods, Hart, LeVel, Parker, etc.

We Predict Concentrates

QFF then made a prediction in print that has been referred to since. We said: "Frozen, concentrated orange juice is *coming* and will be available every morning for the entire family, thus obviating the necessity of squeezing oranges." How true this became!

I must now recount a phase which, so far as I was concerned, added up to an opportunity lost. Around 1945 I went to Florida to investigate the potential of the concentrate business. I was convinced of its eventual success and had even so predicted in QFF. Here, oranges were rotting on the ground, and faced over-production and limited markets. You could buy good producing orange groves from $300-$500 an acre. I was sorely tempted to buy then, but was disuaded. I have always regretted not following my own inclination; groves now are selling *from $2500 up.* I have since learned to pay more attention to my own judgment.

Knight & Middleton of Clearwater, Fla., was the first company I can remember which actively produced a concentrate. Dr. Arthur Stahl of the Florida Citrus Commission and Dr. McDowell were active in experiments which began in 1944. They perfected a method of concentration by cold rather than by heat. Vacuum Foods, which started in Boston, later Minute Maid, were also perfecting a process. Public reaction to the new concentrate was first tested in a few selected stores of the People's Drug Company, Washington, D. C. chain. Here, the new juice, converted to its original state by the addition of water, was served to each customer without comment. For two weeks the test went on but during the whole time there was only one complaint. Later, when fresh fruit was actually squeezed to order, there were many requests for the concentrate. Other drug chains tried the new product and were enthusiastic about it. Next, the juice was introduced in some stores with an equally good response. But during the first two years of introduction the juice moved slowly.

Labor was still short. In the summer of 1945 the Army rushed soldiers to help harvest the big Washington state raspberry crop.

First FF TV Show

September of 1945 saw the production of the first television show featuring frozen foods. The show was sponsored by Marshall Field in Chicago, who demonstrated frozen foods at station WBKB. The telecast emphasized the fact that in the world of tomorrow the housewife will want more time for better living, hence would need frozen foods.

Warnings on Quality

Now more ominous warnings were sounded about poor quality. In October, 1945, QFF ran a full page editorial entitled "A Plea for Quality." We pointed out that consumer grades were not established and accepted by Mrs. Housewife and a brand had only its reputation to go on. Frozen foods were being taken "on trial" by many who had never heard of them before. It was essential to make a "good impression." Many leading packers and distributors signed the editorial which was widely distributed. So serious had the quality situation become.

At this time the USDA conducted transportation tests of frozen foods across the country. The tests showed that shipping frozen vegetables in a refrigerator car then cost slightly more than 1¢ per pound, including refrigeration. We kept pushing for mechanically refrigerated cars which actually did not come in any quantity until several years later. Dry ice cars were already in the experimental stage. However, the truck lines soon became impressed with the industry and immediately took steps to provide good service.

With paper somewhat easier we printed bigger issues. Many now ran over 160 pages. We told our readers that we were using the additional paper to *enlarge* the book and give present subscribers more material, instead of diverting this paper to printing more copies to obtain new subscriptions. We felt that our first duty was to our regular readers.

This period saw many new distributors entering the picture from all walks of life. Some were ex-servicemen, others had worked for packers or food companies; some had been auto dealers or appliance salesmen, one I knew was a stock broker and many came from the ranks of meat, seafood, fresh produce or the ice cream field. One firm which started after the war was Snow Kist Frozen Foods in Jersey City. Jack Karger, its head, had been a Birds Eye salesman before the war and after a stretch in the service he began to operate. Others to follow were Nassau-Suffolk Frozen Foods on Long Island under Morris Bahar, and Global in New York. George McRoberts was another who started originally in the butter and egg business, as was Allen Black.

Direct Selling Starts

But now some distributors were all ready becoming worried about *direct selling*. "Where can the line be drawn between selling a corner grocery and a chain?" We asked in QFF. "Certainly the carload buyer has an advantage over the case buyer." This issue was to flare up much more violently several years later, when dual pricing was recommended as the answer. About brokers, we had this to counsel: "The future of the successful broker does not lie alone in the sale of a car of merchandise—it rests on his all-around *ability to advise his packers* about marketing, merchandising and production. It lies further in the development of a special type of knowledge which will become increasingly in demand when the present period of easy selling is over." There are few "bulk" brokers left. Since then many, almost monthly, ask QFF for recommendations of good items, and we always try to oblige. Over the years, QFF has been responsible for helping many packers get brokers and brokers, packers.

In 1945, QUICK FROZEN FOODS joined the Audit Bureau of Circulation. Of 7,800 readers we then had more than 5,200 paid subscribers.

Industry meeting in the late forties, A. E. Stevens speaking.

E. J. Watson

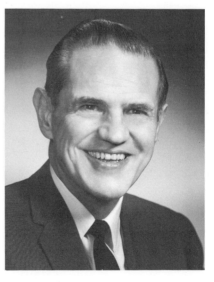

F. G. Lamb

Price Controls Story

Despite the fact that the war was over, food price controls were still on. As more merchandise came upon the market (the army had cancelled 50% of its proposed frozen vegetable take), retailers became more choosy. During the war they had taken everything they could get but with the war over they wanted items that had a good turnover record.

To satisfy demands we published an article and made it into a reprint entitled "How to Get Started in Frozen Food Distribution." We talked to successful distributors; Mazo Lerch in Washington; Lerman Bros., Shedd in Chicago, Frozen Food Distributors in Oakland, Jester in Wilmington, Good Bros. in Philadelphia and many others.

The late Sol Rosenthal, who took over Ed White's brokerage business, was an active figure in those days, a man known and liked for his excellent sense of humor.

First National Convention

Up to this point, the only frozen food conventions the industry had held were the two we ran in Chicago, in 1941 and 1942. The war had prevented further meetings. But now, with the industry expanding, many felt the need for a national convention, and we started our first campaign toward this end. We pointed out that for years the industry had met as a small part or appendage of the huge National Canners Convention. But we also said that more and more new packers were not in the canning business, and even those who were operated their frozen foods business separately. There was also a growing list of freezers putting up poultry, seafoods, meats, cooked foods, specialties. The problems of the frozen foods industry, then as now, are peculiar to itself. Thus the time had come for a separate convention. Packers decided to meet during the Canners Convention in Atlantic City in February, 1946. As the convention drew near many packers found it impossible to get accommodations. The canners had allotted the frozen foods industry very minor space and some of the largest packers were lodged in the Fox Manor hotel behind the boardwalk. The convention committee was dismayed and angered; at the time it included Courtney Seabrook, Ralph Dulany, Carl Kolb, Mary Drumm, Keith Burr of the National Association, and the writer. This unfortunate and overcrowded week, I think, did more than anything else to push the industry into its *own conventions and away from the canners*.

The temper of packers was such that a separate convention was inevitable and it was scheduled for San Francisco the following year. Ed Huddleson, a Stokley official, now was the new president. He had worked with Ed Gibson during the war and had attended many Washington conferences. We wrote at the time: "Mr. Huddleson, a southerner by birth, is a Californian by nature and has a frank, clear and logical approach to industry problems." Many spoke up now against poor quality. One was Ed Gibson, president of Birds Eye, who said: "One dead apple may spoil a whole basket, so one opportunist may not only bankrupt himself but grievously hurt *the rest of* the industry." Good packers in those days weren't afraid for themselves—but of the *other fellow!*

Pratt's Frozen Foods was another operation which attracted much attention in New York. It had a good start, backed by a stock issue which was widely sold. Pratt Thomas, formerly Navy man, was a pioneer frozen foodster and, together with Ben Smith, ran the operation. The company later ran into trouble and finally liquidated.

Snow Crop Enters

In November, 1945 a new firm bowed its way modestly into the industry, but made a tremendous splash later on. This was Snow Crop Marketers. Jack Moone, a former Birds Eye sales manager, and before that an Armour meat salesman, announced the new company whose purpose was the marketing of a complete line of fruits and vegetables under the Snow Crop label. The first office was established in San Francisco, though later the headquarters moved to New York. Associated with Moone were Nat Barclay and Marty Mathews who had also been with Birds Eye. A group of non-competitive producers had been organized to furnish a complete line under the Snow Crop label and distribution, it was stated, would be through selected wholesale distributors in key markets. Sales expanded quickly, almost from the start. However, Snow Crop did not adhere to the distributor as a means of selling. If I remember rightly, SC was the first of the big packers to sell direct to large retailers and sparked off the movement in this direction. But this came later. Both Moone and Barclay are now dead.

Anhydrous Foods

Toward the end of 1945, that versatile genius, Clarence Birdseye, had turned his attention to a new method of food preservation which he presented under the name of anhydrous foods. Just as he applied the principles of quick freezing to low temperatures, so he now turned these same principles to use in drying—a rapid extraction of moisture at high temperatures. The result was the best dehydrated, or anhydrous products yet produced, which the American Home Products Co. tried to introduce for retail distribution. I remember visiting Birdseye in his New York hotel where he exhibited some of those foods. Broccoli, for instance, thus preserved under his special process, maintained a fine color, though shriveled in appearance. Mashed potatoes looked good, carrots also. But even this superior method of dehydrating failed and frozen foods considered it no threat. The quick freezing method was still able to beat all comers— and by the same token I don't think irradiated foods will ever be a major threat to the home market. Quick freezing is a natural method of preservation, not an artificial one. Freezing does not *destroy* nutrients, as does high heat or radiation, it merely *suspends.* After defrosting, the original composition of the food remains, but in the more violent methods of preservation often radical changes in taste and appearance result.

In emergencies freeze drying and irradiated foods will undoubtedly play important roles, but where consumers enjoy a high standard of living I think always the best will be demanded.

Distributors' Association Formed

In December, 1945 a new association was formed which promised to have a great influence upon the industry. This was the National Wholesale Frozen Food Distributors Association which met for the first time at the Yale Club in New York and set up its organization. The meeting had been called at the instigation of Burton L. Prince of Food Distributors, Inc. of New Haven, who was elected the first president. Other officials were George McRoberts and William Walsh of Morrison, McCluan in Pittsburgh, vice presidents; Peter Jenkins of the General Ice Cream Corp., treasurer, and Carl Seaburgh of White Plains, secretary. The new association outlined as its objectives the resolve to promote production, consumption and distribution of frozen foods, and the interests of the wholesale distributor, and to standardize and generally improve business practices between wholesalers, packers and retailers. Others on the first board were George Bickley, George Boynton, Raymond Buck, Stanley Fenton, Joseph Gaudio, Arthur Greason, Howard Jester, Henry Landau, Albert Richards, Jr., and Israel Sky, Altoona.

A Potato Prediction

Another new freezer on the scene was Simplot, who had started as a dehydrator. The firm now installed freezing equipment and the first product was in corn, followed by peas, strawberries and lima beans. A French fried potato plant was in the experimental stage and this turned out to be most important of all. Leon Jones, who leads the operation, early predicted that one day potatoes would outsell peas. How right he proved to be!

QFF was now widely quoted by the press: CBS, *Christian Science Monitor, New York Herald Tribune* (we were mentioned in a *Times* editorial), the *New Yorker, Journal of Commerce, Wall Street Journal, Tide, New York World-Telegram, House Beautiful, Outdoor Life* and many other media. Boldly we launched a campaign to improve the industry. Among improvements we first suggested bettering the original product. We outlined the need for better vegetable varieties, the need for a stronger strain of strawberry in the Northwest (which has come about). We urged the development of machinery for better grade separation and continuous quality grading. We stressed the need for a superior blanching process so that fruits would remain firmer. We demanded the *zero ideal*. In packaging we cried for quicker filling equipment and more economical packaging of consumer sizes. We asked for an improvement in descriptive labeling since many packages lacked necessary information; some packers described cooking periods as shorter than they actually were. We stressed the need for self-service store cabinets and many other reforms. We always strove for a higher industry goal.

Importance of Warehouses

None of us can underestimate the importance of cold storage warehouses to the industry. Indeed, without them there would have been no beginning to frozen foods. Such organizations as Quincy Cold Storage in Boston, Quaker City in Camden, Merchants Ref. and Manhattan Ref. in New York proved to be among the first to act as depots for frozen foods.

More recently a group of leading warehouses joined together to offer a concerted service program to the industry. They operated under the name Trans-American Refrigerated Services, or "TARS."

In California, some early warehouse operations included the Union Ice, Calif. Consumers, (the first processors to build their own storage,) and the National Ice & Cold Storage Co. In the Northwest, Terminal Ice and Northwestern Ice were other early warehouses.

Today warehouses receive competition from changing methods of distribution in the industry, with emphasis on storage at producing and distribution points; some chains are putting up their own zero space though later experience seems to indicate that public warehouses are the most economical. (More on warehouses later.)

Seafoods Grow

The fish industry began to grow now. Booth Fisheries was one of the first to develop pre-breaded fillets, and General Seafoods had a fish cake on the market. Portion control fillets, also were being sold by O'Donnell-Usen who, together with Atlantic Coast Fisheries, were leaders in New England. Improved filleting machinery was being introduced, which reduced costs.

About this period Howard Johnson Restaurants were conducting tests on precooked foods with the aim of supplying a large number of their restaurants with these items. Development of the idea has been gradual, and now a selected line of entrees under this well-known name enjoys excellent distribution.

Here, I would like to pay tribute to a few others who contributed greatly to various facets of this expanding industry. One was Fred Deutsch of Marathon who promoted higher speed packaging equipment and who worked closely with packers, especially during the critical deflation period. Carl Wuestenfeld of Western Waxide was another packaging pioneer—there were many more. Dr. Frank App of Seabrook Farms was an outstanding frozen foods technician and gave QFF much information. Another was Joe Guinane, head of BE production and Ken Eberts of Stokely. There are many, many more technical men who rendered and continue to render outstanding service though many are now retired. I hope they will forgive me if space does not permit me to mention them all.

Whip Topping

In 1945 a new and important product was introduced by Bob Rich—a Whip Topping, which was to become very successful. A soy bean whipped cream, it revolutionized the use of dessert topping; originally it had been born during the war when the sale of whipping cream was forbidden. After the war, when real cream was released, the new company faced a crisis. But the original idea proved sound and it now seems that the soy bean cream has permanently taken its place and that its non-fattening advantage guarantees it a permanent niche in the American diet. Bob Rich is one of the younger frozen food pioneers who, through his persistence in sticking to his original idea, has provided frozen foods history with a real success story.

An Avalanche of Prepared Foods

The avalanche of prepared foods gained in size and momentum. All kinds of stews, meat balls, spaghetti, ravioli, shrimp creole, oyster stew, frozen bread dough, etc. Few of the sponsors of these products stayed in the business, although many of these products have since become successful. They just weren't timed right.

Right here I want to say something about *timing*. After observing this industry closely for well over 25 years it is, to my mind, of the utmost importance. Over and over I have seen the failure of good products just because the timing was wrong, though later, others who brought out the same products at the crest of the wave rode on to success. Just what is "timing?" Orange juice is an example, complete dinners another. The latter item was available years before it clicked. Of course, vigor of promotion and advertising often put over a product which had hitherto been a "sleeper." One example is frozen soups which Campbell made a best-seller, though good soups had been on the market at least ten years previously. Today there are more and better yardsticks for measuring public acceptance than there were 10 or 15 years ago. But timing is still *the prime factor*.

In 1945 QUICK FROZEN FOODS gave its first luncheon at the Advertising Club in New York for various agencies and food accounts. Clarence Birdseye was QFF's guest of honor and speaker. The menu consisted entirely of frozen food specialties shipped from all parts of the country.

This year saw the start of another important eastern packer—Southern Frozen Foods. The late Phil Rizzuto had been in the produce business and a frozen food distributor since 1938 and, together with Ted Delson, started the first plant at Plant City, Fla. The company began to specialize in string beans and strawberries, and was the first to freeze vegetables in Florida. Later, other southern and winter vegetables were added. In 1956 Delson left the organization and Rizzuto took over as president with Herman Kennery, an outstanding production executive, as president and Charles Rizzuto as executive vice president. This company is continuing to expand, as are other eastern and southern packers. I have always believed that packing operations located near the big population eastern markets, with their consequent freight rate advantage, will continue to grow larger as time goes by.

Original Boil-in-the-Bag

During this period I became interested in the "boil-in-bag" process of which I have been a strong advocate ever since. I must give original credit for the idea to Ken Singer, who formerly had been in the ice cream business and who was a descendant of the Singer of sewing machine fame. He first came to our office around 1945 and brought samples of crudely sealed parchment bags in which he had packed a number of meat entrees and similar dishes which could be cooked. His difficulty was in the closure; he was then using a rough metal collar. He later established a plant in Bronxville, N.Y. I was impressed with the fact that by reheating in the bag, (1) all of the original juices and flavor were retained, not possible in any other way of heating, (2) no cooking utensils had to be used other than a pot of hot water. Later, Clarence Birdseye told me that he had been using the bag method since his earliest days in Gloucester. He exhausted all air from the bag, froze the products and then stored them in the same bag. "These bagged products," he said, "were very readily prepared for the table merely by dropping the sealed bag in boiling water or steaming them in a covered pot. In this way there was no danger of scorching and no escape of aroma."

I think we were right in our appraisal of this system; today there is widesperad interest in it. Seabrook has marketed a whole line of excellent prepared dishes in the bag form. Others followed; more lately Green Giant has marketed a complete line of prepared vegetables in boilable bags and the idea has caught on institutionally. Birds Eye, whose prepared vegetable line has been very successful, is reported to be going to boilable bags. In Europe, boilable bags are very popular and are used in almost every country. Also there arc far better materials available which stand the pressure, such as polyethylene and various adaptations. I think in the future the "boil-in-the-bag" process, advocated in QFF in 1945, will become an *important method* of reheating.

Buyers on the West Coast

In June, 1946 we witnessed what I think was the greatest congregation of buyers ever assembled. They flocked to Seattle, all determined to get strawberries. The result was a fantastic upbidding and berries were sold from 32-34¢ a pound, and in retail packages around $4.50 a dozen. QFF wrote: "This is further confirmation that the times are out of joint in this present strange postwar economy. In 1941 growers were getting 5-6¢ a pound. Today berries are retailing from 50¢-60¢ a package and the institutional trade will pay 37-38¢ a pound. Yet the opportunity is here for the industry to give the public a good product at a reasonable price." We saw that this was the result of an accumulated demand on one area, then the only suppliers of frozen berries of any quantity. Again we wrote: "In QFF's opinion there is no power on earth that could have stopped this price spiral and it is just as well to let the trade gct it out of its system and start fresh next year at prices which will appeal to the masses."

Expansion in Canada, West

I mention this because it now became evident that new areas for strawberry production had to be opened if the coming demand was to be filled. We began to run editorials urging that new centers be opened to relieve the concentration on the Northwest. We recommended California, Texas and the Rio Grande Valley. Everyone knows how California has since developed as a strawberry producing state!

During this period I visited western Canada where Delnor Frosted Foods had just started. I want to pay tribute here to one of Canada's pioneers, W. H. Heeney, president of Heeney Frosted Foods in Quebec. He started about 25 years ago and did much to promote the frozen foods idea throughout Canada where he operates several branches. Heeney is also a distributor of several American brands and opened a plant on Prince Edward Island. He started with the freezing of strawberries, after considerable research. Heeney's first distribution was through milk wagons in Montreal and Toronto. Later, he installed freezers in retail stores and branched out into vegetables. The first pack of retail peas was launched in Canada about 1936.

Another important developer of Canada's FF industry was C. B. Powell of Montreal. He did so much to encourage new processing and distribution in the Canadian market and travelled widely in the U. S. and Europe, bringing to Canada many of the ideas he found abroad.

A new packer in the Northwest that year was Evergreen Frozen Foods. Another was Alderman Farms in Oregon, since purchased. Birds Eye installed its new plant at Walla Walla. This was the biggest pea plant up to that time, and it was to play a very important part in the future production of peas.

In California, Mario Ielmini started Patterson Frozen Foods which has been outstandingly successful since. His first products were peaches, apricots and lima beans. Ielmini had come from Italy at the age of 17 with no knowledge of English and little money. He eventually settled in California. Originally he went into the baking business but soon began to freeze peaches, apricots and lima beans. Through perseverance and adherence to sound packing policies, Patterson Frozen Foods gradually became one the leading plants in the state. Early, Ielmini was convinced that a packer should own his own zero storage space and continued to work in this direction.

Few Stick

Of every 10 plants opened in those days only three or four are still in business. Associated Frozen Foods, an over-expanded plant, was taken over about this time. In Modesto, the Modesto Refrigerating Co., a new freezing center, began to rise and it was occupied by several packers. In

Sanger the Glacier Packing Co. was organized by Harold Loeffler, formerly of the USDA. John Inglis, later to become one of the largest volume producing independent packers in the state, was operating in Stockton.

A frequent contributor to QFF then was Leo Young, formerly of the U. S. Fish & Wildlife Service and now a prominent seafood broker.

On my third trip to California I wrote this about the Los Angeles of 1946: "This is a fast moving area where everyone wants to make a million dollars—and *sometimes* they do!"

Cans were making their appearance for the first time in the retail pack. Both American Can and Continental Can were supplying tins for berries and other fruits and the fibre, metal-end containers were also available.

"Battle of Brands" Begins

And now began an era often described as "the battle of the brands." Chain brands had not yet become a factor, but the demand for frozen foods was increasing and cabinet space was still limited. Whereas, before and during the war, there had been only one national company, with several other brands as light competitors, now there were new ones struggling to share the space: Libby, Snow Crop, Stokely's Honor Brand and others. The easy selling days were coming to an end and contracting margins were approaching. But many frozen foods were still high in cost, over-inflated. In August 1946 we ran an editorial entitled: "Who Will Hold the Ball When the Whistle Blows?" There was a picture of three basketball players, labeled packer, distributor and retailer. They all played with a ball entitled: "High Cost Frozen Food Items." The text read: "Sometimes, perhaps soon, the whistle, in the form of fixed consumer resistance to over-priced, under-quality frozen foods, is going to blow. When it does, the game stops and the player who holds the ball is stuck with it."

Shades of a Recession

The whistle was to blow soon and *everyone* was to be stuck with it. Time and again we clearly warned the industry that an adjustment was under way, and so did many leaders.

We did much at this time to get better attention from the railroads. Railroad men and the industry were still 15 degrees apart in their thinking on temperature protection. The answer, of course, lay in more super-insulated cars. In order to stimulate the carriers QFF ran an editorial entitled: "10,000 Railroad Cars—Not Chicken Feed." We estimated that 10,000 cars would be needed for frozen foods during the coming year. There were then only about 1500 insulated cars. The result was that the Department of Agriculture took an interest and ran more frequent tests. The Pacific Fruit Express responded quickly and built many cars, as did Merchants Dispatch and the Union Pacific.

Some Southern Packers

At Knoxville, Tenn., a new company was started by Ed Booker, a former auto man. Other southern packers were starting up then, the late Cliff Bateman, a large peach grower in Macon, Georgia, had by 1946, already reached an eight million pounds production. He developed in southern vegetables, peaches and shrimp. Another was Marion T. Fannaly, who died several years ago. Friendly and enterprising, he started from scratch in Ponchatoula, La., and built up one of the largest storage and freezing plants in the south. Another old timer was A. Montz of La Place, La. The firm specialized in winter and southern vegetables, as well as shrimp and okra gumbo, a native product.

Concentrates Start—Fox

I have spoken briefly about the beginning of concentrating in Florida. Now, actual large scale operations began to go up. The first was the Pasco Packing Co., formerly a cooperative, but now run as a private enterprise company. L. C. Edwards, Jr. was in charge of frozen juices and I think the first pack consisted of a four-ounce concentrate.

It was expected that the following year Florida would produce a concentrate which would cut the price of whole frozen juice by 30-40%. In 1946 Snow Crop introduced orange juice concentrate in the New York and Philadelphia markets and at the same time another company which was to make a great splash in the industry got its start—*Minute Maid*.

It was announced in QFF in April 1946 that John M. Fox, president of Vacuum Foods Corp., an outgrowth of the National Research Corp. of Boston, had completed the company's first plant in Florida. At the beginning both concentrate and an orange powder were produced. The new Plymouth plant was equipped to handle 20,000 gallons of fresh orange juice per day.

Jack Fox started his career at Colgate University but, desiring to get into the business world he quit school. He sold shoes and insurance; he ran a filling station. He then joined International Business Machines and soon became a senior salesman. His next venture was with National Research Corp., Boston, where he became interested in high vacuum studies, one of National Research's specialties.

Laboratory experiments were getting under way in application of these principles to orange juice. A Florida pilot plant was considered, but finances were needed. Fox interested Whitney, the New York financier, and William Coolidge, a Boston banker, in the project. After some early difficulties, financing was arranged.

Stock was sold and the company's first plant at Plymouth, Fla., was ready to produce for the beginning of the 1945 processing season.

Orange powders and institutional concentrate were the first products. At that time Snow Crop was getting started, too, and Minute Maid's

R. P. Fletcher, Jr.

W. M. Walsh

This building, completed in 1945, in Plymouth, Fla., was Minute Maid's first national headquarters. Since that time, the structure has been added to until it has tripled in size and is now used as the administration building for the Plymouth plant.

first contract was to produce for this label. Fox subsequently developed Minute Maid into a $100 million business which has since been sold to Coca Cola. Fox is now chairman of the board of United Fruit.

Ambrose E. Stevens joined Minute Maid and was elected vice president, a position he held for the next ten years. He later became manager of the National Cranberry Association in Hanson, Mass. and is now a prominent consultant.

On the West Coast Twin City Foods, run by Arne Lervick, was incorporated in Stanwood, Wash. From modest beginnings, this operation has become one of the most important in the Northwest. As time went on, new mechanical equipment was added until the plant was a model of efficient production. Under able management it has progressed far.

Tips to Readers

In April 1946 we announced a new high circulation of 8500 copies on an ABC basis. We said at the time: "QFF has patterned its circulation to fit the contours of an expanding industry. In short, there is no waste in QFF's circulation for each copy of the magazine goes to *someone* who is actively engaged or shortly to be associated with some phase of frozen foods."

Since the magazine was growing pretty large, we published some tips on reading. In tip No. 1 we told subscribers: "You can't read a magazine like QFF in a hurry any more than you can digest a fine well-cooked meal in fifteen minutes. You can't read this magazine in one sitting. But make up your mind to one thing: QFF is well *worth* reading and it is necessary that you set an adequate time aside each month for its perusal, preferably two hours. We guarantee the time will be well spent."

Tip No. 2—"don't open the magazine haphazardly, starting at the back or in the middle. You can't get much out of a magazine that way. Start on page 1 and you'll want to continue right through. *Read it like a book.* If interrupted, put a mark where you left off and continue later. Finish one article at a time. We don't expect you to read every article, only the ones in which you are interested, but read them through."

We also told readers to familiarize themselves with the layout of the magazine—it is generally the same. Thus, they would know immediately in which part of the magazine to look for the section in which they were most interested. And these suggestions on reading still hold true today!

As early as 1945 QFF offered a Readership Guarantee to its advertisers, one which I think has never been equalled in the publishing field. We offered (and still offer) to let any advertiser make a mailing to any legitimate list of frozen food packers, distributors, chain buyers, etc., at our expense, inquiring which publication in the frozen foods industry they prefer and read. We guarantee that QFF will come out at least 5 to 1 ahead. About 32 such tests have been made in recent years by advertisers and agencies and *in no case* has QFF emerged with a lead of less than 5 to 1.

"The Frozen Food Critic"

In 1946 we introduced our readers to a testing kitchen operated by Miss Laura Track, whose page, "The Frozen Food Critic," became and still is a regular feature in QFF. Miss Track is an experienced home economist and each month she analyzes various new products as they come upon the market. These comments, whether favorable or not, are always frank and constructive and have been very valuable to many packers. Products are given numbers, companies are never mentioned.

Fish Expands

The frozen seafood branch of the industry now began to become very active. A large number of new labels made their appearance; many came from Nova Scotia and other parts of Canada, and fillets were coming from Iceland and the Scandinavian countries. In one year U.S. fish imports jumped from 10 to 42 million pounds.

In frozen seafoods several brands were now becoming popular. In Gloucester, Gorton's was introducing new items: fish cakes and new fillet packages. This company, under the direction of Paul Jacobs and Fritz Bundy, has done much to lead the fish industry to higher levels. It was the first to adopt inspection and grading.

Blue Water, managed by Bob Gruber, another leader in the National Fisheries Institute, and an exponent of portion control seafoods, was emerging. The company is now owned by Gorton's. Forty Fathoms was an important brand, too, and, at Atlantic Coast Fisheries, a new filleting machine was installed to reduce labor costs and increase yields.

Precooked Seafoods

Filleting machines soon became standard equipment in most plants. Earlier, another firm, started by Louis L. Libby had, in 1943, introduced the first precooked frozen codfish cakes, scallops and shrimp. Later the firm became the Red L Corp. Onion rings, crab cakes, fish dinners and complete seafood and fish dinners were made. Gorton's also own Red L.

The first packer to freeze Alaska King crab was Lowell Wakefield, who marketed the first 12 ounce retail packaging carrying his name in 1947.

Meanwhile the craze for prepared and cooked foods was stronger than ever. New items were coming out all the time and some were rather far-fetched—and, I might add, shortlived. Examples: franks and sauerkraut, banana whip, pea soup and ham chips, Brunswick stew and other dishes for which there was no adequate market. I would say that of hundreds of prepared food companies that started up at that time, only about five per cent remained in business. By October 1946, there were already 737 packers of frozen foods. Most of them were fruit and vegetable processors, but there were 163 seafood freezers and 100 packers of cooked foods and specialties.

In 1946 the industry had packed over 800 million pounds of fruits and vegetables. Continuous U.S. inspection was beginning to be adopted by many plants. In California, John Inglis Frozen Foods announced inspection; so did California Consumers.

In California in 1941 there were about eight packers—in 1946 there were eighty! In 1941 California produced about 13 million pounds; in 1945 the pack had grown to over 200 million pounds or 30% of the national pack. Burt Harrison was then, and for many years thereafter, secretary of the Western Frozen Foods Association. He did an outstanding job in the industry and got together the first regular production figures from his state which he sent regularly to members. This provided some curb on overpacking. He retired in 1958.

Gradually at first, but later with accelerating speed, the industry's big blow-up was approaching. By the end of 1946, tonnage had boomed to 1,300 million pounds, almost double that of the year before. Much of it was in weak hands and of subquality. Inventory losses were threatening as prices dropped.

Large retail markets began to advertise sales and price levels were forced down. Many banks, which had loaned money indiscriminately up to 90% inventory, were beginning to cut drastically in the other direction.

Up to that time the industry had been standing on the edge of a cliff and what probably pushed it over the edge was a story that appeared in the *Wall St. Journal,* Dec. 12th 1946, headed "Frozen Food Drop—A Glut on the Market." Holdings in cold storage were then *860 million pounds* in fruits and vegetables alone. The article had an immediate damaging effect on credit and confidence in the industry.

Since 1945, QFF had constantly warned its readers that a slow-down was at hand, the natural outcome of a cycle of price deflation. At this time we wrote: "The present trend will just have to run its course," which it did. A number of firms were eliminated but, surprisingly, not as many as had been expected. Most held on.

One that didn't was the S. A. Moffett Co., Seattle, which had one of the finest distributor set-ups in the country. While inventories grew, Moffett continued to construct new buildings and enlarge capacity. By 1946 his sales were almost $6 million, large at that time. The crash swept the business away. Moffett became a broker, but died not long thereafter, one of the tragedies of that era.

In New York, another firm, Pratt's Frozen Foods, started by Pratt Thomas, was to fail for similar reasons. It had been financed for expansion on a stock issue, but its annual report in 1946 showed a $200,000 loss. The late B. P. Smith was then president of the company, which later closed its operation.

Our Wall Street Meeting

When the industry was at its lowest ebb, we decided to do what we could to help the situation. The financial fraternity was very important, because in their hands rested the financing of the coming pack. It was vital that their confidence in the industry be strengthened.

I suggested that a meeting be held in early 1947 between leading bankers and leaders in the industry. I was put in charge of the affair and QFF gave a luncheon on January 28, 1947, at the Wall Street Club in New York, which was attended by some 50 frozen food and financial leaders.

The packers were represented by E. T. Gibson of Birds Eye, Ed Huddleson of Honor Brand, Charles Seabrook of Seabrook Farms, Ted McCaffrey, National Fruit Canning, C. L. Snavely, Consumers Packing, E. J. White, Sacramento Frozen Foods, Robert Arneson, North Pacific Canners, Ted Delson, Southland, Burton Prince, then president of the distributors' association, and William Walsh, its board chairman.

I opened the meeting and announced its purpose. Ed Gibson told the bankers that there were not enough good quality frozen foods to meet the demand, and that many people had come into the industry who were not equipped to produce quality merchandise.

He said that banks were at fault, to a degree, for some excessive inventory loans that were unwarranted, but he also emphasized the long-range potentialities of the industry. He did a good job of convincing.

Another speaker, Ed Huddleson, then president of the National Association, pointed to the cabinet bottleneck and he predicted that in another year the industry would be well out of its congestion of merchandise. I gave some pertinent figures on the current inventory, as compared with immediate and future demands. Charles Seabrook and others spoke.

The bankers listened gravely, asked a few questions, and came away from the meeting with renewed confidence in the industry's future. They had met the industry's top men and were satisfied.

The Tide is Turned

The bankers who attended represented Lehman Bros., Irving Trust Co., Bank of Manhattan, Industrial Bank of Commerce, Marine Midland, Empire Trust, Chase National, Corn Exchange, New York Trust, Chemical Bank & Trust, Brown Bros., Harriman, Commercial National Bank, Manufacturers Trust, National City Bank and many others. I received many letters from these bankers after the meeting and they thanked QFF for giving them a clearer picture of the industry.

I think this meeting was one of the industry's *milestones,* for shortly thereafter credit began to loosen, prices firmed and the industry was on the way to recovery. It was also one of the most useful contributions QFF made to the trade in those days.

The industry learned one very important lesson from it all—the *quality* lesson. Never again did producers become as careless about quality as they had been, and since then frozen foods have maintained a consistently higher quality in all items.

Handling Large Inventories

We learned another lesson, too. Big inventories aren't always bad. The danger is in *whose* hands they are held. If stocks are in weak hands there is danger ahead, but if they are in strong hands the situation is not too serious. In this respect, the gradual improvement of the financial position of many packers in more recent years has had much to do with stabilizing situations which might have proved disastrous a decade earlier.

Our Foreign Visitors

We had many visitors from abroad and they made QFF their head-quarters. Attracted by the growth of the American frozen foods industry, investigators from foreign countries came to the U.S. and we were able to give them much help. I remember several. One was Wallace Smedley who represented the second largest packer in England. Another was the late George Muddiman of Birds Eye of Great Britain, later president of that country's packers' association.

Louis Lowenthal, head of the frozen food department of J. Lyons & Co., one of Britain's most important food operations, was another visitor. He was then establishing "Frood," a line of prepared foods which have had great success in England.

I made many friends in England and always enjoyed greatly the friend-liness and hospitality so prevalent in that country. But more on this later.

From France came M. Bamberger of Maison Olida, a large meat firm interested in complete meals. A frequent visitor to this country is Louis Vaudable of Maxim's restaurant in Paris. Vaudable put up a very fine, but expensive, complete meal employing some of Maxim's finest French recipes and he still supplies some airlines.

At this point, frozen poultry production began to expand rapidly, especially in the Delaware, Maryland and Virginia areas and in the Shenandoah Valley. Georgia soon became the second state in broiler production. Utah, California, Washington and southern New Jersey began to produce large quantities of frozen chickens. Birds Eye opened up a modern plant in Maryland, still one of the finest in the country. In Omaha, Swanson began to sell cutup turkeys.

Annual Yearbook

In March, 1947, in conjunction with the San Francisco convention, really the industry's first national convention, excepting our own in 1941 and 1942, we issued our first year-book. It ran almost 300 pages and contained industry information of all kinds, including our first production map, a packaging section, an equipment directory, production figures, a cabinet section showing the latest in boxes, a list of refrigerated truck lines showing terminals, market prices and about fifty other features—plus a few predictions. We were very proud of this issue which was the biggest in our history up to then.

A Rebirth of Confidence

The San Francisco convention was held at a critical time: The industry was just coming out of its first crisis. But the industry had plenty of vitality. Registration was over 5,000, and there were 100 beautiful exhibits in San Francisco's Civic Auditorium. Over 1,000 attended the banquet.

Gone was the wave of pessimism that had recently swept the industry. There was a rebirth of confidence everywhere. Courtney Seabrook was elected third president of the association which, in a few short years, had built up a very substantial treasury and was enlarging its Washington staff to permit a program of intensified consumer research.

The association also developed tentative standards. The convention was supported wholeheartedly by the National Frozen Food Distributors' Association and, as I look back at it now, I firmly wish that the unison which prevailed then could have continued *permanently*.

At the suggestion of one of our readers, we then adopted a slogan "The magazine that grew up with the Industry."

An interesting sidelight during the convention gave rise to the following story. During the meeting there occurred an unusual and brief snow flurry. The quick-witted mayor of San Francisco immediately issued a statement that he had "ordered it especially for the frozen foods convention."

Start of Big Scale Price Cutting

About the middle of 1947 real price-cutting among packers became apparent. There had always been competition, but big scale price cuts among national packers, and fiercer competition for cabinet space, started with the entrance of Snow Crop and Libby into the field.

This immediately *increased* the complete lines available to retailers. Snow Crop was responsible for ushering in direct selling and by-passing the wholesaler, though I suppose it would have come sooner or later, anyway. But Snow Crop was also responsible for starting the trend toward a smaller 10 ounce package, which the rest of the industry had to follow eventually.

Package after package shrank, following the dictates of competition.

The situation gave rise in one of our issues to the following ditty:

I hope that I shall sometimes see,
That mythical, gaunt family,
Whose appetites are models for
This recipe "serves four or more."

Our Tenth Anniversary

In August, 1948, we celebrated our tenth anniversary. We had achieved a circulation of 10,000 copies a month, the largest in the field. There were now 700 packers, as against 200 in 1938, 250 brokers against 40, and 50,000 stores handling frozen foods compared with 10,000 which was the number when our first issue was published.

We predicted in our tenth anniversary issue that during the next ten years prepared foods would become stabilized, that chains would come heavily into the picture and with their own brands, and that mergers would increase. All of this came about not too long thereafter.

We found that the "shakeout" of packers, which the *Wall Street Journal* had so vociferously predicted a few months previously, had *not* materialized. Of the eighteen fruit and vegetable packers who had gone out or been in difficulty, ten had been reorganized and were still in business.

New packers were coming in, too. The American Fruit Growers of Los Angeles, a large and well-financed company, had been studying the industry for several years. Their Blue Goose label was nationally known to housewives and they decided to spearhead a complete line of frozen fruits and vegetables with this brand.

For awhile the brand went well but soon it was being buffeted about in the price wars between older national brands. About three years after its inception, American Fruit Growers decided to withdraw from the frozen food field.

Another who started early was Borden, who had put its "Elsie" label on a line of frozen foods. I think this proved that size and strong finances are *not enough* to put over a brand in this industry, which is indeed a complicated one. However, Borden later re-entered the industry through the purchase of Henderson's and others.

An extra "fifth" sense is needed and history also shows that most successes have been made by those who had some previous experience in frozen foods. Companies who later entered the field and who were successful generally *hired or took over* an organization with frozen food experience.

New Conservatism on Coast

When I went to the coast that year I reported that real conservatism had hit the Northwest, and in some cases packers have not yet recovered from this severe reaction. But there was a reason: Where banks previously had been lending 85% and even to 100% on the dollar, the figure now had been reduced to 50%. The California situation was somewhat shaky.

Incidentally, at this time a new threat presented itself, pre-packaged fresh produce. It appeared with a flourish but, while pre-packaged vegetables are still sold, they are available in season only, and never really challenged the industry.

In California I attended the opening of a large new plant, Ventura Farms Frozen Foods at Oxnard. This was a corporate set-up, backed by a cooperative, and run by the late Bill Salter. Geo. Rees is now manager.

Automation Takes Over

I noticed for the first time how automation was beginning to take hold. Forklift trucks were employed in greater quantities in the industry. Fast filling machinery became almost universal in a short period of time. Roller conveyors were installed in many plants, and the main objective of all packers was straight line production.

Frigidinner in Philadelphia, under the late Jack Fisher, had started to pack the first complete meals, some of which were going to the armed

Bing Crosby signing his first contract with Minute Maid Corp., 1948. Looking on are Donald Clifford (left), president of Doherty, Clifford & Shenfield advertising agency, and Ambrose E. Stevens, vice president of Minute Maid.

Industry woes were depicted in this QFF cartoon showing a car labeled 1946-47 ff carryover stalled on the tracks. Industry representatives are desperately trying to push it out of the way before it is hit by the train ("1948 pack season"). It was captioned, "Will they get the car off the track in time?"

J. Fox

J. I. Moone

forces. Twenty Minute Dinner Co. also had meals. All kinds of baked goods were coming on the market: Cup cakes, cream puffs, angel loaf cake, blueberry muffins (by Little America), custard pies, nut cake, baked alaska, chocolate chip cookies, devil's food, mince pie, orange dinner rolls and more. Some, not many, have stayed.

First Micro-Wave

In the late 1940s, the Raytheon Corp., together with General Electric, introduced the first electronic oven. The Radarange, developed by Raytheon, attained an unprecedented speed in cooking, and heating was accomplished in a matter of seconds.

Frozen meats were cooked in minutes, though searing had to be done separately. Meals were reheated in seconds. I have always believed that quick re-heating is one of the most pressing needs of the industry today. How convenient are "convenience foods" when it takes a half-hour or 45 minutes to re-heat them?

QFF runs several articles each year aimed at encouraging manufacturers of this equipment to build inexpensive, high-temperature heaters for the home. When a compact, moderately priced, high-frequency heater, that cuts cooking to minutes, is available for the domestic kitchen, I think the sale of prepared foods will double.

Frozen Meat's Future

About meats, QFF then wrote: "Fresh, pre-packaged meats are a development of the retailer, frozen meats are a development of the packer. Fresh packaged meats represent no fundamental advantage besides facilitating the handling of these meats at the retail source.

"But frozen cut meats mean a *real saving* all down the line. The packer gets the offal and by-products. He is able to identify each cut with his brand. He saves on shipping rates and he eliminates the necessity of maintaining a costly branch house structure. The meat packer can keep inventories throughout the year and thus control price fluctuations."

I believed then, and still do, that fresh cuts in pre-packaged form retarded the acceptance of frozen meats by many years, but frozen meats will come eventually, as indeed they must. Some, who recently have been burnt in marketing frozen meat cuts may eye this statement with some skepticism, and they have every right to do so. But again—it's a matter of *timing!*

More New Companies

In this period several companies were born and later made important successes. One was Mrs. Paul's Kitchens, begun by Ed Piszek in Philadelphia. The first items were deviled crabs and oysters, to be followed by fish sticks, onion rings, shrimp, scallops and other products. The firm has made money for years and has a firmly entrenched position.

In Maine, freezing of french fried potatoes was launched by an old New England firm, H. C. Baxter & Co., through a subsidiary, the Snow Flake Canning Co., which also froze vegetables. Baxter was a dehydrator during the war, but when he saw that dehydrated potatoes were going out of favor after the end of hostilities, he switched to frozen french fries which were originally packed for Birds Eye. Genial John Baxter Sr., later became president of the National Association and has always been an appreciative reader of QFF.

First Chain Brands

About this time, here and there, the first chain brands began to make their appearance. One of the first, Penn Fruit Co. of Philadelphia, was beginning to market a line of vegetables in 12-ounce cellophane bags under its own label. Safeway was still studying the field.

We made a survey among leading chain officials and 70% reported that they were buying most of their frozen products from local distributors at that time. Another 15% reported buying 100% from packers and this was the beginning of the direct-to-packer-trend.

Almost daily new uses were found for freezing. In Jackson, Miss., the garbage of many hospitals was frozen as a sanitation measure. The medical profession was freezing blood plasma. We also now announced that bones, taken from patients, and which had been stored in freezing cabinets at temperatures as low as —13°, were being used for grafting in surgical operations.

The rabbit business also was coming up. Pelphrey in Los Angeles was introducing quick-frozen rabbit and turning out 40,000 lbs. of dressed meat weekly. While the domestic rabbit market was principally on the West Coast, it has spread since then to the South and Midwest. I remember visiting a rabbit freezing plant at that time and I can never forget how snowy white rabbits went into the plant at one end and frozen cartons came out at the other!

Another company established about then, which was destined for big success, was Milady's Food Products, organized in 1947 by the late Hy Epstein. He was one of the pioneers in prepared foods, in blintzes and potato pancakes. Through consistent application, hard work and advertising, Milady's has become the foremost name in that field: it is now owned by Pet Milk.

Chains Begin to Advertise

In January, 1948, we ran reprints of advertisements by chains in which frozen foods were featured. This was worth talking about at the time. Albers Supermarkets, for instance, was devoting considerable newspaper space to frozen products and was one of the first to embrace this line; two or three modern cabinets were installed in each store. The chain was one of the first to buy in carload lots from processors.

As we had anticipated, locker plants, which had reached their peak immediately after the war, began to decline. From a high of 12,000 plants, the industry declined to 9,000. These plants received their greatest competition from two sources: One, the increasing availability of all commercially packed frozen foods in local stores, and two, home freezers. Shortly thereafter we dropped the subtitle, "The Locker Plant," from our mast-head, though we continued to carry some information about Locker Plants in each issue.

In February, 1948, the first Minute Maid advertisement appeared in QFF. The label was very different from what it is today. The advertisement read: "Minute Maid Concentrate Orange Juice has only been on the market a few months with its 6-ounce retail size, but retailers say it is the most popular and profitable frozen item they ever handled. It does away with the messy business of squeezing, yet it costs less than whole oranges."

Almost from the beginning, and right up to the present, Minute Maid has delivered the "better for your health" theme. Shortly thereafter, in order to hasten introduction, Minute Maid and Snow Crop placed thousands of small display cabinets in retail stores. Sales were stimulated, as well as retailer interest, but the idea proved too costly and was later abandoned.

In 1948, the Florida Citrus Canners began operation at Lake Wales, Fla., and first packed for Birds Eye; later they developed the Donald Duck brand which has occupied the unique position of "an advertised private label" ever since. Marvin Walker, now head of the organization, is one of the citrus industry's outstanding figures and has been a commissioner of the important Florida Citrus Commission.

During this period we noticed that many packers were putting on their labels the rather disturbing admonition: "Do not attempt to refreeze after thawing." It was good advice, but after we did some research we found that housewives were intimidated by the phrase. We suggested that it be toned down a bit and came up with, "After defrosting, treat as you would an unfrozen product," or "consume immediately after thawing." Eventually this instruction was no longer found necessary as consumers became more accustomed to handling frozen foods.

A frozen food cook book was published by the Frozen Food Foundation in Syracuse and served as a model for many food recipes.

QFF Absorbs Rivals

About 1945, two competitive magazines came into the field. One was called *Food Freezing,* published by the Ogden Publishing Co., also owners of *The Glass Packer.* The other was *Frozen Food Industry,* put out by Reuben H. Donnelley Corp., major printers and publishers. Both magazines secured some business but found the going rough. They were, however, good competition.

In this connection I must relate an interesting story which might be entitled "poetic justice." I had an advertising man working for QFF at the time, who was doing well and earning a good income. Moreover, his future looked bright. But sometimes the next pasture looks greener and one day he came to me and blithely said: "I'm leaving you and going to *Food Freezing.* I think they are going to make better headway."

I urged him to stay but to no avail; he had made up his mind. Only six months later, in February, 1948, the publisher found his magazine was losing money and asked me to buy it. I did, and the advertising man who had left QFF in such a hurry was out of a job since we had replaced him. The acquisition of *Food Freezing* increased our circulation, though we *did not* advance advertising rates.

In December of that year I received a phone call from the then president of Reuben H. Donnelley, publishers of the other magazine, *Frozen Food Industry:* "What will you ask," he said, "to take over *FFI* and service our subscribers and advertisers?" We came to a prompt agreement and *more readers* were added to QFF's list. We started serving them the following month. Other competition was to come later and that is to be expected. It helps keep everyone on their toes!

Volume Up—Prices Down

1948 was a year in which volume climbed and prices and profits sloped downward, a trend which has continued to this day. It was the natural outcome of growing competition plus tightening cabinet space. More advertising and sales promotion appeared during that year than in any previous year. Per capita consumption had risen to 5½ pounds. Practically all new stores were installing frozen food cabinets and about 60,000 stores were then handling frozen foods.

A reduction of a few cents a pound had increased sales sometimes as much as 400%. Some large chains and supermarkets were averaging from $200 to a high of $800 a month; smaller retailers were averaging about $35 a week. The SAP (subject to approval of price) method of buying was beginning to prevail over the "firm at opening" system.

I must mention Watson Rogers, president then as now of the National Food Brokers Association. He was outstandingly instrumental in helping the industry and in pushing frozen to the Brokerage fraternity. Bill Dalton, secretary of the National Association of Refrigerated Warehouses, did a good job over the years, in furnishing the frozen foods industry much information on warehouses. He has since been succeeded by R. M. Powell, C. E. Jackson, secretary of the National Fisheries Institute, was a valuable source of needed information on seafood.

QFF always has had a big circulation among bankers, investment analysts and financial houses and many in the financial fraternity refer to it monthly as a guide on trends and prices, as well as the activity of various packers in the field.

Snow Crop Changes Policy

I have written earlier of Snow Crop's beginning in 1945. I should now bring my readers up to date on this volatile company. Though at first the firm held the theory that a good merchandising and selling organization, using a group of non-competitive packers as a source of supply, could succeed without operating plants, the late Jack Moone by 1948 had changed his thinking.

He said: "It was obvious to the management that the company had to entertain the idea of *controlling* its own production under the Snow Crop label from start to finish. In order to accomplish its major objective, which was the production of prime quality products.

In order to achieve this end more money was needed and Clinton Industries, third largest corn refinery in the world, purchased a 67% interest in the company. The firm moved into imposing new offices on New York's Park Avenue. Charles W. Metcalf, a former General Foods vice president, became chairman of the board. "We're in this to stay," said Jack Moone, and QFF commented, "Whatever the outcome, it is an exciting experiment in merchandising."

By now QFF had full-fledged sections on Seafood, Meats & Poultry, Prepared Foods, Transportation, Freezing, Warehousing, and others. There were plenty of developments to keep all the sections filled.

The Amerio Manufacturing Co., later known as Amerio Contact Plate Freezers, was organized by Pat and Helen Amerio and became an important factor in freezing equipment. Its pressure plate freezers and, more lately, its automatic continuous freezing process, are widely used both in this country and abroad. New types of freezers failed to supplant them.

Packer-Distribution Rift

A rift between packers and distributors was becoming more apparent. Many distributors thought that nothing was being done to help them move merchandise. Whipped into a white heat of determination to increase per capita consumption of frozen foods, several hundred distributors went to the 1948 Chicago convention, grimly set on putting over an advertising campaign.

A "council" was formed including Burt Prince, Bill Walsh, Alvin Langfield and Carl Seabergh. The new president of the packers' association was Fred Becker and the council included processors, distributors and brokers to study the subject of industry advertising.

The council hired Harry Schauffler, then a public relations man, and since executive director of the distributors' association, to make a tour and report on a plan. He reported that out of 400 pounds of fresh fruits and vegetables consumed per capita, 82 pounds came out of cans and only 5½ pounds were frozen.

The distributors recommended a million dollar advertising appropriation for the first year, the money to be charged to the cost of the product at the packers' level. But the idea proved too rich for the industry's blood and was firmly, though none too tactfully, shelved. Coming as a letdown to the distributors, this served to widen the rift.

Otherwise, the 1948 convention proved a success. The distributors took over more of its functions, ran a cocktail party, a luncheon and a few other events, all under the direction of Bill Walsh, who that year was elected president of the National Frozen Food Distributors' Association.

A "Rough and Tumble" Industry

Around then, QFF published a rather timely editorial in which we said: "This is a rough and tumble industry, lusty, full of confidence and with a bold front. This is as it should be and those who have no confidence in frozen foods are better out of it."

Our April, 1948, issue suffered from the first and only strike we had in our history, and, I hope, the last. This was a typographers' strike which forced the curtailment of a good portion of the issue.

Packers were beginning to worry about increasing freight rates. QFF pointed out that claims on frozen products were considerably less than on fresh. The association's committee endorsed an overhead bunker type of railroad car, using either dry ice and salt or dry ice, and many of these were constructed.

In 1948 baked goods entered the frozen food field. There were several apple, cherry and fruit pies on the market, produced by companies no longer active: Ma Sommers, Liberty Baking, Cease's, etc. But here again it was a matter of timing. The consumer was not yet ready for fruit pies.

French fried potatoes, which had been introduced a few years back, were beginning to gain in volume under the Birds Eye, Brock and other labels. Eventually, all national and regional as well as chain brands were to include this item.

New Time-Saving Equipment

I have mentioned the new Marapak packaging equipment which speeded production. In addition, the Package Machinery Co. developed a wrapping machine for handling up to 160 packages a minute. Chisholm Ryder had developed a carton filler, designed to fill end-opening rigid types of containers.

Thermo King, a fully automatic defrosting system with a mechanical timing device, was becoming widely used in transportation.

Another firm that consistently served the industry and whose products are in wide use is the Niagara Blower Co. At the time QFF started, Niagara Blower was developing its "No Frost" refrigeration method which used an organic liquid spray. The modern unit is widely used in maintainng below-zero temperatures in large frozen-food warehouses. Kramer-Trenton, another firm, began to sell packaged refrigeration plants.

The mechanically refrigerated car was one of the outstanding developments at the time. The first fully equipped car was placed in general service by Fruit Growers Express in February, 1949 and they now have over 1700 such cars in service. Pacific Fruit Express operates some 2700 mechanical reefers and Sante Fe has added another 500 to its frozen food fleet.

W. Rogers   H. Schauffler

First meeting of Honorable Order of Zerocrats, an organization of outstanding workers in behalf of the frozen foods industry. Left to right, seated: C. L. Snavely, Joseph Gaudio, M. K. Spiegl, E. T. Gibson, Ralph O. Dulany, Burton L. Prince. Standing: Fred M. Deutsch, William M. Walsh, Lawrence S. Martin, W. L. Pavlovski, Watson Rogers, Harry K. Schauffler, Alvin Langfield, E. J. Watson, A. J. Rogers, C. Courtney Seabrook and E. J. White. Other charter members are Clarence Birdseye, Fred J. Becker, William Dalton, E. E. Huddleson, T. E. McCaffrey.

Early meeting of the NAFFP Nutrition Research Committee with K. G. Dykstra (center), Birds Eye, as chairman.

We Urge More Diversification

In 1948, according to QFF's Processors' Directory, there were 900 packers.

At that time, I felt that there was too much selling concentration on one item—strawberries—and that many other important frozen products were being neglected.

Consequently, QFF published the following editorial: "Many industry members seem to fall into the thinking that the frozen food sun rises and sets on strawberries and a few other leading items. This is *narrow thinking* and does little to broaden the industry's scope. New products are coming to the fore. (With the decline in strawberries in recent years, this proved good advice.)

"Soon, concentrates will probably outsell many leaders. Winter vegetables, seafoods, prepared foods, meats and poultry are all increasing in sales, some at a greater pace than the old standbys. The point is that the industry must be regarded in a *broad* aspect, rather than as an industry made up of berries, peas and cherries. The preservation of foods by quick freezing is designed to cover a multitude of foods—practically *everything* we eat."

A FF Fiction Story

Up to that time little basic change had taken place in the industry. Practically the same products and techniques were used. Of course, there had been great growth in companies and sales. But many problems remained: in transportation, LCL shipments; in industry, harmony; in distribution, financing and marketing.

In short, we said, the industry was in a rut. What it needed was more daring, courage and experimentation. The industry was too self-satisfied, so we took it on ourselves to do some blasting. A number of articles ran in each issue designed to inspire new ideas and new methods. Many of these have been adopted and are being used in some form or other.

In June, QFF ran its first experiment in fiction, a frozen food murder mystery. It was called "Cold Comfort" and concerned a husband who, in his spare time, raised vegetables in his garden, froze and stored them in his freezer.

This absorbed all his attention and did not receive the sympathy of his nagging wife, who finally plagued him to the point where he killed her, freezing the body and putting it into the freezer, as he did in his other freezing experiments. As an epitaph he wrote: "If you can't please 'em—freeze 'em!" The story was reprinted in 1962 in *The Saint's Mystery Magazine*.

One of the industry's leading marketing men was M. C. Pollock of C. A. Swanson, later with Campbell Soup and recently with Green Giant. He contributed a great deal during this period in merchandising ideas. He is now with the Weyerhaeuser Paper Co.

There was a movement afoot to install lockers in the basements of apartment houses. One company actually put in quite a few in Westchester County, but the idea never went far beyond this stage.

Cooperatives Start Up

The retailer cooperative began to be an influence. In Los Angeles, Certified Grocers, a big organization buying for many large supermarkets in southern California, began to purchase direct.

"Does this move, which is being duplicated less dramatically in other parts of the country, signify a new trend?" we wrote. "Will pressure from now on be more and more in the direction of lower percentages of operation? Are we at the point where large chains will buy direct?" The answer was yes—and this proved to be the trend from then on.

In that year California began packing strawberries in large volume. Driscoll put up about 10 million pounds. Lima bean production grew to around 35 million pounds.

Thus ended the first ten years. In this era the industry was on its way to maturity. It faced new, and different problems and *change* was the order of the day.

4

The Creative Years

By the end of 1948, chains were bringing out more of their own labels. We speculated that if one large organization such as Safeway, with 2,500 stores at the time, went wholeheartedly into frozen foods, the industry would not have sufficient production facilities to supply them with a complete line and at the same time satisfy its own customers.

First National Stores were already going strong with their own brand "Yor Garden." And we didn't figure on the A & P! One of the obstacles to chain expansion then was the cost of refrigerating equipment. Grand Union was among the first to expand in frozen foods. Jewel Food Stores, Chicago, National Tea, Fishers, Cleveland, Loblaw in Buffalo and others were becoming increasingly interested in the new industry.

Top Frost was being distributed to smaller chains and supermarkets. At that time, Certified Grocers, Los Angeles, made the astounding statement that it could handle frozen foods on a 12% markup, which it has lowered considerably since. Other chains were working on markups ranging from 15 to 22%.

The IGA stores got into the picture. Few chains then had regular departments set up to handle frozen foods, the management of which was generally left to the head of the produce or the meat department.

We began to emphasize the fact that *75% of all American foods are perishable*. The goal of the industry, we said, should be to convert 65% of all perishable foods to preservation through quick freezing which, if accomplished, would yield a business of $50 billion a year! We did not include prepared foods in this estimate.

The industry was now on a much better basis. The introduction of concentrates and other products eliminated the once feared "summer slump." Production was being decentralized, packaging costs were being reduced and already 30% of frozen foods were transported by truck.

The "Halved" Berry

On the West Coast, Brussels sprouts were becoming popular and Birds Eye opened a new plant at Santa Cruz. Dole began producing frozen pineapple chunks. In San Jose, two brothers, Don and Ken Hartman, operated the Hartman Ranch which controlled 150 acres of apricots and beans. The operation grew, but finally the encroachment of real estate developments forced the ranch out of business. Nevertheless, to Hartman belongs the credit for having developed the first "halved" strawberry machine and he produced halved berries for several years.

PictSweet, which had received bank backing, continued its promotional program and covered 20 markets. The New Washington variety of raspberry was becoming increasingly popular and proved hardier than the Cuthbert.

When I was on the west coast that year, several packers asked me to visit some banks and alert the bankers to the future of frozen foods. I did what I could and wrote in QFF: "Northwest banks, particularly, do not seem to realize that they are sitting on top of a segment of the industry that has a great potential.

"From this area comes the Marshall strawberry which for years will have a continually greater value in this country. The Northwest also produces other leading items. Instead of holding this part of the country down—and other parts as well—bankers might be wise to pump more money into the operations of good, substantial packers so that they can produce more of the needed items, not less."

Stir About Research

About this time I published a rather bold editorial on research which brought many letters, of both approval and protest, from colleges, laboratories and experiment stations. We had been receiving papers for years from universities, and while we published many, we found that fewer and fewer were showing any new results.

Consequently we wrote: "For some reason or other very little practical work has emerged from government or university-controlled institutions during the past ten years. While it is true that such laboratories have proven invaluable for testing purposes, for weighing properties of certain materials under specific conditions, or for testing relative merits of packaging materials—such work is being *duplicated* over and over again.

"And, in too many instances, research work never seems to get out of the experimental stage. There is much theoretical and too little conclusive work. There is too much dabbling in unimportant aspects of the industry while the important projects are ignored."

We went on to say that many universities and government stations suffered from lack of imagination and guidance and that important problems were crying to be solved. We made a particular point of the fact that, so far, all the important developments in the frozen foods industry had come out of *private* research in the laboratories of commercial operations.

From Rutgers University we received a letter of complete approval.

M. A. Joslyn of the University of California, together with H. C. "Dutch" Diehl, agreed that the industry would get more and better research when it created a permanent technological organization or liaison with research agencies. The Western Research Laboratory, Albany, Calif., wrote, "We found much to agree with in the editorial."

But there were others who protested. The editorial was not written with any malice, but rather to blast away the indifference, and perhaps self-satisfaction, which then existed in this type of research. I think it accomplished its purpose. Since then I am convinced that the only way to get results in research is to work on grants for *specific projects.*

More Pre-Cooked Foods

A new precooked packer at the time was Gretchen Grant Kitchens, started by Lou Midler who brought out a line of hors d'oeuvres, which have done very well ever since. It is now owned by the Glidden Co. Every conceivable prepared item was being brought out and each issue of QFF mentioned the names of at least 15 or 20 new packers. Very few stayed in business.

There were Neapolitan cakes, cherry flips, biscuit tortonis, lemon, chocolate and other pies, Scotch scones, pecan muffins, crepe suzette, apple brown Betty, and the like.

However, one of the pakers who started then stayed in the business. About this time, a new company, Roman Ravioli, Inc., was started in New Jersey by two brothers, Joseph and Cy Settineri. The first items were ravioli, tomato sauce and pizzas. There has been a big expansion of the firm since those days and from small beginnings, the company built a new, modern plant. Later, Joe Settineri was to play an important role in the National Prepared Frozen Food Processors Association. The last five years have seen the most phenomenal growth in Roman's history. During the past five years, Roman merged with the New England firm of H. P. Hood Co. Advertising has increased many fold. The line has grown to include products such as manicotti, lasagna and cavitelli. A new and larger plant housing the most modern equipment available has been built in South Hackensack so that today the Roman brand frozen Italian dishes are found throughout the country in almost all leading chains. Since that time, both Settineri brothers have retired from the firm and are in other businesses.

The Welch Grape Juice Co., a famous national "name" brand joined the frozen food ranks about here. The company began putting up quick-frozen grape juice concentrate in the New York area. It clicked right from the beginning and is one of the few products in the industry which has been able to maintain a fairly steady price. Jack Kaplan, former head of Welch, was successful in selling the company to a growers' co-operative.

Distributors Reduce Costs

Many distributors were then working on a margin of from 16-24%. We started a campaign of information on the mechanization and streamlining of distributing plants and cost-cutting in make-up rooms and in the

An early meeting of the Eastern Frosted Foods Association, about 1953. Directors and guests at head table.

Early days in Chicago—a 1950 meeting of the National Distributors Association.

delivering of orders. Within a few years, many distributors were able to reduce their costs considerably. More than one distributor, after modernization, was able to reduce his expenses by as much as 7 or 8%.

On our best sellers' list orange juice now had edged strawberries out of the number one fruit position.

In New York, the institutional business was expanding and such companies as Waterman, Boker, Peltz and others were expanding in frozen foods. In 1949, Thorman, Baum, an institutional wholesaler, opened a new, 40,000-foot plant and operated 17 trucks. Max Treewater, the firm's manager, was well known in the industry for his wit; he rarely made a phone call without telling a joke.

New Florida Concentrators

In Florida, more concentrators appeared. One was Plymouth Citrus Cooperative Association, a co-op which has gone into private label packing. Another was the Adams Canning Co. Ridge Citrus Concentrate also began the operations at Davenport, Fla., with late Harry DiCristina as president. He has since built up a premium valencia pack. Lou McKnight is now president.

Minute Maid now had two plants. Advertising was on the increase. By this time a keen rivalry had sprung up between Minute Maid and Snow Crop for control of the juice market, although at the time each was working in the other's plants. I remember buying a can of Minute Maid juice, under which label was a Snow Crop wrap.

Snow Crop took newspaper advertisements in 25 cities as well as advertising in the *Saturday Evening Post, Ladies Home Journal* and on the radio. Minute Maid was featuring Bing Crosby, then a director of the company.

New developments were beginning to march apace. In our March, 1949, convention issue we said, "As the frozen food picture continues to unfold it becomes increasingly apparent that changes are coming with increasing momentum.

"There are no fixed rules or regulations about this industry and the frame of mind which includes a readiness to accept changes as they come along, and to adapt oneself to these changes is probably the best asset any member of the industry can have today."

In Pittsburgh there were two important distributors at the time. One was Morrison, McCluan, a partnership between the late Malcolm McCluan and William Walsh; the latter was to become active in association and convention work, as well as in industry activities.

Another important distributor was the late Frank Blum who took on frozen foods enthusiastically, which led to expansion for him. He introduced many new products in Pittsburgh and is 100% institutional.

Buyers' Labels Grow

By 1949 a new trend became evident: More and more packers were beginning to produce for buyers' labels. Individual independent packers labels, of which there were many, began to diminish. This trend has continued up to the present, with the difference that then, smaller freezers were packing for national brands, and today they are packing for chain labels.

In March, the 1949 convention came and went, and it was noted that packer-distributor relations seemed to have improved. There was a good attendance and more than 80 exhibits.

The "battle of the brands" was being fought vigorously. There were many price skirmishes in various distribution centers and we wrote at the time: "The smoke has not yet sufficiently cleared to render a decision."

We brought out the first directory of Wholesale Distributors, listing all wholesalers handling frozen foods, their original businessowners, brands carried, proportion of business in retail and institutional, zero space if any, number of trucks, etc. It was a thorough compilation and proved useful to many packers. It has since been published every 18 months.

In our packaging review of that year we noted another important change—a swing to more attractive varicolored labels. Gone were the Eskimos, the huskies and icebergs and, in their place, came lifelike color pictures of the foods themselves. Printed cellophane continued to be the most widely used overwrap, but improved printing on waxed papers was now beginning to make this material more popular. Several foil wraps were appearing on the market.

Average Age Is 42

By 1950 concentrate output was beginning to absorb 25% of Florida's oranges; later the juice can was to take over 70% of the crop.

With the continued placement of home freezers, more opportunities arose to sell case lots to home owners. In order to stimulate the sale of quantity assortments of frozen foods through retail channels, stemming from the packer and distributor, we started a campaign entitled: "Stock Your Home Freezer."

It immediately received the enthusiastic endorsement of distributors and appliance manufacturers. We printed and distributed banners bearing the message "Stock Your Home Freezer Here." These streamers were put up by distirbutors in the stores of their retail customers. The campaign was a *huge success;* it was repeated the following year and won many new friends for QFF.

Following a survey we noted the interesting fact that the average age of executives in the industry was about 42, and that many active heads of packing and distributing concerns were even younger.

B Labels Start

By 1950 another new trend had begun. Many packers were beginning to bring out second, or B grade labels. We wrote at the time: "It will be interesting to see if the industry is ready to digest the first and second labels. Distribution today is bigger, chains are more in the picture, and pricing is more sensitive." Actually, the move didn't succeed then, though it was revived. More will be mentioned on this later on in the story.

It seems that through the years the frozen foods industry has been lucky. On many occasions it avoided obstacles which might have felled a stronger trade. When over-production threatened, as it often did, Mother Nature stepped in to lend a helping hand in the form of droughts, rains or freezes. Time and again a crop failure has proved a *blessing in disguise.*

At the time of my seventh annual West Coast trip, the concentrate front was active in California. New firms such as Realgold, Ventura Coastal Lemon, Mutual Citrus Products and others were producing both orange and lemon juice. At the same time Sunkist, a large and dominant growers' cooperative, entered the picture.

They froze orange juice, which later became secondary and was over-shadowed by lemonade and other "ades." In this production they held a commanding position, since Sunkist Growers controls close to 70% of California's lemons. Since then, lemonade has been marketed at very low prices.

Nationality Foods Come

In Texas, Mexican foods were growing at an astounding rate. Patio Foods was freezing such favorites as hot tamales, chili con carne and beef enchiladas. Moreno became active in Los Angeles, as did Cuellar Foods in Dallas, and Rosita Products in Arizona.

Other nationality foods were cropping up. To the Chinese and Italian dishes I have mentioned, there now were added kosher foods. Zion Kosher Meat in New York marketed a line of chopped meats, skinless frankfurters, cocktail sausages and similar items.

Chinese Landmark

A new company in Brooklyn, Temple Frosted Foods, which was to make its mark, was started by Sidney Schwartz and Bowden Goon to produce a Chinese line. Later, won ton soup and complete dinners were added to the line.

Expansion continued in the Northwest. New packers were Umatilla Canning and Jory Packing. The Pacific American Fisheries bought Cedergreen and began to operate from Bellingham, Wash. Norman Cedergreen was put in charge of the operation; he later became a broker in Seattle. In 1962, Cedergreen Frozen Pack reverted to its original owners—the Cedergreens; Another new arrival on the packing scene was Prosser.

Price Wars Flare

During this period Snow Crop announced a new policy, establishment of its own branches in key markets to operate on a non-profit basis. The trade was set back on its heels when Snow Crop further announced that all the company's distributors would be expected to operate on a margin of

10%. This created quite a stir and soon other packers were obliged to cut distribution corners.

QFF noted that in the midst of the "battle of the brands" distributors were caught in the middle. As price wars began to flare in different markets, chains also were beginning to "special" various items, often below cost. And let me say here that I have never understood one practice to which this industry seems to be given: The reduction of prices on products which are short in supply.

To reduce a price when an item is long is quite understandable, but to cut it when production trails demand, as happens occasionally in this industry, seems senseless.

Birds Eye announced their policy of 16⅔% of cost. Meanwhile, the Distributors' group was trying to keep its members on a profitable basis. A cost accountant was hired and exhaustive studies were made of distribution costs. Shortly thereafter the membership set up a uniform accounting system which proved of great value to them.

Coupons Start

The coupon give-away now entered the picture. Snow Crop was the first to give a ten-cent premium on its labels and others soon followed. The distribution picture became more complicated when Jack Moone of Snow Crop, who had been castigated for months by distributors because of his policy toward lower margins and direct selling made a surprise appearance before the distributors' organization.

He presented a new program in which he stated that his company was through with wholesaling via its own branches and was handing this business back to the distribtuors. He announced a dual price policy, a single price to chains and independents, and an FOB warehouse price.

Mr. Moone said that the FOB selling price structure would have to come into being before chains would push frozen foods. At the same time, Minute Maid decided to deliver direct to stores through a fleet of trucks operated by driver-salesmen, the distributors in the areas receiving a fixed margin.

Start of Lower Prices

There is no question that the policies which Mr. Moone inaugurated resulted in increased volume and gradually lower prices. But, in many instances, prices went too low, as evidenced by the low profits made in recent years. I think that if strong leadership had been exercised at this point, and if the industry had been able to agree and stick to a more conservative price policy, profits would be higher today.

At the same time South African lobster tails were being introduced in the U.S. and quickly became popular. It is one of the few frozen products whose supply has always trailed demand. Soon, other lobster tail importations followed, coming from Cuba, New Zealand, Australia, South America and other countries.

Orchard Hill Farms, Redhook, N.Y., introduced a deep-dish pie and for the first time an aluminum container was used in which the pies could be baked. This was a milestone, and foil has played a big role in reheating and cooking ever since. The company has since become an important factor in private label.

Armour, about this time, introduced a line of specialty meats, including beef steaks, hamburger patties, sweetbreads, pork cutlets and similar items.

Monosodium glutamate was coming into use in the industry and QFF ran many articles endorsing its advantages, since it emphasized the dominant flavor in many foods. It was much needed, we felt, especially in prepared foods, and today, MSG is widely used in many of the industry's products. I think it should be applied to vegetables to point up flavor, and I feel that its use would give many a product a "plus" which should help sales.

The Florida "Gold Rush"

In 1950, I went to Florida and reported that "the gold rush is on." The price of land had tripled in one year. There was a *250%* increase in concentrate output. The whole state was humming with activity, just as had the west coast directly after the war.

There were 17 plants in operation. The potential market scarcely had been scratched and 50,000 juice cabinets were in stores on liberal financing plans, as well as a number of automatic coin machines placed in strategic locations.

Even mighty Coca-Cola expressed concern at this growing competition, but they consoled themselves with the thought that even if all available oranges were diverted into concentrates there would be only enough for an eight-day supply, if figured on the basis of the rate at which Coca-Cola was then consumed! Since then Coca-Cola has gotten a great deal closer to orange juice—they *own* Minute Maid today!

Retail prices were then from 25-29¢, though later competition was to lower this level greatly. Minute Maid bought 4,700 acres of grove land for about $5 million. Cross & Blackwell was in the picture, and Pasco, Winter Garden and B & W were all increasing output.

In Florida, the price of raw fruit was shooting up and the trade was worried. Many processors were paying up to $3.50 a box. The National Frozen Food Distributors' Association ran advertisements in Florida newspapers addressed to growers, entitled "We Think You Are Too Smart to Kill the Goose that Is Laying the Golden Egg."

Snow Crop now was sponsoring Sid Caesar on TV and Minute Maid had the Kate Smith show. About this time Winter Garden Citrus Co-operative in Florida began to expand its plants. The late Robert Mairs, the head of the marketing organization which sold for Winter Garden's growers, numbering some of the finest in the state, urged the trade to "buy direct from growers."

The state's second largest independent concentrator, Winter Garden packs for many of the country's chains and private label owners, and also promotes its own "Whole Sun" label. Jim Bock is general manager and Buck Thompson sales manager.

Key Men

Pasco, about which I have already written, now was under the direction of Bill Edwards. It should be noted here that he plays a very important role in the direction, not only of Pasco, but of the concentrate industry as well. His evaluation of the industry's inventory and price position from year to year has proven generally right.

I have mentioned B & W earlier, but want to add that Tom Quinby, who became a good friend of ours, formed his own selling organization, Processors Sales in Orlando, Fla., which represented B. & W. Quinby, former sales manager of Pasco, is himself a grower with considerable acreage. I have always found his analysis of the often complicated concentrate outlook keen and generally correct.

Since then, Snively Groves has become a factor under its brand Cypress Gardens, and Adams Canning has launched its Adams label. Hood, Griffin and others started about this time. One of the pioneers in the growth of lemonade since 1948 is Ventura Coastal Lemon Co., and its sales director, Louis Soulan, former Chicago broker.

Birth of Breaded Shrimp

One of the industry's most unusual success stories is the story of breaded shrimp. Around this time I visited the small town of Thunderbolt, Ga. Here I met William Mullis, "father" of the breaded shrimp industry. Originally he ran a small grocery store and often took shrimp home to his wife, who fried it for him. But he didn't get it often enough and he asked his wife the reason for this. She told him it took too long to prepare. Mullis reasoned that if shrimp could be cooked quickly, as quickly as frying bacon for instance, people would eat it more often.

He tested his theory by putting up a batch of shrimp, dipped in a light batter. This he froze, packaged and sold. It was called fantail, because when split, the tail assumed the shape of a fan. With the money he got from selling the first batch he made several more and thus expanded, slowly.

Capitol Fish Co. of Atlanta was the first distributor to give him encouragement. Local capital was obtained through Louis Ambos, a local shrimp producer. (His son, Henry Ambos, is now president of the company, since Mr. Mullis sold his interest several years ago.) Mullis now runs Neptunalia Seafoods.

From this $5,000 original investment the project rapidly grew into a $10 million business, and Mr. Mullis made a tidy fortune. Many others got into this business later. The shrimp business boomed, but it had a temporary setback when the percentage of breading and shrimp meat became too close. Since then, the industry has adopted regulatory measures and sales are going up again.

We ran several articles on the potential market for sub-tropical fruits such as avocado, mango, guavas, etc. None of these fruits ever caught on excepting avocado, which I think has certain possibilities when frozen, possibly in paste form.

San Juan Fishing Co., Seattle, was offering a one-pound consumer package of halibut and steaks. This company made great progress, both in its retail and portion control business, and is now the biggest on the west coast.

Incidentally, the first breaded shrimp gave rise to another industry, breading mixes, which came to be widely used in other products such as meats, poultry and fillets, etc. Breaders include Modern Maid, Meletio, Downyflake, Ward Baking, General Baking, Greer, DCA, Burns, Stein, etc.

In February, 1950, QFF published its biggest issue to date, more than 300 pages, including four special inserts and eight complete sections. This reflected the industry's upward trend. I might say here that it has been my experience that the size of QUICK FROZEN FOODS *reflects the condition of the industry,* just as the stock market reflects business. When the industry is up, QFF is up, and vice versa.

More on Shrimp

Seapack Corp., which had been started by Jack Hice, a former newspaper man, was beginning to offer a frozen seafood dinner in addition to its shrimp line. This company, of which Tom Pearce is president, has now became a division of W. R. Grace.

Grand Duchess Steak Co. of Akron, O., opened their doors at this time and began to put out a line of steaks and other ready-to-cook meats. Operated by Harry Snyder, the firm has expanded considerably: it has since been taken over by the Stark, Wetzel Co.

We Cover Europe

In the summer of 1950 I made the first of many subsequent trips to Europe, in the course of which I visited almost every country this side of the "iron curtain." I became acquainted with most packers and distributors in England, Ireland, Holland, France, Belgium, Western Germany and the Scandinavian countries.

England has made the biggest progress, led by Birds Eye. I will say this, from my own observation: Frozen foods have succeeded in countries only where there was strong leadership in the form of at least one company with financial resources to spearhead promotion of frozen foods. Without such leadership it is very hard to get an industry started.

QFF now has a big international circulation, reaching almost every country in the world. More than 1,000 copies go abroad each month; two even go to the Department of Agriculture in Moscow—on subscription of course!

Southern Vegetables

Firms like Southland, McKenzie, Winter Garden, Bateman, Ark-Homa, Dulany, Seabrook, Phillips, Trappe, Colonial Cannery and others began to enlarge on their packs of southern vegetables, such as yellow squash, whole okra, turnip greens and blackeye peas. These products soon received wide acceptance, not only in the South but also in other parts of the country.

Georgia was becoming an important poultry state. (Today several million broilers are hatched each week.) Jesse Jewell was the first to expand in frozen poultry. He discontinued all processing of ice-packed poultry and devoted his entire production to frozen chickens.

This excellent organization added many new products during the next few years, including fried chicken, portion control poultry, fruit and pot pies, cloverleaf rolls and many other products. J. D. Jewell later acquired Southern Frigid Dough. Standard Packaging Corp. now owns Jewell.

Georgia Broiler was another firm that showed fast growth. Meanwhile, Caroline Poultry Farms was offering a complete line, as was Shenandoah and Plus Poultry. Youngblood's in Texas soon offered whole poultry and in parts, as well as breaded chickens.

The Trucking Deal

Now another new wrinkle in distribution cropped up—the "drayage" or trucking deal. The first was Howell Trucking Co. of Jersey City, working in conjunction with Merchants Refrigeration. This was a direct to chain service of which we said at the time "something new has been added."

Proponents of the idea claimed it could operate at 5% of the chain's cost. Similar operations started up in Philadelphia, Boston and in other cities. Some distributors started direct routes to service their large retail customers. The idea, however, never went beyond a certain stage.

Sara Lee Starts

Cheese cake, an item which was to prove outstanding, made its debut on the market. I believe the first cheese cakes were marketed by Dutchland bakeries in Chicago and by Mother Hubbard, as well as some others.

Then Sara Lee entered the market. Originated by Charles Lubin, this brand soon was distributed nationally. I have often referred to the "Sara Lee type of merchandising" as an example of what can be done with a top quality product which can be sold at a fair price, and maintained there.

I think the success of this company flouts the commonly held beliefs of many in the industry, 1) that you have to have a complete line to get in cabinets, 2) that you have to give constant "deals" and 3) that you must give away to price cutting. Of course Sara Lee is nationally and heavily advertised and its product is made of the best materials.

Despite some competition the product, from a price standpoint, has remained in a *class by itself*. Later, the company was bought by Consolidated Foods. Among the products in the firm's line are pound cake, chocolate cake, brownies, coffee cake, etc.

Most Profitable Dept.

QFF started a series of articles, aimed at giving the trade ammunition to show retailers why frozen foods could be their most profitable department. Among other arguments, we showed that in many stores, frozen foods' share of profits was 50% greater than its shares of sales.

When, in 1951, tension over the Korean situation was at its peak, we ran an editorial "If War Comes" which pointed out that the industry had built up an arsenal of frozen food "fortresses" across the country which, in case of a breakdown of transport facilities, were capable of making most communities self-sufficient.

New Association

In early 1951, a committee representing prepared frozen food packers met in our Wall Street office and plans were laid to form their first organization, later to become the National Prepared Frozen Food Processors Association. The charter members include Sid Schwartz, Joe Settineri, Hy Epstein, Lou Midler, Jim Thomas and W. F. Morgan.

The first meeting of the newly-formed group was held at the New Yorker Hotel in January. Sid Schwartz, then of Temple Frosted Foods, became first president. Functions of the association were announced to be 1) the furthering of prepared frozen foods, 2) the development of better means of transportation and warehousing and, 3) the interchange of ideas on packaging, standards and distribution.

Lime juice and limeade was introduced at this stage. Parman-Kendall became the prime packer, being situated in southern Florida where limes grow. This juice later claimed a position in the concentrate lines of most packers, and I think it will grow in favor.

In order to prove to ourselves that QFF was maintaining its position as the leading trade publication in the industry, we hired the Recording & Statistical Corp., an impartial organization which had made many surveys for such publishers as McGraw-Hill and others, to make a survey in the frozen foods industry.

Readership Study Shows QFF 9 to 1

This was accomplished by sending out 2,700 post-cards, returnable to their offices. Over 90% of the respondents said that QUICK FROZEN FOODS was their principal publication and more than 86% reported that QFF was the only magazine they read for frozen food information. We published this report in our March 1951 issue. Similar surveys have been made each year since and the percentage has always remained the same.

Safeway & Frozen

After several years of cautious study, Safeway Stores decided to go all out on frozen foods. Alan Young, who was and still is in charge of this development, did an outstanding job. Safeway was also experimenting with its own Bel-Air line of peas, which it was to expand later to a complete line.

Seafoods still were expanding. Frozen trout was introduced by Xman Trout Ranch and, later, others such as Snake River Trout Co., "State O' Maine," and Empress Fisheries developed good distribution. Robert Stix, a broker and importer, brought trout in from Japan, and Danish trout also was offered on the U.S. market.

Town Square in Pittsburgh, started with strawberry shortcake and later expanded its baked goods considerably.

Enter Morton

Morton Packing Co. was organized in Louisville and elected George Egger president. This was one of the first companies to promote chicken and beef pies in a big way. Its "Kentucky Colonel" became a familiar TV figure. The company branched out into entrees, fruit pies and cakes and later was bought by Continental Baking Co.

In Chicago, Fox de Luxe Foods expanded into poultry, pies, complete dinners and portion control items. Swift introduced a line of sandwich and luncheon steaks.

Excitement began to grow in the industry about Grade B labels, an important trend in this direction having developed. QFF wrote at this time: "For years the primary concept of frozen foods was based on the fact that only top-grade merchandise should appear in the retail package, and Grade B quality, or quality that did not pass the rigid standards of the consumer package, should go institutional sizes. But perhaps times have changed."

19¢ Splurge

The trend became evident when several packers offered staple items at retail prices 20% below other brands. Among such lines was one called "19¢" brand. It had quite a flurry at the time until competition from first grade brands became more intense, forcing down many Grade A labels to prices below 19¢, which hurt this label. Eventually the idea petered out.

San Francisco again hosted the industry at its fifth convention in 1951. The industry was relatively prosperous and the convention was fairly well attended. Since the Korean War was in progress, the Quartermaster Corps announced that it would purchase 6 million pounds of fruits and vegetables and 11 million pounds of concentrate.

Ted McCaffrey of National Fruit Canners was elected president of the packers; Alvin Langfield headed the distributors. Georgia's former governor, Ellis Arnall, who later became chief of OPS, was appointed general counsel for the distributors' group. He became active in industry matters, especially in framing codes for better industry operations.

Waffles Appear

Another new product which was later to become a staple item made its bow. The item was frozen waffles. Though frozen since the war, the product never was mass-distributed until Waffle Corp. launched its Downyflake brand. Herb Koff did a superb job in marketing the product, which was first introduced in Philadelphia and New Jersey. The waffles were pre-baked and frozen but required no defrosting and could be heated easily and quickly in an ordinary toaster. Soon thereafter we ran an article entitled, "Frozen Waffles Seem to Have Caught On," since over 700,000 were sold weekly.

The company later brought out pancakes and French toast. While other waffles since have come on the market, Downyflake still holds the national franchise. More lately, Quaker Oats has entered the field.

While on this subject I would like to stress the importance of *consistency* in advertising. Many a good venture has dropped from the market for lack of "follow through." During the years, I observed new products, introduced with fanfare and fireworks. For a while each lit up the sky like a meteor, only to disappear and be forgotten. A national franchise is *only* possible through consistent advertising, year after year.

Onion rings now came along, introduced by firms like Red L., Mrs. Paul's, Sky Valley Foods and, more lately, by Dulany.

QFF had acquired a new editor, Joseph Fletcher, who had been executive editor of *Chain Store Age* for 15 years. On our staff he succeeded Mun Innes who went to the National Frozen Food Distributors where he now does an excellent job of editing the distributors' News Letter.

Benefits to Farmers

As the industry grew, the farmer and grower benefitted tremendously, especially in certain areas. In Florida, for instance, concentrates proved a bonanza and transformed citrus growing from a haphazard, and often losing, business to a highly profitable one, increasing the value of both crops and property.

In other areas, farmers received unprecedented prices for berries, asparagus, broccoli and other vegetables. The shrimp industry gained new success with quick freezing, and the seafoods and poultry industries were aided greatly. Freezing, in the long run, brought much stabilization to farming and eliminated the peaks and valleys. To the farmer, it added up to a greater market and a more secure existence. In areas such as Maine potato growers got much higher prices with the advent of frozen potato plants such as Potato Service and Vahlsing.

However, in areas where frozen foods brought increased demand, some growers became greedy and short-sightedly pushed up the prices of raw materials. This practice has always boomeranged on growers, because the retail price can never go beyond certain limits. When it is forced down, over-supplies accumulate and, ultimately, the grower himself is forced to take a lower return.

Direct Sales

Birds Eye, at that time, experimented with a frozen tomato juice which I thought was an excellent product, but I suppose its canned counterpart was too strongly entrenched and it was withdrawn.

The biggest packers about this period were Birds Eye, (They still were holding an umbrella over the industry), Snow Crop, Libby, Honor Brand, PictSweet, Cedergreen, Blue Goose, Seabrook, Dulany, Fairmont, and Flav-R-Pak, etc. These were complete line packers, though many others such as Minute Maid, Pasco and the like were building big volume.

By now retailers were doing from 3% to 5% of total volume in frozen foods, and 200,000 stores had cabinets. Production became an all-year-round affair, because packers were putting up more items.

A Thought on Competition

The history of this industry has proved that a successful product does not remain alone for long and that it is always hard put to hold its position. Treading on the heels of every successful product comes a host of others. This was particularly true in the case of prepared foods: waffles, cheese cake, fruit and pot pies, dinners, fish sticks and many other products.

The first packer makes a fair profit, then with competition, the price is battered down, and often the quality as well. Eventually, no one makes a profit! After this, many packers drop out. In the end, if he is strong enough, the *original* producer is left holding the field. It doesn't always work this way, however.

Birds Eye's New Policy

In June, 1951, through the vice president of General Foods, Charles Mortimer, the following statement of Birds Eye's new distribution policy was made: Birds Eye would enter into no exclusive or restrictive selling agreement with any customer and would continue to service any market through a single, direct buying distributor as long as the Birds Eye policy of retail distribution could be achieved.

When a review of the distribution situation in any market, served by a single distributor, revealed that their joint efforts could no longer satisfactorily achieve Birds Eye's distribution objectives, then the company would sell other direct buyers who qualified.

The statement helped to straighten out the already tangled distribution and marketing picture.

G. O. Bailey now became manager of Birds Eye and the company bought another plant at Nampa, Idaho.

Incidentally, we campaigned at that time to have concentrates included in USDA warehouse holdings and shortly thereafter they were added. We since have urged the inclusion in USDA reports of a breakdown between retail and institutional sizes.

Treesweet Products, long a California juice canner, entered the market with the production of lemonade. Later, a plant was established in Florida and orange juice is also being packed.

At this time, Jack Moone suddenly resigned from Snow Crop, the company he had helped establish. In leaving he said, "I leave Snow Crop as the No. 2 factor in the industry, with the annual sales of $60 million, as against zero when I started the company six years ago." With Marty Mathews, he then started an organization called Concentrate Marketers, which contracted with Sunkist to distribute lemonade on a four-year contract.

The new president of Snow Crop was the late Nat Barclay, another former Birds Eye man.

More Restaurant Use of FF

QFF started a campaign to improve the use of a better grade and broader variety of frozen vegetables in restaurants. An editorial said: "It seems incongruous that an expensive meal, featuring a $4 or $5 steak, is often accompanied by C. Grade frozen lima beans, some over-mature peas, or string beans, or cut corn that is as tasteless as straw. Yet these same diners would never tolerate this grade of merchandise in their homes."

We urged the use of more types of vegetables by restaurants, such as spinach, asparagus, broccoli, sprouts and corn-on-cob, etc.

More time-saving equipment was being introduced to packers. New improvements in harvesting were foremost. Viners for peas and beans were coming into universal use. A harvester which cut and loaded peas directly onto the trucks in one operation was being used. A mechanical harvester for spinach and corn reduced costs. A machine was introduced for mechanical harvest of raspberries.

The originator of one of the most beautiful pie cartons I ever saw was George Petritz who began producing cherry pies; later he added others. The company since has been taken over by the Pet Milk Co.

First Chicken Pie

C. A. Swanson of Omaha now launched its first 8-oz. chicken pot pie which was backed by an extensive newspaper campaign. Clarke Swanson also developed a wide variety of frozen chickens, including cut-up fryers, drumsticks, breasts and thighs. More about him appears later in this story.

Ocoma Frozen Foods built a new processing and freezing plant and began to develop frozen poultry. Like Swanson, Ocoma changed ownership and was to develop greatly, as we shall see.

An investigation into the extent of financing needed in the industry at that time showed that investment in plant facilities should average about $5 per 100 pounds of food packed.

More developments came along. Thaw indicators were introduced to determine whether frozen food packages had been subjected to dangerous thawing temperatures. Several such devices now are on the market and, while they are useful for testing purposes, it is doubtful that they ever will be used widely on packages.

This brings us to mishandling of frozen foods, about which the industry was much concerned at the time, as it is now. As volume grew, this problem became more serious. Later, QFF ran posters in its Retail Edition to educate store clerks and managers on proper handling. The National Association of Frozen Food Packers started a program of retailer education.

Two important distributors then became prominent in the South. One was Sam Vogel of Little Rock. Another was Richard Page who established Arrow Distributors in New Orleans and later did much to develop Frosty Acres. Both men contributed much to the industry. The whole South was growing along with frozen foods. There now were 233 distributors and 156 packers in that area. Including concentrates, the South today is second only to the West Coast in total frozen food production. It stands high in the national production of frozen poultry, shrimp, other seafoods, meats, berries, prepared foods and an increasing number of vegetables.

More Fish Imports

Fish imports were growing at an astounding rate. In Iceland, for instance, over 60 plants produced frozen and other fish. Iceland, Denmark and Norway were shipping large quantities of frozen cod, haddock, perch and other fish to the U.S. Later, when fish sticks were introduced, block frozen fish came largely from abroad.

In the West, California Berry Growers, a large cooperative, started producing berries in California. Smith Canning Co. enlarged its Pendleton plant. Milan Smith, who was later to go to Washington in an official capacity, was its manager, Smith is now head of the National Canners Association.

At the March, 1952, convention in Chicago we presented a consumer survey in cooperation with the Crowell-Collier Publishing Co. Over 2,500 personal interviews were held with housewives in food stores in 35 cities. The results were printed exclusively in QFF. There was much pertinent information on the consumer's attitude towards frozen foods, frequency of buying, preferences and dislikes.

Gibson Retires

On January 1, 1952, the late E. T. Gibson retired from General Foods. An "elder statesman" of the industry, he did much to steer Birds Eye through its formative years. More, he acted promptly and, as it turned out, correctly, during the critical early war years. He was responsible for getting packers together into an association, as I wrote earlier. In short, he was the right man in the right place at the right time.

For years QFF has been campaigning for a smaller frozen pea. This campaign at last bore fruit when California began to pack the Wyola variety. Peas from that state have increased gradually, though production is limited.

A&P Moves Into Own Brand

In March, 1952, both A&P and Grand Union announced their own brand of concentrate. This was sweet music to the ears of the independent concentrators in Florida. It sounded more like a dirge to the national brands, however, for this started the swing of concentrates to chain brands.

Today, every major chain, many smaller ones, cooperatives and voluntaries, as well as many distributors, have their own juice labels. Competition from the big chain cuts into national brand sales. A&P also came out about then with its first labels, vegetables. IGA also put its brand in its stores and, of course, many chains already had their own labels. This meant increased competition for cabinet space.

The sixth frozen food convention, as mentioned above, was held in March, 1952, in Chicago and had the biggest attendance of any convention to date. C. L. "Hap" Snavely, of Consumers Packing Co., was named packer president; W. L. Pavlovski of Beatrice Creameries, distributor president. The main question at this convention time was de-control of frozen food prices under OPS.

In early 1952, Gorton's of Gloucester introduced pre-cooked codfish cakes. Gorton's remained in the forefront of many later developments in seafood packing. One of the first to appreciate the need for quality, Gorton's recently adopted an inspection policy, under which all lots of fillet are inspected by the U.S. Dept. of Interior.

Another new packer was Tilghman Packing Co. of Tilghman, Md. The firm owns its own oyster beds and packs breaded oysters and crab cakes. The company has since been taken over by Dufiy-Mott.

Food Clubs Start

Food clubs now entered the picture and began selling home freezers and food. "Are food clubs here to stay?" we asked in a four-page survey. At that time in Los Angeles, these clubs were selling 6,000 freezers a month. But their story of savings was hard to prove, not only in meats but in commercially packed foods.

We found in New York, for instance, that leading food club plans were selling beef at almost exactly the price of the chains. When I went to Los Angeles that year, the high pressure selling of home freezers was terrific, with salesmen getting a high commission on each sale.

I remember reporting at the time that one home freezer plan salesman did such a good job of convincing his prospect that he needed a freezer for a better way of life, that he got the buyer to install the freezer in the bedroom, there being no other space in the house. When delivered, it was found that the freezer was too big to go through the front door, so the purchaser agreed to have his bedroom window removed to permit entry. This left him with an outside door leading to his bedroom, an example of the sacrifices made by those who were sold on a better way of life through food plans.

A Noble Experiment

In 1952, we brought out a pocket edition of QFF which was published on the 20th of each month. It was small in size, easy to read and it condensed industry developments. I always liked the pocket size, which measured 4 by 6 inches; in fact, this little magazine was modeled after "Quick."

The industry liked it too, but unfortunately, we couldn't get advertisers to make special plates for this size, so we had to sacrifice convenience to expediency and the edition was enlarged to the same size as QFF. This is now our RETAIL EDITION, with a circulation of 42,000.

Concentrate Pouches

During early 1952, an individual serving of concentrate appeared. Pasco Packing Co. had developed a flexible film pouch, or envelope type of package, for a single serving of juice. This was a 2½-ounce bag which was used by the Walgreen drug chain. It provided absolute portion control, since a special machine was made for reconstituting the juice, automatically adding the correct amount of water.

This prevented over-dilution, which often happens in the case of counter dispensers. Sunkist also developed a single serving of lemonade, but with indifferent success.

Pink lemonade made its appearance. The product originally was introduced by Mr. and Mrs. Raclin of Chicago and was packed by Sunkist. Today most companies have a pink lemonade, which always has been a steady seller.

In September, 1952, the Chicago Frozen Foods Association expanded and became the Central States Frozen Foods Association under the chairmanship of Charles Peterson who, together with the writer and others, was among its founders. Since then, this association has grown and embraces many mid-western states.

In September, 1952, the Chicago Frozen Foods Association expanded and became the Central States Frozen Foods Association under the chairmanship of Charles Peterson who, together with the writer and others, was among its founders. Since then, this association has grown and embraces many Midwestern states.

The importation of frozen seafood continued to grow. Norwegian Frozen Fish, under the trade name "Frionor," began to sell cod, haddock and other fish fillets here, as did some English and German firms. Coldwater Seafood Corp., which had gone into business only a few years before, was selling 24 million pounds of fish from Iceland in this country.

C. Lubin   H. C. Boerner

A famous QFF cartoon, entitled "The hand that rocks the cradle rules the industry," referred to the growing role of chains in ff distribution about 1951.

One of a series of cartoons which enlivened the monthly pages of. QFF.

First Fish Sticks

The first fish sticks began to make their appearance. With the introduction of this product, the trade immediatey recognized a new staple of major importance. Birds Eye tested its first product in Worcester, Mass. It was a 10-oz. package retailing for 59¢. Others followed: Gorton's, Fulham, O'Donnell-Usen, Blue Water, Red L, Snow Crop, Tilghman and several more. In Boston, Boston Bonnie erected a $250,000 fish plant. Hy Trilling, its president, later greatly popularized fish sticks through a series of unusual ads featuring a "mermaid."

Later, as we shall see, this new star was to have a meteoric rise which was checked for a time by its own errors, but resumed its upward flight once the errors were corrected. I think the fish stick and portion has a permanent niche among frozen food "regulars."

Meanwhile, the big, unorganized, sprawling fish industry, with its haphazard and often uneconomic marketing, was beginning to show signs of more cohesion. Its association, the NFI, through regular conventions and other efforts has accomplished a good deal toward knitting the industry together.

At the same time, consumption around 12 pounds per capita, was at a ridiculously low level. On the other hand, quick freezing had revitalized the entire industry. Shrimp deveining machines, fish filleting equipment and, in some cases, freezing at sea, were increasing volume and reducing costs. Then, with the entrance of breading and fish sticks, the upgrading of fish meat in palatable form, was doing much to increase the consumption of fish.

QFF presented an idea at that time to increase seafood sales. We suggested that the consumer be given a frozen sauce in an envelope which would be packaged with the fillet. All she had to do was to heat the sauce along with the fish. We felt that few housewives knew how to make a good fish sauce which is very important in making a more palatable fish dish. By providing her with it, she could come up with a better tasting piece of fish. The idea was taken up by several packers.

In 1952, orange juice, which the year before had been high, now went to the opposite extreme. Housewives could buy cans at two for 29¢ and often below! We pointed out the danger of this "pogo stick" pricing, which not only prevented price stabilization from the industry's standpoint, but what was worse, also confused the housewife so that she did not know what the price of a can of juice should be.

Since the industry's inception, the concentrate can has sold as low as 9¢ and as high as 36¢.

Packaging Advances

Several packaging manufacturers, Marathon, Western Waxide, Pollock and others, now came out with standard label designs, which enabled many brand names at low cost. This was another important step in packaging.

Al Brackett, who had been Birds Eye's manager of packaging reseach retired at this time. He accomplished much to advance this science. Several articles authored by him appeared in QFF.

We installed a special section on Transportation & Warehousing, which has grown with almost every issue. A careful and constant check is kept on the latest developments in these fields, and the information gained is duly reported. I think this action is of great value to the industry.

QFF had begun to notice that in these later years the industry's basic method of preservation was not being kept before the public sufficiently. We saw that many consumer advertisements seemed to take it for granted that the public knew the featured product was frozen, making no mention of this fact in the ad.

QFF wrote: "Here's an example of failing to put your best foot forward. This industry originally was sold to the public on the 'miracle of quick freezing,' a newer and better way of food preservation. The trade should remain proud of its origin and never forget that quick-freezing is what makes this industry's products different from canned and fresh foods."

With a rapidity born of intense competition, the 10-ounce package pretty well had taken over in most products by 1953, and we said: "Let no one suppose that the final type of frozen food package is yet determined. There is today excellent high-speed equipment on the market, but improvements are still under way. No trade offers as many opportunities to the packaging industry as does frozen foods."

Mass Feeding

QFF early recognized the coming importance of in-plant or industrial feeding, and we said so. Many plants which had cafeterias and restaurants, often feeding thousands of employees, were installing large freezers and beginning to handle frozen foods.

This market, so far as frozen products are concerned, has never been fully developed. The technique of in-plant feeding is still a hit-or-miss affair. I think there exists a golden opportunity to serve this field with a well-designed frozen food plan.

ReaLemon Products arrived on the scene in Chicago and took over a California plant. This company developed quickly in frozen lemonade and other juices. In Pittsburgh, Quaker State Foods began bringing out a line of meals, including turkey dinners, pot roasts, Swiss steaks and a variety of other complete meals.

Midwest Production

Already the idea of brokers doing a retail job for packers was being developed. In 1953 Food Enterprises, New York, had 39 salesmen in the retail field. This trend was to grow greatly in a few years, culminating in many large packers turning over their entire retail organization to brokers.

The Midwest was growing as a production center for peas, corn, and many other vegetables. Strawberries and cherries had long come from this area, but it was enlarging in other products as well, including prepared foods, meats, poultry and seafoods. I believe the Midwest has not come anywhere near full realization of its potential as a producing area, and that in future years it will show a greater rate of production growth than many other sections of the country.

At the industry's seventh convention in Chicago, many new faces were seen at the Conrad-Hilton, emphasizing the industry's continued growth. Most of the talk was about low prices and profits and price wars. "The blood bath isn't over yet," said one packer.

QFF published what was then a rather sensational article showing that, for the first time in food history, frozen peas were consistently *cheaper* than canned peas. Many thought this was an achievement; others thought otherwise, since it demonstrated on how low a margin the industry was operating.

Mel Spiegl was elected president of the packers, and Joseph Gaudio became the distributors' president. The Packers' Association allocated $200,000 to be spent for a five-year nutritional research program.

A Depression-Proof Industry

We ran an editorial which has often been quoted, entitled "Is the Frozen Foods Industry Depression-Proof?" The 1958 recession which brought out reports of profitable operations by many packers who showed small profits in boom days, seemed to indicate that the industry does go counter to recessions. People may cut down on other things, but it seems they continue to spend money on *good foods* when business conditions are tight.

Chicken pot pie sales, starting from zero, were now more than 100 million packages. The item had become a best-seller. Concentrates had, for the first time, reached sales of one million gallons a week. At the same time, fruit pies began to hit the market.

Pies Begin

Everyone jumped in. The argument was that a frozen pie baked in the home would be much fresher than a fresh pie baked 12 to 14 hours before the housewife bought it. It was a *good argument,* as growing sales showed.

Fruit pies proved a bonanza to many packers of frozen fruits. Sales of apples, peaches, berries and other fruits increased, just as pot pies opened a new market for vegetables and potatoes. We called this "remanufacturing."

At this time Fred Otterbein, former president and general manager of General Foods of Canada, succeeded the late Howard Chapin as general manager of Birds Eye. He brought high executive ability to that post, backed by a solid knowledge of costs and accounting. He proved to be a valuable asset to the frozen foods industry.

Do Women Want Variety?

We began to express real concern about the amount of space which chain brands were taking up in their own cabinets. "Such brands as Safeway, First National, A&P and others," we wrote, "are taking up more and more cabinet space in their company stores. In some chain units, the brand occupies as much as 75% of space at prices which are highly competitive.

"It is interesting to note that in no other food category could a chain brand occupy anywhere near this amount of total space. What variety-conscious woman would shop in a chain where 75% of all canned goods were under the company's own label?"

On the other side of the picture, independent packers were benefitting. More and more orders were coming their way. In touring plants that year I reported: "There is hardly a plant I visit which is not packing under the Bel-Air, A&P, Yor Garden or other brands."

A Horror Movie

I might bring in here a funny episode which occurred at the time. There was a movie released, probably the first of a long series of horror and scientific fiction movies, entitled "The Beast from 20,000 Fathoms." The film was about a prehistoric monster which, millions of years ago, somehow got into a quick frozen state in the Arctic north.

Thus frozen, he remained in suspended animation for millions of years, until an atom bomb defrosted him. The monster made its way southward, creating havoc along the way, until he finally arrived in the East River at the foot of Wall Street.

Working his way up Wall Street, the beast destroyed everything in its path except, by some miracle, the offices of QUICK FROZEN FOODS. The movie showed our building standing safe and untouched amid surrounding wreckage.

Our explanation of this miracle, which we offered, was that we at QFF were exponents of a system of preservation which made the beast's survival possible, and we like to think that he *appreciated it!*

First TV Dinners—$1.09

Swanson then introduced its first "TV" dinner in 50 principal cities, backed by a big advertising campaign. The price was $1.09 for a 12-ounce package. Success was almost immediate, confirming what QFF had predicted many years before.

After the first meals were launched by Maxson and Frigidinner, there were many "false alarms." With the introduction of the "TV" dinner we said that "the day of the complete meal has now dawned for good." And so it proved. I think that the platter dinner, though not as yet perfected, eventually will become one of the industry's top sellers. At today's prices, 39-79¢, how can anyone duplicate this meal in a restaurant?

Despite many editorials on the subject and the pleadings of many in the industry, the packers' and distributors' groups split in 1954 with two conventions held. The packers convened in February at the Commodore Hotel in New York; the distributors met at the Waldorf-Astoria the following month.

In March, we announced that QFF had accomplished an unprecedented publishing feat by putting out two larger issues totaling more than 500 pages, plus two Retail Editions, in one month. The February Packers' Convention Issue appeared February 1st and the March Distributors' Issue came out on the 21st of February. It was a job which kept us burning the midnight oil for many weeks.

A Policy on Write-Ups

One day QFF received a letter from an old advertiser who complained that he did not get as much publicity as the companies who never advertised. Therefore, in our next issue we published, under the heading "Editorial Policy," the following:

"In the interests of honest and legitimate publishing, and especially in the interests of both reader and advertiser alike, QFF publishes only what it deems to be *of value* to the reader. How is value determined? What instructs or informs the reader has value.

"We consider the time of our thousands of readers too important to waste with meaningless personality write-ups, unless such information is useful to the greatest number. If a company has *something newsworthy* to report to the trade, QFF will print it, regardless of whether such a firm is or has been or ever will be an advertiser.

"Such a policy promotes confidence in the integrity of a magazine, because the reader knows that an effort is being made to give him *honest information* without bias or pressure."

Frozen Foods—2000 A.D.

In February, 1954, we published an unusual story, or fantasy, called "Frozen Foods in 2000 A.D." It was a big dose of long-range predictions in sugar-coated form, some of which have already come true. (See February, 1954, issue).

We received many letters, two of which I quote. One was from John Baxter of Snowflake Canning Co., who wrote: "Your article fascinated me, it is most interesting and well written. I don't expect to be around in 2000 A.D. and I am afraid that my son Jack won't be here either. Probably his son will follow him in the vegetable processing business. I am going to send your article to Jack to put in his safe deposit box to pass along to his son."

E. T. Gibson, then at Columbia University, wrote: "I appreciate your fantasy of the future. Jules Verne was thought to be crazy when he first wrote his stories of undersea and upper air travel. Maybe you are not really nuts." Yesterday's extravagant fiction is often today's fact.

V. Stouffer   J. M. Biggar

QFF's Retail Edition

Our Retail Edition was growing. It then had a circulation of 40,000 which included all chains from those with two stores on up to the biggest, plus all voluntaries, cooperatives, and 22,000 independent supermarkets—the cream of America's retail buying power.

The Retail Edition is the only publication devoted entirely to the retail merchandising of frozen foods. It also was designed to carry to retailers the regular promotions of packers. Each issue featured a detachable poster. Several of these were devoted to educating retail clerks and store managers on the better handling of frozen foods, a permanent problem of the industry. The RE has since been translated into Dutch, German and Swedish. QFF also produced a film strip, with an accompanying sound track, titled "What Every Grocer Should Know About Frozen Foods." It ran about 15 minutes and was widely distributed not only in this country, but abroad. It was designed to show the retailer why frozen foods can be one of his best departments.

Soups Appear

In March, 1954, Campbell Soup began to market its first four frozen soups in Philadelphia. This was followed by perhaps the most powerful advertising campaign the industry had ever seen. Advertising appeared in *Life, Saturday Evening Post* and other national media. Result was that Campbell got immediate space in the country's cabinets, not only in chains but in independents and in delicatessen stores, as well.

Rarely before or since has any company been able to obtain retail acceptance as fast as did Campbell; often it was out of proportion to the importance of the product. But the soups were good, and today the products can be found in most stores. Wisely, Campbell froze only those soups which did not can well, such as shrimp soup, clam chowder, oyster stew and the like.

More interest was being shown by the bakery people in freezing. Speakers at a bakers' convention predicted that the major portion of all bread soon would be frozen.

Another speaker said that unless baked goods manufacturers employed quick-freezing on a wide scale, regular frozen food processors would extend their lines to include baked products. This is what actually happened, though in a few cases bakers did go into the business, including Continental Bakers, Johnston, Ward, Dressels, Pepperidge, and Arnold, etc.

Many bakers use quick-freezing to prevent staling. Arnold Bakers, for instance, built a large warehouse for the storage of baked goods. The company's president said he hoped eventually to freeze and store at least one full day's bake in the plant. He added that much of the products being produced on holidays and double time would then be done on a straight time basis.

Howard C. Boerner, who had been sales manager of Minute Maid, resigned about this time and formed his own brokerage organization in New York. He went into retail merchandising and was successful following a trend started by Food Enterprises several years before.

I paid a visit to a growing shrimp center, Hooker's Point in Tampa. This port has grown greatly as a receiver of Gulf shrimp. A new plant, Ocean Products, was established here by Leo Levinson of Chicago, and was soon to show phenomenal growth. The operation, also run by two capable sons, Robert and Marshall, started with breaded and other varieties of shrimp, and branched out into other seafoods. Another packer there is Shoreline Packing, a subsidiary of J. W. Horses, operated by Day Wood.

Stokely Buys PictSweet

In a surprise move, Stokely-Van Camp bought controlling interest in PictSweet Foods, Mt. Vernon, Wash. Both labels were continued and through this absorption, Stokely acquired nine additional plants. In its last fiscal year, PictSweet had grossed $17½ million and was understood to be showing a profit. Later E. J. Watson resigned. He is now president of Lamb-Weston. This was the beginning of a new merger trend which was to be followed by some startling developments.

During the same month we honored our 40,000th subscriber who was Sabin Meyer, 27-year-old New York broker.

5

The Volume Years

In 1954, per capita consumption of frozen vegetables, fruits and concentrates was up to 12 pounds, but this did not include other foods which have brought the figures well within the 13-pound range. While vegetables other than frozen in the period from 1949 to 1953, rose only 19% in consumption, frozen vegetables increased 85.5%!

The industry's vigorous promotions of the previous ten years had shown *results.* Frozen food stores had an estimated 50,000 cabinets in 250,000 retail outlets.

QFF now began to quote monthly retail prices in 26 cities. This showed the high and low advertised prices, by brand, of 45 items and proved a yardstick of retail price movements.

Were too many items being packed? QFF's 1954 Processors' Directory showed more than 1000 different frozen food products being packed, with twice as many individual freezers packing each item as there had been a few years before. In some individual products there were from five to ten times as many packers duplicating the same product.

Prefabricated meat cuts were beginning to hit their stride. New firms like L. B. Darling, Wyandot, Goren Packing, On-Cor, Frigid Meats, and others previously mentioned, were able to offer consumers quick-cooking, low-cost meats in convenient form.

But now a new field opened up—the portion control institutional market. Exact portion control savings in high-wage kitchen labor began to make good sense to many hotels, restaurants and kitchens. Within a few years, portion control meats were to account for a good slice of frozen meat production.

Another new star now rose, the rock cornish game hen. First introduced by Jacques Makowsky if Idle Wild Farm, the product had quick acceptance, not only in the institutional field, but in retail stores as well. Others became prominent: Victor Borge started his Vibo Farms.

In October, 1954, both Southern associations merged into one convention, a practice which was to continue yearly thereafter. These were the Southern and Southwestern groups thcn headed respectively by Clyde Barrington and Frank Hicks. These conventions draw from the entire south and serve to mix hospitality, relaxation and fun in equal parts with business and work.

For National Brands

In the midst of an avalanche of new chain labels, a voice spoke out that gave heart to national packers. At a convention in 1954, Val Bauman of the National Tea Company said: "We do not believe in private labels, we used to have them but got rid of most of them. We believe completely in nationally advertised frozen food brands.

"When people walk down our aisles we want them to meet *friendly labels,* labels they see advertised every day. We want to take advantage of the money being spent to advertize frozen foods." I hope Mr. Bauman still feels the same way.

We were still concerned about the lack of cabinet space and QFF offered cash awards for the best design for a cabinet, that would overcome the floor space shortage existing in many retail stores. We estimated that approximately $100 million in sales were lost by the industry each year, because not enough products could get to consumers. As a result of the contest many elaborate drawings and designs were received, some of which were of unusual merit. Our contest served to stimulate thinking towards improved cabinets. The winning design remarkably resembles 1968 models!

We also encouraged the wiser spread of multiple packaging. A start already had been made in the concentrate field where two, three or four packages were being offered in a multiple container. Experimental work is being done by some packaging companies in multiple wraps for vegetables and other packages. The public long has been accustomed to multiple sales in the frozen foods industry. Peas at four or six for a certain price, or strawberries in multiples up to five and so on, is a common occurrence in many markets.

QFF Predicts Prepared Vegetables

We continued to plug for progress. "What frozen produce needs," we said, "is a jazzing up—a new look. The public wants a change once in a while. But how can you change an agricultural product? Just a little imagination, the application of new ingredients such as MSG, the development of different varieties, the use of sugar or precooked vegetables. Nothing stays new forever." Seven years later prepared vegetables were introduced by Seabrook, then Birds Eye and Green Giant.

We pointed out that the worst judge of a product is the industry itself, and I believe that more firmly than ever today. The industry is too close to the forest to see the trees. When bringing out a new product, many packers allow the testing to be done by their own sales force, brokers, or customers.

Marathon Corp. produced an unusual film called "Time for Shopping," which is worthy of mention here. It was taken in supermarkets without the shoppers' knowledge, and showed something which ordinarily misses the eye—the extreme care with which people choose frozen foods out of a cabinet. Women, men and couples were shown examining packages closely, picking them up and putting them down again; some actually inspected packages up to 10 minutes before buying. The moral of this film demonstration was that people *do* pay attention to labels—and what is on them.

Fried foods were starting to show a strong upsurge. French fried potatoes, fried shrimp, fish sticks, prefabricated meats, breaded seafoods and poultry, oysters, crab cakes, codfish cakes and other items were becoming popular in all parts of the country.

Deep-fat frying in the home was increasing. This, of course, encouraged the use of prepared breading and batter mixes and also encouraged manufacturers of bread crumbs to enter the field. I think there are strong possibilities in the breading and frying of certain vegetables. For instance, okra, green beans, eggplant, tomatoes and other types of firm vegetables. Many people certainly find fried fish much tastier than broiled or baked fish.

MM Buys SC

In 1953, QFF predicted that big mergers were "close at hand." The industry was electrified when, in November, 1954, Minute Maid bought Snow Crop from Clinton Foods for more than $39 million. This brought MM a complete line of 61 Snow Crop vegetables, fruit, fish, poultry and others items, three more concentrate plans in Florida and three processing plants in the West.

Now MM had a complete line. But the move was to cost MM dear. It entered the vegetable field at a time when chain brand competition was becoming stronger every day. Though Minute Maid made money for the first year or two on Snow Crop lines, it lost thereafter until it finally divested itself of that label to Seabrook Farms. Today, Minute Maid is back in the juice business. Changing conditions had obviated the necessity for a complete line.

The second big merger within a year hit the industry. Campbell Soup took over C. A. Swanson & Sons in an exchange of stock. At the time, William B. Murphy, president of Campbell, announced that the changing pattern of eating habits makes the market for frozen foods, especially precooked meals, very attractive.

Campbell Soup gained Swanson's 10 plants and its "know-how" of the manufacture and marketing of prepared foods. Swanson originally entered the field in 1934 as a Birds Eye distributor and began packing frozen eviscerated poultry a year later. Since then, the company broadened out into frozen poultry parts in 1948, followed by chicken pies, beef and turkey pies and complete dinners. Sales at the time of the merger were around $100 million.

Dinners Catch On

Campbell had shown what its powerful advertising and merchandising guns could do with frozen soups. Now, its full strength was to be turned on dinners, pot and fruit pies and other items in the prepared line. Large sized advertisements appeared, and still do, in leading magazines and other media. Meanwhile, Campbell constantly improved its products and reduced prices until today, a very satisfactory frozen meal can be bought for 60¢. Campbell-Swanson is now a household word in prepared foods.

Consolidated Foods Co., Chicago, which had almost obtained control of Libby the year before, now purchased E. A. Aaron & Bros., veteran Chicago wholesaler firm. This was the beginning of Consolidated's expansion program which was to bring Ocoma, Sara Lee, Booth and others into its fold. At the same time, Swift & Co. bought Holiday Food Co., and Stoaway Sales, which put this meat packer in the pot pie business.

Retailer Rules

By this time it had become clear to everyone that the big-volume retailer now ruled the frozen foods industry. In QFF's March Year-Book there appeared a leading editorial, with a cartoon of a hand labeled "the large retailer," rocking a cradle labeled "the frozen foods industry." Underneath was the caption "The Hand That Stocks the Cabinet Controls the Industry."

We said, further: "Over the limited zero space through which must siphon the multitude of products of several hundred packers, the large chains and supermarkets now hold almost absolute sway. Their edicts dictate what goes into what valuable and coveted cabinet space, for how long, and what the price shall be. The industry wanted big volume and got it—but *at a price*. Is the industry being sacrificed upon the altar of volume?"

While profit had been cut almost in half in the past 14 years, sales had increased 650%! But things were different from what they had been ten, five or even three years before.

Many paradoxes appeared. Frozen foods often were selling for less than their canned counterparts. Competition to get into cabinets was warlike. The differential between advertised and non-advertised brands was not as great as it should have been. The national brand packer was not getting a sufficient premium for his brand.

Now a "Group of Industries"

Chain brands were crowding many a packer. Volume grew, but the strongholds of power were shifting. The whole frozen food picture was in a state of flux. Independent packers, however, were benefitting, temporarily at least, by the growth of chain labels.

We said at the time, "There should be enough business around for years to come to keep the private label packer busy."

Far-seeing brokers realized that they could profit by offering packers a distribution service which would reduce the processor's cost.

Thus, with more people than ever entering the industry, more confusion reigned. We said that this was no longer one industry but a group of many:

First officers of the Southwestern FF Association, organized in 1953.

The tempo of mergers really speeded up on Nov. 30, 1954, when Mark Candee of Clinton Foods (left), packers of Snow Crop, sold that division to Minute Maid. John M. Fox, then MM president, signed to close the deal.

L. D. Levinson

W. B. Murphy

frozen produce, prepared foods, concentrates, baked goods, meats, poultry and seafoods. The frozen foods industry was indeed reaching vast proportions.

In vegetables the best sellers were now peas, lima beans, broccoli, spinach and green beans, with french fries a rival for third position in many markets. In fruits, strawberries were still the top selling item, followed by raspberres, peaches, cherries, rhubarb and pineapple. In concentrates it was orange, grape, lemonade and grapefruit juice, in that order.

In March, 1955, QFF brought out its biggest issue to date—520 pages. "It weighs three pounds and cost $1.50 a copy to produce," we said. More than 50% of the issue was devoted to solid editorial material. There were 12 sections, 50 features, 22 departments; it contained maps, statistics and information on every possible phase of the industry.

The issue had its lighter side. In it we ran a section of humorous material ribbing the industry. About packers QFF had this to say:

> *You have to admire the packer,*
> *   With him it's always a struggle,*
> *'Twixt under-and-over-supply, it seems,*
> *   He's taught himself to juggle.*
> *When over-supply pulls prices down,*
> *   And then the picture reverses,*
> *The packer keeps right on muddling through,*
> *   No matter what the purse is!*

And about distributors:

> *You may think YOU have worries.*
> *   Well, maybe so.*
> *   But distributors' lives are filled with woe.*
> *With chains and margins and selling direct,*
> *   Any fun in this business is hard to detect.*
> *Be that as it may he keeps right on going,*
> *   There's one thing to say about him:*
> *The industry hopes he'll stick around,*
> *   They sure couldn't do without him!*

Nor was the broker neglected:

> *Confucius say that everyone*
> *   Goes broke except the broker—*
> *He keeps his inventory in his hat,*
> *   From fruits to fish to mocha.*
>
> *His chief expense is his telephone,*
> *   But when all's done and told,*
> *A good solid broker of frozen foods,*
> *   Is worth his weight in gold!*

More truth than poetry perhaps.

For the first time QFF published an "International Section" which covered frozen foods around the globe. It also carried ads from England, Belgium, France, Japan, Germany, Norway and other countries.

New variations of frozen potatoes appeared. Patties met with instant success, originally having been brought out by Ore-Ida. Other potato variations, in addition to french fried and whipped, are puffs, au gratin, creamed, diced, hash brown, stuffed, "krinkle cut" and sweet potatoes. Some companies introduced frozen French toast, but success was negligible.

The national convention in Chicago in 1955 was vast. More than 2,500 attended and there were more than 200 exhibitors. United again after the split of the previous year, packers and distributors convened once more under the same roof. George Mentley was elected president of the packers; Sam Vogel of the distributors.

What astounded everyone was the scope and breadth of the industry, made apparent by the numbers and variety of people who attended, and the great array of new foods and equipment. The convention was indeed a milestone. But convention dates had been erratic, jumping from early January to late March. QFF consequently took a poll of its readers on both time and place. The results strongly indicated Chicago for the site and late February or early March for the time. We suggested that at least the *same time* be fixed for each convention.

It was a great privilege for me, about this time, to receive an award given by the Marketmen's Association of the Port of New York. The citation read: "Always willing to subordinate personal interests to over-all progress, his untiring efforts have made an estimable contribution to the food industry with its ever-changing and expanding problems." John Q. Adams, chairman of the board of directors, awarded the citation.

Another packer was Mariani Frozen Foods of Santa Clara. Originally in fresh produce, the firm installed several berry lines and became an important packer in strawberries and melon balls.

Thoughts on Meat—Swift's Experiment

Swift now made its famous full-line debut. Expensively and handsomely packaged in aluminum foil were 17 cuts, including beef, pork, veal and lamb steaks, chops and roasts. Each cut was carefully boned and trimmed. Millions of dollars were spent to introduce the line, which in a very short time was able to obtain a surprisingly large amount of cabinet space.

Sales were not up to expectation, because of the sizable difference in price between the fresh pre-packaged meats and the new frozen and trimmed cuts. Later, the line was cut down and revised; new prepared meat and poultry items were added.

I think Swift's original foil-packaged effort was a little too rich for the average consumer, taking into consideration the availability of fresh meats. The boned and trimmed feature was not sufficiently understood to make up this difference in price.

But, the fundamental idea is *sound* and as brought out earlier in this history, frozen cut meats mean a real saving all down the line—IF they are universally frozen and accepted!

A meat packer estimated that if frozen meats were sold at fresh meat prices, packers would net about 5¢ a pound. At present, large meat packers net a fraction of 1% on sales.

Again it is all a matter of timing. Success will come, I believe, to the degree in which meats are produced by *all packers,* for this will reduce costs to a competitive degree with fresh meats.

I think the reason frozen meat acceptance is inevitable with time is the basic economies it offers to meat packers: Reduction of weight, retention of offal, bones and other by-products, uniform trimming, identification, control over production and distribution, reduction of costly branch house maintenance, as well as other reasons.

Armour, too, dabbled in heavier cuts, Del Love, I might add, has done much for both his company, Armour, and frozen meats in general.

More for Less Trend

Now fish sticks and pot pies were to run the gamut of cheaper packages and low prices—the same thorny trail that many other products had traveled before. Both items were selling for 30% less than in the previous year, even with smaller-sized containers.

The whole trend was to offer more for less. Not only were prices lower, but quality had also decreased. The cycle spun to its inevitable conclusion, sales went down instead of up, and several packers left the scene.

Then a revival got under way, quality improved, prices firmed, standards were adopted, and today, both fish sticks and pot pies are on an upward trend again.

By this time, many large chains and supermarkets were reporting that from 7-10% of total sales were in frozen foods. What was more important was the fact that all large retailers now recognized the need for adding low temperature cases and, when planning new markets, allowing for an adequate frozen food department.

What had long been awaited became a fact at the end of 1955 when A&P came out with its own vegetable line in eastern markets. Prices were lower than on nationally advertised brands. This was only the beginning; the squeeze was on!

Howard Johnson entered the market with a line of prepared foods, including some of the restaurant's specialties, such as frozen fried clams, scallops, lobster newburg, chicken fricasse, fish chowder, pies and other items. The company has since greatly expanded its line.

I was invited to address the National Food Brokers Convention in Atlantic City that year. On this occasion, I pointed out the need for brokers against the background of changing trends in frozen foods.

Chains Battle, Too

QFF now pointed out that the battle between chains was in full swing. All over the country chains were trying to outdo each other with low-priced specials. Chains themselves, caught up in the squeeze for *more and more volume,* were fighting to attract the housewife's dollar to their markets.

New supers opening up were geared to do not $100,000—but a quarter of a million dollars a week! To move such volume, low prices were indeed needed. Are there *too many* supers?

We also bemoaned the lack of executives in the industry. In an editorial headed, "Wanted—Executives," we said that the biggest shortage in the industry was not in cabinets, or production men or salesmen, but in good executives.

"Unfortunately," we said, "true executives are born, not made, though training helps. Too many frozen food firms are being run by production men or salesmen." Many firms were finding it to their advantage to reach out into other fields to hire proven executives, even though they had no experience in frozen foods.

The 1956 convention was jointly sponsored by both packers' and distributors' groups and held at the Waldorf in New York. It was vast and overcrowded with an attendance of over 3,000. Brokers, we noted, had multiplied noticeably. At that time, QFF ran lists of room numbers as a service to convention-goers. F. G. Lamb was elected packer president. Richard M. Page was made president of the distributors' group .

The National Prepared Frozen Food Processors Association was now in full swing. Declaring that one-third of the housewife's frozen food dollar now went to prepared foods, the association was not functioning as a separate body and had its own banquets and meetings during national conventions.

Nutritional Survey

In 1956, the National Frozen Food Packers' Association published its long-heralded $250,000 nutritional survey. The findings were made by the Wisconsin Alumni Research Foundation. Vitamin and mineral contents of 30 vegetables, 14 fruits and 7 juices were established.

The highest in vitamins and minerals were found to be asparagus, broccoli, collard greens, orange juice, peas, spinach and strawberries. Harold Humphrey was chairman of the nutrition committee. However, QFF went a step further; we published a comparison of the nutritive values between *frozen and canned goods* and reprints of the chart were widely distributed.

The comparison showed canned foods at a considerable disadvantage in a number of items, especially when compared to frozen vegetables, fruits and juices in B1, Riboflavin, Vitamin C, Vitamin A and Niacin.

The Association could not make these comparisons but we did, and many packers and distributors found them to be an added "sales tool." In view of all the money spent to make this nutritional survey, I feel it has never been as widely used by the industry as its importance indicated.

Pendulum Swings to P.L. Packers

Many private label packers, around 1956-57 had been worried about the loss of private label business from advertised brands and the squeeze on the independent packer's own label.

But the pendulum had swung in the opposite direction. Chain brands were proving the salvation of many packers. That year there was a record strawberry pack and for the first time, California *took the lead* away from the Northwest.

With a previous year's carry-over, the industry had to move around 350 million pounds before the end of the year. In 1957-58 there was a heavy pack of berries to move, also, but it was done.

When on the West Coast I made it a point to investigate the *quality* going into chain brands. I talked to many plant superintendents and executives and I watched production lines. There was no doubt that most chains were favoring Grade A merchandise and were determined to have their own brand of frozen foods *match* the quality of advertised labels.

As QFF had long advocated a smaller pea, I was glad to note a new, hybridized pea being developed in the Northwest, known as 633 and 637, or "Freezer Perfection."

North Pacific Canners & Packers had just moved into a large new plant in Portland. Since then the direction of this able organization has been turned over to George Robertson and Bob Birkeland. Northwest Packing Co. also has been re-built.

About this time, Edward J. White, who had a long and brilliant career in frozen foods, retired; he was given a testimonial dinner in San Francisco.

Stouffer Starts

Another large processor now entered the picture—The Stouffer Corp. of Cleveland, large restaurant chain and catering organization. Under the directory of Vernon Stouffer and Wally Blankinship, the firm built a new and modern processing plant and brought out 24 attractively packaged items. The products received good distribution, though the line has been somewhat altered since and great strides have been made in restaurant feeding and vending.

Sara Lee Sold

The merger trend was still on the march. Consolidated Foods, which had recently taken over Ocoma, Aaron and American Frigid Dough, now plucked a prize—Sara Lee. The transfer was made through issuance of 160,000 shares of Consolidated stock and Charles Lubin remained in charge of the subsidiary. Up to the time of the sale Sara Lee had grown from $400,000 in 1951, to $5 million.

Campbell-Swanson entered the entree business, launching a line which included beef and gravy, meat loaf, seafood au gratin and chicken with noodles, followed later by more items.

Birdseye Dies

Known as "the father of quick freezing," Clarence Birdseye died in New York in October, 1956. We have related his story earlier, and I can only add that he was a good friend of QFF and was our technical adviser for many years. He used to liken the frozen foods industry to a small infant—plenty of noise on one end and an absolute lack of control on the other—a very apt description even today.

When the industry had its crises, he confidently asserted, "the industry, like the phoenix, will rise again from its own ashes."

Pot Pie Crisis

At this time pot pies were under fire. Less than 25% of the total weight of the average frozen meat pie was made up of meat and vegetables, according to a survey by a consumer group. On the average, 40% of the total weight of the pies was in crust; 14% meat and 4% to 10% in vegetables, the rest of the pie being made up of various gravies and fillings.

The pot pie industry which had risen so phenomenally to the tune of 375 million units sold in one year, was now undergoing readjustment. Prices ranged as low as 17¢ for an 8-ounce pie. Poor quality by some operators, who since have been shaken loose, was threatening to put the item in eclipse.

"Plenty of gravy and little meat" was coming to be the consensus of opinion. Some packers attempted to raise prices and market premium pies, but with little success, excepting in limited markets.

A growing line of entrees, too, was cutting into pie business. Prices have been so low that most consumers seem unwilling to pay *more than 25¢* for a pot pie, no matter how good.

Minute Maid-Seabrook War

A curious incident occurred during this period in price cutting, which I am sure all participants will want to forget. In an effort to find cabinet space for its new, and short-lived, premium line of vegetables and fruits, Minute Maid launched a fierce assault to elbow out two competitors, Seabrook and Birds Eye, in the upstate New York State area.

MM's weapons were: 60¢ a dozen under the regular price, 10¢ vegetable sellers, coupon give-aways. The other two packers were not hesitant in retaliating. Housewives had a field day. Retailers, confused and bewildered, went along with the show. Seabrook was offering concentrate at 5¢ a can, if purchased with a Seabrook vegetable.

"We're waiting," said one retailer, "to see if they'll give away a package with each free one." Many pondered on this example of mass-hysteria merchandising, which, fortunately, died down just as quickly as it had flared up.

Exempt or Not

Toward the end of 1956, the U.S. Supreme Court ruled on a subject which had been the object of many debates on QFF's pages. Frozen fruits and vegetables were ruled exempt products. The decision added to the general confusion of the whole transportation problem.

Annual banquet of the Distinguished Order of Zerocrats.

Directors of the National Frozen Foods Association, standing, left to right: Harry K. Schauffler, New York City; H. M. Holland, San Antonio, Tex.; Donald E. Dover, Elkhart, Ind.; Lee S. Sweptston, Greensboro, N. C.; A. E. Langford, Jr., Pensacola, Fla.; A. L. Robertson, San Francisco, Calif.; Arvel Kamman, Evansville, Ind.; Stanley Langenthal, Boston, Mass.; Robert Grant, Saginaw, Mich. Seated, left to right: Frank Hicks, Austin, Tex.; Gordon Griffith, Miami, Fla.; Arthur Boone, Austin, Tex.; H. D. Jester, Sr., Wilmington, Del.; Willard Richards, Boston, Mass.

Opponents of the trend to more exemptions had warned that it would only divert more traffic to unregulated carriers which, in turn, would reduce the incentive for regulated carriers to invest in improved equipment. In the absence of published tariffs, they had also warned that the industry would be left without a first-class transportation network.

The packers' association had gone on record to support regulated carriers, though later they adopted a neutral attitude. Others in the industry contended that it didn't matter whether the trucker was regulated or not, as long as he had adequate equipment.

Distributor Future

QFF, and many others in the industry, continued to debate the future of the wholesale distributor. Partially crippled by the direct deal, what was his future to be?

He could concentrate on institutional business or a retail label of his own, which none could take away. Many distributors did sponsor their own brands. The principal distributor-owned brand was Frosty Acres, controlled by Frozen Food Forum, Atlanta, Ga.

A complete, well-chosen line of specialties, which even the largest chains do not buy direct, is another answer, particularly with even the higher profit margins on specialties and prepared foods. I think eventually, mergers between wholesale grocers and frozen food distributors in certain areas are feasible for the purpose of operating a voluntary chain of independent retailers.

Not long after New Year of January, 1957, what was probably the most *relaxing* of all frozen food conventions took place in Miami, at the swank Fontainebleau Hotel. QFF called it an "expense account" or "cabana" convention, since many delegates brought their wives and families and everyone ended up with a nice sun tan to show for the trip.

Minute Maid's then president, John Fox, said that "management which is not optimistic should be fired . . . the survivors will make good profits, but it will be a rough, tough business."

David Levitt of Downyflakes Foods declared that creeping inflation could be blamed on labor.

The subject of a service fee for distributors was gaining ground. Many insisted that where a distributor was expected to give merchandising and introductory services, such a fee was essential.

The USDA predicted that frozen foods, alone of all the principal food groups, would increase in greater proportion than the growth of the population, thus making further inroads into the overall food industry. This was certainly shooting for QFF's long-cherished goal to convert the 75% perishable bulk of all foods to preservation by quick freezing!

Mishandling Problem

As frozen food volume grew, the problem of mishandling frozen products grew along with it. Zero temperature was not being maintained at all points down the distribution line. A check by one packer of 156 of the 220 public warehouses whose services it employed, disclosed that 54% of them were deficient in at least one respect; 9% had storage temperatures of about 5°.

In distribution warehouses the percentage was considerably higher. The Florida Citrus Commission had purchased 1,408 samples of concentrates in various stores throughout the country. Only 23% had been stored at zero or lower.

State legislation against improper handling practices was imminent and this was something the industry did not want. Consequently, a Task Force to improve handling of frozen foods was appointed by the National Frozen Food Packers Association, with Sterling Doughty as chairman.

All related industries were on the committee. A widespread educational campaign at all levels was adopted and meanwhile the NAFFP was to make tests in stores throughout the country.

In many stores, packages were observed above the frost line. Large super markets were no exception. QFF, through a series of educational posters inserted in its RETAIL EDITION, did much to instruct clerks and store managers on proper handling. One such poster we published read: "Exposure is Murder—*Get Frozen Foods Off The Floor Fast.*"

On Seafoods

I was invited to address the annual convention of the National Fisheries Institute in May, 1957, and I urged seafood packers to stress fully the really outstanding nutritional elements found in seafoods. To implement such a course I suggested that the nutrition story be printed on small inserts and placed in every package of frozen fish marketed.

I added that 40% of all frozen seafood business is done during the Lenten season and that the prime object of the industry should be to level out the peaks and valleys and lift fish out of a seasonal category. A markup similar to that taken by retailers on other frozen food would help sales.

"The only way to increase per capita consumption of frozen fish is by improving the *taste* of such products. The consumer's mouth must be made to water for seafoods.

"This means prepared seafoods," I said. "Per capita consumption could be increased by (1) the rise of portion controlled seafoods; (2) the increase of precooked and prepared seafoods; (3) the growing emphasis upon branded products; (4) more realistic pricing, and (5) realization of better quality through inspection and grading."

Service Brokers

In a sudden move to win more retail cabinet space, Birds Eye went to brokers in the New England and Chicago areas. This was a major policy change and one which was to sweep the industry.

Up to that time Birds Eye and most other large packers had sold retailers exclusively through their own branch sales offices. Gene Merkert of Food Enterprises took over the account in New England and Robert Mitchell, formerly of Libby, set up his own brokerage organization to handle Birds Eye in Chicago.

The service broker was becoming the most important cog in frozen food distribution. It simply meant that a good brokerage organization which has "ins" with the right chains and big retailers can do a *better* job than many a packer's own sales organizations.

It also meant that brokers could operate on a fixed expense. QFF said: "So vital and valuable has big chain cabinet space become, national packers have thrown aside all preconceived methods of distribution in favor of anything that will get them into the life-giving space, and keep them there."

Meanwhile, other packers followed suit. Minute Maid also went to brokers all over the country. So did Libby, Morton, Swift, Armour, Sara Lee, etc. The merchandising broker, with a staff to retail salesmen, began to occupy a *new* niche. Now he had something to offer which packers needed!

On a Better Industry

In June, 1957, QFF published 10 points for a better industry. Briefly, some were: (1) More careful prior-to-planting analysis of probable sales by packers. Development of marketing studies on leading items. (2) Don't sell just to make a sale—*sell to make a profit.*

(3) The presence of an ample supply of raw material alone should not be the basis for greatly increased production, without sound knowledge of what the market will take. (4) More advertising dollars should be spent for advertising, rather than diverted to rebates and allowances. (5) More business morality and higher ethics; more sound, courageous and imaginative business leadership.

QFF kept plugging away for *premium brands.* "With many products down-graded, with prices low, the time is ideal for premium brands of frozen foods," we said. Several came out. Southland Frozen Foods marketed a whole green bean in an aluminum wrap.

Seabrook put up a similar premium bean in a gold foil package. A premium product, properly advertised and promoted, is bound to pay its way many times.

On my 1957 West Coast trip I found that many packers were taking a more sober look at production. Acreage was being pared. Meanwhile, California strawberry production was shifting from the San Joaquin Valley to the Salinas-Watsonville-Santa Clara area. Farmers Frozen Foods opened a large new plant in Salinas.

Minute Maid Moves Brokers

In the fall of 1957, Minute Maid went through a renaissance. First, to cut expenses, its offices were moved to Orlando, Fla. Ambrose E. Stevens, a vice president, resigned. So did MM's treasurer, Robert Bender, its advertising manager, and others.

Sales managers in various areas set up as brokers, included Eugene Bruce in New England, Robert McCarthy in Chicago. Gay Pryor and his organization set up in the Philadelphia-Baltimore area. Colony brokerage in Philadelphia, headed by Al Barrison, now covers 5 states. Other "old timers" besides those already mentioned elsewhere, include: Meier-Morrow, Lutgens & Reichenback, Aris Brokerage, Bill Forbes, Ken Pezrow, Velma Lee, V. C. Arguimbau, Oceanic Sales, Dudley Slocum, Kirstein, Kennedy Menke, Ben Soloff, Mattlage, Stanley Marcus, G. L. Morrow, Davenport-Webb, Zino, Byron Carlson, one of the first bulk brokers; Moore Food, C. Hagerty, Koff & Smith, W. J. Hasselman, Gene Lichter, John Lutz, Daniel Mordecai, Jack Carpel, Marketing Assoc., Food Enterprises, Cobb & Cobb, Cunningham, McCormick, Ja-Son, Battle, Sessa, A. C. H., Ira Samelson, Bill Amos, Marshall Goldberg, E. Skinner, Harry Schierholz, Car-Dave, Frank Finnegan, R. H. Shaw, Flick-Byrne, Otto Kuehn, Tom Trump, Walter Meier, Fist Brokerage, Desnick & Association, Oscar Bank, J. H. Fleming, Stover & Clark, Maffry, United Food Brokers, Bob Glazier, James Brokerage, Hagan-McGuire, R. M. Sloan, Hall-Roepke, Ayres & Roberts, Clyde LeBaron, C-M Sales, W. G. Swanson, William Dooms, Pacific National, Valley Packing, N. W. Cedergreen, Harold Barrett, Food Associates, and others. In Canada three brokers stand out: C. B. Powell, A. R. Clouston and Foodwell, Ltd.

Snow Crop Spin-Off

Admitting that its frozen Snow Crop produce line didn't pay, MM finally decided to dispose of it through a Seabrook take-over of the label. Seabrook, which acquired a nationally advertised brand and some 10 new markets, seemed to be happy with the deal.

Meanwhile, MM divested itself of this burdensome brand and decided to go back into the exclusive business of processing juices. Holman Cloud was made executive vice president. Hamilton Stone, now a leading broker, became vice president in charge of sales. At the same time, Minute Maid formed a growers' cooperative to supply it with fruit.

Expansion continued apace. Zero holding space was, and still is, springing up everywhere—in packing plants, distributors' warehouses and in chain and cooperative organizations. Three suppliers playing a part in this expansion are Jamison, who developed a special door for use with power trucks and an aluminum-clad door, the Clark Door Co., suppliers of an automatic opening door and Butcher Boy with a light weight horizontal sliding door.

In its August, 1957, issue QFF asked its readers to guess what the average American consumed in all foods in the year 1908, and what they thought current per capita consumption was. The correct answer is *600 pounds of food per capita*—both in 1908 and now!

All of which showed that the human stomach can hold just so much food. The point is that times change and, while people may eat the same amount, they eat *different* foods.

An early meeting of the NAFFP board, around 1954.

Founding officers of the National Prepared Frozen Food Processors Association made their first official appearance on the stage of The Carillon, Miami Beach, Fla., immediately before kicking off their 1964 annual Night Club Party. Reading from left to right: William Lipton, Modern Maid Breading Mixes (director); Warren Friedman, Mrs. Kornberg's (director); Hy Epstein, Pet Ritz (vice president); Ernest Schoenbrun, Sau Sea Foods (director); Tom Ascher, Temple Frosted Foods (vice president); Bernard C. Zipern (executive director); Joseph Settineri, Roman Products (director); Louis Midler, Gretchen Grant Kitchens (vice president); Nat Friedson, Meat-O-Mat (president); Sidney Schwartz, Sidney Fox Poultry (director); and George Wexler, Original Crispy Pizza Crust (director).

The All-Industry Task Force to Improve Frozen Food Handling meets in 1958.

1956 Directors of Eastern FF Association. Earl French was chairman.

Founding members of the Frozen Potato Products Institute, Chicago, which heralded tremendous growth of that phase of the business, are seated (left to right): H. F. Lochrie, Birds Eye; F. Nephi Grigg, Ore-Ida Potato Products; R. S. Farish, J. R. Simplot Co.; W. E. Buechele, Brock & Co.; W. W. Carpenter, Bryne Marcellus Co.; E. J. Rollins, Taterstate Frozen Foods; D. Langley, Taterstate; T. C. Waterman, W. H. Foster, Stokely-Van Camp; John Baxter, Snow Flake Canning Co. Standing: G. R. Squires, Cedergreen Frozen Pack Corp.; M. A. Peterson, Idaho Potato Growers; A. Oppenheimer, Idaho Potato Processors, Inc.; L. C. Jones, Simplot; Byrne Marcellus, Byrne Marcellus Co.; D. B. Berelson, Ore-Ida; W. H. Mosely, Ore-Ida. Not pictured: M. L. Waggoner, Jr.; Olney & Carpenter, Inc.; George Mick, Chef-Reddy Foods; Manning Exton, Seabrook Farms Co.

First meeting of the All-Industry Frozen Food Committee and directors and officers of the National Frozen Food Association.

During this period, Stokely-PictSweet moved its offices from the Northwest to Oakland, Calif., and a man who had exerted considerable influence upon the industry, E. J. Watson, resigned. He was succeeded by William H. Foster.

Coupons, Giveaways

In its December, 1957, issue QFF ran a leading editorial entitled: *"Packers Caught in a Welter of Coupons and Giveaways."* We said that if the number of coupon offers made by any one industry in the U.S. were tabulated, the frozen foods industry would lead them all.

Most packers were against give-away promotions and all claimed they were forced to match their competitors. One said, "We have a tiger by the tail and can't let go!" The practice still persists.

For instance, a Morton coupon, clipped from a newspaper advertisement was good for 10¢ toward the purchase of a pot pie, representing one third to one-half of the price.

Birds Eye was offering four cans of juice for 59¢. Upon receipt of these four can tops the consumer got a refund of 25¢, a saving of better than 40%. Minute Maid offered a coupon worth 10¢ against the purchase of five cans of its juice. Swift gave consumers back a silver dollar if they bought five pot pies in New York for $1.19 and mailed the labels back.

Swanson had cut-out coupons worth 15¢ against a purchase of casseroles, and it gave a package of frozen fruit pies free to a purchaser of a TV dinner. Libby gave a 10¢ allowance against the purchase of two packages of strawberries. These were but a few.

Low-Price Psychology

Of course, coupon redemptions are generally low, but we questioned whether it was sound business. Did it not set up a *low price psychology* in the consumer's mind? It also developed fickleness on the part of buyers, many of whom shifted from brand to brand, depending upon the attraction, without ever becoming very conscious of the value of any one of them.

The First Florida Freeze

By May, 1957, a 10¢ retail orange juice price was seen as prices tumbled. FOB prices dropped to $1.00 a dozen. A record inventory was on hand. In order to give growers the true picture on concentrates, the Florida Canners Association distributed widely a reprint of a QFF article entitled "Determination to Keep Prices Low Rules Orange Concentrators." It was hoped that the same determination would rule growers as far as fresh fruit prices were concerned.

Florida was beginning to worry about an over-pack of juice. Like the sword of Damocles, the fear of a 110-million-box crop of oranges hung over the state. The industry was carrying more than six million gallons.

The score the previous year: FOB prices were $1.25 a dozen, and a big pack was coming up.

However, several months later, an unexpected "Act of God" was to lift the concentrate industry out of its predicament and, in a few short days, reverse the situation.

Meanwhile, worried by a current drop in sales, a campaign was adopted to improve the quality of concentrates.

In December I went to Florida on my annual concentrate tour. There was considerable nervousness on the part of the industry about the prospect of moving the 102-million-box crop. There was talk of cutting the price. Could the nation absorb the estimated 70-80 million gallons?

On December 12th everything changed. A severe freeze, which some said was ten years overdue, hit and hit *hard*. Driving to Lakeland it was so cold I had to put antifreeze in my car radiator! Many areas were wiped out, young trees particularly were hurt.

We immediately predicted a 30% cut of the estimated pack and that is exactly what happened. Those caught with big inventories benefited, such as Minute Maid, whose stock gradually rose from 4½ to 12 points.

I stayed in Florida right through the freeze, visited all concentrators and attended hectic meetings of the Florida Citrus Commission. This group took immediate and courageous steps to protect the quality of concentrates. But the danger of poor quality hung like a cloud over the industry.

As it turned out, however, more freeze-damaged fruit could be used than was expected at first. The quality also was *above expectations*. Thus, standing upon the brink of possible price chaos, the whole industry, by an "Act of God," was saved from possible over-production.

Prices shot up to unprecedented heights and many concentrators went on allocation.

Chains were taking more concentrate under their own labels. We estimated that during the 1957-58 season ten leading chains took 40% of Florida's pack.

H. P. Hood became the latest to join the ranks of Florida concentrators, acquiring a large plant at Dunedin.

Mexican Plants

Mexican strawberries were becoming a factor on the American market. Several new and modern plants had been built in Mexico and all berries were in institutional sizes. Among the leaders were Congeladora de Irapuato, whose president is J. I. Mendoza, and Del Centro, run by Manual Moran. Mr. Moran is now in another business.

In 1963 the U.S. imported about 30 million pounds of frozen strawberries from Mexico. By 1968, an estimated 60 million pounds were brought in, all frozen, but in addition another 30 million pounds of fresh were exported. Mexico in five years had not only doubled its production of frozen berries, but had grown to important stature as a shipper of fresh product. One of the leaders in the importation of Mexican berries and orange juice is George Bernhardt of San Antonio Trading Co. Also, many plants were beginning to produce frozen vegetables: peas, broccoli, green asparagus, green beans, cauliflower, etc. One such operation, set up by Findus (Nestle), is producing a line of frozen vegetables which are distributed in Mexico City, Vera Cruz and other centers. I tasted some of these Mexican vegetables and they were excellent. I think there is a great potential here for frozen produce.

Co-op Advertising

QFF ran an editorial, "Just How 'Cooperative' Is Cooperative Advertising," in which we maintained that advertising allowances were draining millions of dollars yearly from the coffers of frozen food packers, who sorely needed that money to promote their own labels to the consumer and to lower their operating costs.

As a result, many large retailers who insist on such allowances, often as a prerequisite to stocking a brand, are reducing their own costs of advertising. Not only that, we said, but some retailers are benefiting by the difference between the national rate charged by the packer, and the local rate which the retailer pays.

The whole practice is *questionable* and is coming under the scrutiny of the FTC. We claimed that retailers should *pay* for their own advertising and the whole system of cooperative advertising should be made illegal.

A Slight Recession

As the recession arrived, many packers were going *counter to it*. We had predicted years before that the industry was practically "recession-proof" and so it now turned out to be. Packers such as Seabrook, Minute Maid, Dulany, Morton, Booth, Swanson and many others were showing better profits than they had when business boomed.

One reason was that somewhat higher prices were prevailing in various items, due to crop shortages. This was particularly true in citrus, green beans, some vegetables, and in the prepared food field, which, though still highly competitive, was becoming more stable.

However, one thing was evident! Many firms were showing higher profits on the *same* volume. This proved that more volume, as many had earlier maintained, was *not* the answer to better profits.

Sales by Packers, Chains

In 1958, QFF estimated that 14 leading packers were doing about $580 million worth of frozen foods business; among the first six were Birds Eye, Minute Maid, Campbell-Swanson, Stokely, Booth and Libby.

At the same time, we figured that 16 leading chains were selling 802 million dollars in frozen food products.

While the government was issuing price indexes showing that foods had hit new highs, a QFF study revealed that in the five years between March, 1953 and March, 1958 prices of frozen foods had *declined* 18%. This information was released by QFF to the press.

A Study on Pizzas

Another leader making phenomenal gains was pizza. QFF made a study of regional preferences and found that different parts of the nation had distinct preferences about sizes and types of pizzas.

The four major categories were: the hors d'oeuvres size, served as an appetizer or snack; the individual portion size; the medium-sized pizza, serving two to four and the large-sized pizza.

The best selling pizza is the medium group, 5 to 10 inches in width and 5 to 10 ounces in weight. There were preferences, we found, in the type of crust and in the shape of the pie, which is generally either round or rectangular. QFF's directory lists 57 makers of frozen pizza.

It Isn't Quite Fair . . .

In June, 1958, there appeared in QFF an editorial that brought many letters from all over the country, both pro and con. Entitled, "It Isn't *Quite* Fair, Is It?", the editorial suggested that chains be *limited* in the expansion of their own brand labels.

More than one large packer of a nationally advertised line has been forced to turn over some of his production to feed chain labels. The editorial brought more comment than any run before or since. Brand packers were happy about it, but private label processors less so. Two processors who packed for chains cancelled their advertising (later reinstated). However, of the many letters we received, most of them recognized the justice of our position.

I am well aware of what the chain has done for the frozen foods industry and for the consumer, through volume selling and improved methods of marketing. Nevertheless, the picture can be lopsided at times.

Recently a speaker at a meeting of the American Bankers' Association predicted that the time was coming when farmers would grow chiefly to fill specific orders, placed under long term contracts with giant retailing organizations.

"Such foods would go into private labels, controlled by food stores, which are fighting a *winning* battle with national labels on the food shelves and in cabinets," the speaker pointed out.

6

The Trend to
Big Companies

And now, the era of consolidation had begun. Competition, as we have shown, became even more intense; nevertheless, surprisingly few companies went out of the business and a great many came in. But the new ones were coming from other fields. Firms like Pet Milk, Seeman Bros., Green Giant, Ward Baking. American Home Products, Coca Cola, Wilson, Morrell, Rath, Pepperidge Farms, were all getting into frozen foods. Management and personnel changed with great rapidity. Many small companies, especially in the prepared food and seafood fields, which had started right after the war, were now becoming firms to be reckoned with; many plants were expanding and new advertised names appeared before the consumer. By the end of 1958, frozen food sales were close to $2½ billion, there were 1600 frozen food processors and the investment in the industry was reckoned to be around $5½ billion. There were over 1000 distributors and 400 brokers. Financial strength of most packers was greater, too, and the relation of working capital to sales was higher than at any time.

Net profits, still low, were moving up slightly. In frozen produce the average ranged from 1¾% to 2½%; in prepared foods from 3%-6%, sometimes higher.

Shortly thereafter, the Federal Trade Commission decided to investigate the "concentration of power in the chain store field." I want to say here that QUICK FROZEN FOODS, all during its career, has followed a courageous and far-sighted editorial policy absolutely unequalled by any other publication in the food field. It has been our aim to stay ahead of the industry, never behind it. This fearless policy will be continued as long as QFF serves the industry.

Swing Toward Institutional

There began to develop a strong swing on the part of distributors toward the institutional business. Many wholesalers were being squeezed by direct selling and independent stores were becoming less and less. The institutional route beckoned, and at least 300 distributors who had hitherto been exclusively retail, opened up institutional departments. QFF ran many inspirational success stories about distributors. One was about A. W. Huss in Milwaukee, which had increased volume to $5 million through good management; another concerned Frank Blum & Sons of Pittsburgh. QFF took a keen interest in distributors' problems; one of our editors spent several days with a distributor, riding his trucks and accompanying his salesmen in order to learn the problems of distribution.

QFF made a survey of frozen food brokers and found a distinct trend away from the 100% frozen broker and toward the addition of grocery and non-food items. About half of the country's frozen food brokers had now taken on additional lines. Many had turned to institutional business. One broker said it was becoming increasingly difficult to add volume by merely taking on new lines. New frozen lines frequently levered one of his own principals out of the cabinet. An important New York broker was Howard C. Boerner, former sales manager of Minute Maid. He formed his own brokerage company, retaining Minute Maid and obtaining other leading brands. He employs 110 people and does a business of over $50 million annually. Hamilton Stone in Los Angeles does $45 million and Gene Merket in Boston of Food Enterprises does between $40-$45 million. These are just a few brokerage organizations with corps of salesmen. There are many others.

Bakeries and Baking

Baked goods began to advance quickly. Pepperidge Farm introduced its line of turnovers and patty shells, Sara Lee its new coffee cake. A precooked starch which cut the preparation of frozen pies was developed; Buitoni entered the field with macaroni and cheese and new cream pies were brought before the consumers. Chock Full o' Nuts came out with frozen doughnuts. QFF ran an article which suggested retail bakeries as outlets for frozen foods. We ran pictures of several bakeries which had put in frozen food cabinets and pointed out that these stores had been losing ground to supermarkets. A large line of frozen baked goods was suggested; just how far this idea went I don't know but it does have possibilities.

Fruit Pie Price War

Now the industry found itself in the grip of a deadly price war. The fruit pie, a popular item with the consumer was the target. 22-oz. pies sold three for $1; 39 cents for a top selling 8-inch frozen apple pie began to look high. Fruit pie packers had gotten themselves into an impossible situation and money was being lost by every producer. Worse, consumption was not increasing because there was no margin for advertising or promotion. To add to the confusion, some chains planned their own frozen pies. Starting on the West Coast, the price war soon became national. One or two packers tried to stick to top quality and a firm price, but the going was hard. Actually, chain *unfrozen* pies were selling at a higher price than the frozen. I am sorry to say that unsettled fruit pie prices still persist, although there is one bright spot—quality remains high.

In the field of distribution, companies which rendered a full service; warehousing, transportation, retail and institutional distribution were expanding. One such was Plantation Foods in Miami headed by Gordon and Walter Griffith. The firm covers two-thirds of Florida and has expanded with new warehouses and services.

Poly Bags Come

Started in Canada, the idea of selling frozen foods in bags hit the U.S. with a bang in early 1959. Back before the war, several packers tried to market frozen vegetables in cellophane bags without success. Now however, with the development of better films, bags became a reality. The "pour and store" idea for free-flowing vegetables was catching on. Safeway was the first chain to go in—with a 2-pound bag. Today, the wide variation in sizes has narrowed down to a few; principally one, 1½ and 2 lb. sizes. In March, 1959, QFF was worried about the plateau which frozen vegetables had apparently reached. No important increase was evident since 1957. The reason, QFF said, was because frozen vegetables were no different than they were ten or twenty years ago. But, we hoped, the new prepared or "pepped up" vegetables might change the picture, (which they did soon thereafter). We also felt that the new poly bags which pushed out more merchandise in one and two pound sizes to consumers, would move more product and help surpluses—which also happened.

This was a period which might be compared to an express train which slows down momentarily at a railroad crossing. But the frozen foods express didn't slow down for long. Volume soon resumed its upward curve.

Boilable Bags Grow

As has often been stated, I am a firm believer in the boilable bag as the best means of re-heating many products. By 1959, bags began to get popular, as well as aluminum pouches. Meat and gravy, beef and sauce, stews, casseroles, seafood and poultry items, prepared vegetables and sauces and a great many other products, especially in the institutional field, now began to appear in pouches. In Europe the idea caught on particularly well. In my trips abroad I saw soups, pot-au-feu, and even a complete boiled chicken in boilable bags.

Seabrook was an innovator, having launched the first vegetable line which included such items as asparagus cuts in hollandaise sauce, creamed spinach, broccoli au gratin and lima beans in sauce. Minnesota Mining's "Scotch Pak," Du Pont's Mylar, Kordite, Spec-Fab, and later, Standard Packaging's "Flex-Vac" boilable bags have proven of great value. While on the subject of packaging, I would like to add that Ekco

Containers' aluminum trays are popular with the prepared foods industry; Kaiser, Chicago Metallic, and Alcoa have all contributed to the aluminum field. At this time Crown Zellerbach and Marathon brought out sealed poly-paper pouches for strawberries. All kinds of new packages were coming on the market. Such pioneers as Marathon, Pollock, Container, Mead, Schoettle, Weyerhaeuser, Crown Can, Lord Baltimore, Muirson, U.S. Industrial Chemicals, R-C Can, Continental and American Can, Package Machinery, W. Virginia Pulp, Union Carbide, Du Pont, Gordon, Sefton, Haekin, Fibreboard and many others all had something to offer the industry. In the plastics field, Eastman, Formed Container, JE Plastics, Koppers, Milprint, and others began to offer special packaging for the institutional field and for vending. Indeed, QFF commented, there were now plenty of packaging systems to choose from!

Fish Portions Come In

By 1959 fish sticks had climbed to over 60 million pounds, but at the same time a new product began to emerge—fish portions, mostly uncooked but breaded. Their rise was spectacular. Fishery Products, now owned by Gorton's, was one of the innovators. The firm also introduced a "fish sandwich" and other variations. We suggested that fish sauce in a separate pouch be included with fillets to save housewives the chore of making a sauce. Some packers adopted the idea.

Zero, Zero

The theme of the 1959 packers' convention was the AFDOUS code and the industry rushed to frame its own frozen foods code to offset legislative action by states. Harold J. Humphrey of Birds Eye was elected president. Nothing developed by the Association of Food and Drug Officials was beyond the ability of the frozen foods industry to meet, was the general contention. A great deal of publicity has since been engendered in every branch of this industry about mishandling, with the result that the proper treatment of frozen foods has improved at least 100% in the past four years. Nevertheless, several states *have* passed zero laws which in the end, may be all to the good.

In April, Edwin T. Gibson, a frozen food pioneer, died. As previously mentioned in this History, he had played an important, if not vital role in the industry's early days.

Southern Vegetables

Other parts of the country besides the South were now beginning to eat southern vegetables; blackeye peas, okra, squash and greens. New southern vegetable recipes were beginning to appear in newspapers, and they were playing a more important part in private and advertised label lines.

Packer profits began to rise. Birds Eye, Consolidated Foods, Libby, Seabrook, and others enjoyed a better return. QFF commented: "It is too bad that profits in this industry are only made when *firm prices* prevail, generally due to shortages, rather than because of natural growth and volume increases."

Poly bags fostered the "pour and store" idea for free-flowing vegetables. Safeway was the first chain to go in with a 2-lb. bag.

E. Merkert

D. Whitley

L. Jones

We reported that the U.S. Senate was an enthusiastic frozen foods user; the Senate restaurant buys 70% of its vegetables frozen and 50% of its fish and seafoods in frozen form.

Eruption of New Products

An avalanche of new prepared foods now paid tribute to the vivid imagination of packers. Among them were shish-kebab, pizzaburgers, casseroles, garlic bread, rolls, hero and submarine sandwiches, hushpuppies, yeast rolls, candied carrots, chocolate souffle, baby foods, barbecued meats, and many more. In an editorial headed "Go For Broke," QFF said: "Naturally, not all of these new products or companies will succeed. However, some of them *will,* and past experience teaches us it's as likely to be the fellow with the wildest, most unlikely product—as the one with the apparent 'natural.' " Sau-Sea Foods also expanded its line of shrimp cocktails and built a new plant.

The south and south-west groups got together and held their regional convention in Dallas. Every year these conventions have grown and the last one took place on a Nassau cruise boat. QFF ran special sections covering these conventions and for my part, I can only say that the southern hospitality that abounds at these affairs makes them the most enjoyable to attend of all frozen food conventions. The same is true of the regional New England groups which have their meets each fall at some famous New England hostel—with golf accommodations. Sometimes more is accomplished at a section affair than at a national one.

In June we started our *International Edition,* printed in three languages. The issue, which has been very successful since, was aimed at the growing frozen foods industry in 60 nations, but more on this later.

We discovered that the frozen food failure rate for the previous year was only .0306% per thousand, *below* the national average. In 1958 there were only six failures with total liabilities of less than one million dollars. This was heartening.

Outstanding Editors

Sam Martin now became editor of QFF, having served for some years as managing editor. He contributed a wealth of frozen food experience and enthusiasm and has done an excellent job since. He is a frequent speaker at conventions and meetings and has a sound knowledge of frozen food developments. During its 30 years, QFF has had outstanding editors. Among the outstanding ones were Galina Hopkins, who has since married and retired to England; Joseph Fletcher, now on the west coast; and Munro Innes, presently editor of the Food Distributors' news bulletin.

The Seabrook Upset

In March, 1959, QFF ran a "profile" on Jack Seabrook entitled "Four Years at the Helm." As president, he had brought a bold, new look to the company. Head of the world's largest frozen food farm, the firm showed a profit, on its $35 million sales in 1958. Seabrook introduced new products, acquired the Snow Crop line from Minute Maid and had upped sales under the Seabrook label against private brand packing.

Now, with a suddenness that astounded the industry, Seabrook was sold to Seeman Bros., Inc., New York grocery wholesalers of which John Fowler was then chairman for $3 million. The sale of 448,000 shares of stock, about 98% of Seabrook common stock, marked the end of a family battle for control of the company. The strife was between Charles Seabrook, the father, and his sons, Jack, Courtney and Belford. In 1954, facing a loss of $1,600,000, the elder Seabrook placed his stock into a trust, which was headed by his son Jack, who operated the firm to new prosperity and profits. When, as a requisite for a bank loan renewal, C. F. Seabrook would not renew the trust, the family fight developed. The father had long differed with his sons in operating policy but a climax was reached when the sons sought to have him declared mentally incompetent. Legal action was started. In the meanwhile, C. F. Seabrook's release from a mental hospital was obtained by his attorneys, and he filed a counter suit against the sons for one million dollars each. In evident pique, the father then sold the control to Seeman Bros. Though not asked to do so, the sons left the company. Jack Seabrook has since made an eminent career as a bank director and chairman of the board of Frick & Co. Courtney has stayed in the frozen foods business as a consultant and in other capacities. Seabrook has had its ups and downs since; lately it has made money and most recent reports show an encouraging trend back to profits again. (Later Seabrook developments in next chapter.)

During the same month a noted figure, John I. Moone, founder of Snow Crop Marketers, died. He was only 46, but he had made Snow Crop a household name. Another event that month was the retirement of George Mentley after 25 years of service with Birds Eye.

Dinners—Our Prediction Fulfilled

An interesting incident took place at that time. The industry was startled one morning to read an advertisement of Air France which said: "Nothing's frozen except the ice cubes. Frozen foods? Impossible. Sooner starve or live on bread and water! Gourmet cuisine, freshly prepared and served." We were besieged with phone calls and hastily sent a reporter to interview the French airline, whose officials expressed chagrin when the full import of the caption was explained to them. "The ad was prepared by our N.Y. agency who were apparently carried away with enthusiasm for our French cuisine," said an official, who added that he had many frozen food packages in his own freezer. An apology was made.

Of all prepared food items, we announced that frozen dinners had shown the greatest advance, an increase of 35% in sales in one year, fulfilling an old QFF prediction. Entrees were next, followed by fruit pies, baked goods and nationality dishes.

Automation Takes Over

On my 17th annual west coast trip I reported that *automation* had taken over, because, while labor and other costs continued inflationary, frozen food prices remained low. Such equipment as automatic tray loaders, pneumatic pea cleaners, electronic check weighers and metal detectors produced by the Brilmayer Co., were becoming widely used. At one plant a package, rejected three times by the metal detector, upon investigation, was found to contain a very small sliver of metal in a pea. Distributors were automating too. Jerseymaid in Los Angeles had installed the first fully automated warehouse which included the controlled ordering of pallet loads, the use of an IBM card punch system and other innovations.

A great boon to economical operations proved to be the Porter-way Harvester, in common use on such basics as peas, spinach, lima beans, broccoli and elsewhere in the country on Southern vegetables. This machine had a flexible cutter bar which cut close to the soil and a shaker system that left hearts and other matter on the ground, loading only sorted leaves on the truck.

Vegetable sales still remained static. We urged a cooperative advertising campaign, to be undertaken by vegetable packers, aimed at making Mrs. Housewife conscious of the fact that she was depriving her family of nutritious, high-vitamin foods by not serving *more* frozen vegetables. QFF also emphasized the need for bigger package units and more extensive use of the Nutritional Survey. Poly bags were helping move more poundage, too.

Concentrators Spend $3.3 Million

What QFF had advocated for years now came to pass—the Florida Citrus Commission, under the able direction of its then aggressive young head, Homer Hooks, decided to promote concentrate rather than reduce the price of juice. $3,300,000 was pledged and by the end of the season, the campaign had proven a tremendous success. It was clearly demonstrated that more consumers could be won—not by a cheap price for the can, but by good, sound merchandising. We estimated the campaign saved concentrators $10 million.

QFF's 100 Leading Markets

We now introduced a *real milestone* in QFF's service to the industry— the publication of marketing data in 100 leading markets, broken down 21 ways. The survey, made by Harold L. Franklin for QFF, gave actual dollar sales in each market, from New York to Stockton, Calif., and thus, for the first time provided packers with a yardstick against which to compare their own sales in their markets. The study covered vegetables, fruits, meats, poultry, seafoods and other items. Since then, the studies have been enlarged each year so that they now cover at least 15 leading items. In 1961, QFF published something that was hitherto thought impossible, the *institutional* sales in 100 markets. These Surveys have now become a standard marketing tool for the industry.

About this time the trade was saddened to learn of the death of W. C. Mitchell who had shortly before retired from Libby, McNeill & Libby after 38 years of service. He was Libby's first frozen food manager and was later succeeded by H. R. Mathis and Dave Whitley. Libby has continually forged ahead; today it has one of the most complete lines in the industry.

We published the "Simplot Story" which graphically told how this former dehydrator developed into the country's largest potato packer. Leon Jones, former president of the NAFFP, is general manager; Starr Farish is sales manager.

In January, 1960, we published an exclusive article on freezing fish in Russia. We ran pictures of Russian trawlers and factory ships, showing designs and giving figures. No such article had ever appeared anywhere before.

Price cutting continued unabated. QFF published an editorial without words. Under the heading, "Need We Say More?" we ran clippings from newspaper ads. Some read: "frozen peas, 13 cents; french fries, 10 for $1; fruit pies, 29 cents; meat pies, 6 for $1; orange juice, 10 cents; dinners, 3 for $1 and fish sticks at 29 cents.

Year of Mergers

This was a year of mergers. Seabrook took over Bateman Frozen Foods, Santa Clara Frosted Foods and the Lewiston pea plant after it had itself been acquired by Seeman Bros. Mrs. Paul's bought Braddock Frozen Foods, Minute Maid acquired Tenco, Jesse Jewell was bought by Standard Packaging Corp., H. P. Hood bought Bella Products and Gorton's took over Fla. Frozen Food Processors. But this was only the beginning—a wave of more mergers was to follow, as we shall see.

By early 1960 frozen vegetable packers were feeling good. Prices were firm, especially in peas, corn, lima beans, green peas and winter vegetables. Rarely before, had this branch of the industry been in so enviable a position. But already, the heavy hand of the PATS method of buying by chains was being felt. Meanwhile, in the shrimp industry, exports were coming in at a great pace and American producers were becoming worried. Tariffs were proposed.

The American seafood industry, from a production standpoint, lagged badly. It needed government recognition. It lacked modern fishing boats and proper equipment. Efficient trawlers can be bought in several countries for one-half of their cost if built in the U.S. Hy Trilling, president of Boston Bonnie Fisheries appeared before the House Merchant Marine Committee in Washington. He pointed out that few new trawlers had been built since 1948 and that imports of semi-processed fillets amounted to 62% of the American market. Russia, he said, had 30 vessels with 70 more being constructed.

Prepared Foods First

We announced in 1960 that prepared foods now took 30% of the retail frozen food dollar, frozen produce, 22%, concentrates 20%, meats and poultry 18% and seafoods, 10%; the balance in other products. Including institutional however, vegetables were still No. 1. Frozen potatoes moved up to first place among vegetables. 15 packers now did $745 million dollars; 12 leading chains about $860 million in frozen foods. In 1960, frozen food sales averaged from $20-22 per linear foot and we estimated that additional business from the expansion of new supermarkets alone should be around $250 million in that year. New supermarkets were averaging 100 lineal feet of display cases for frozen foods. In March 1960, QFF enlarged its marketing study to cover 200 leading metropolitan centers.

A Pricing Policy

Libby now offered a streamlined pricing policy which would eliminate all cooperative advertising. An FOB pricing plan, with buyers paying the freight was introduced. "There will be no more payola," said Mr. Mathis, then general manager. This move created quite a stir in the industry.

In 1960 we surveyed the Negro market, concentrated heavily in the nation's urban areas. We found that Negroes bought most heavily in frozen vegetables, the average household in the $4000 income group spending 73 cents per week. Next came fish, poultry and meats, then meat and fruit pies. Sugared strawberries were popular.

Fruit Sales Down

The sales of fruit were showing a downward trend, with the exception of some fruits and berries used for the fruit pie industry. There were several reasons. One was that preservers, big users of frozen fruits, were concentrated in fewer hands and many preservers now packed their own fruits. Ice cream users did not buy as they once did; strawberry ice cream for instance used to be a leader, it is now well down on the list. There are also fewer bakers than ten years ago and less fresh baked goods are sold. In the retail cabinet there are few dozen fruits today, compared with a decade ago when one could find plenty of berries, peaches, and apricots. Today, there are only strawberries, raspberries, mixed fruits and melon balls. Yet, QFF reasoned, frozen fruits were better, fresher tasting than canned but somewhere along the line the frozen product had missed the boat. We suggested experiments with vacuum-packed frozen fruits. The freestone peach, I still feel, if properly packed, is an excellent item and someday someone will make it popular.

Aluminum, followed by composite cans, now hit the concentrate industry with a bang. Almost overnight, many processors switched to aluminum in order to save shipping weight. Since juice is sold on a FOB basis, the principal demand came from the large chain buyers. Can manufacturers also announced a thinner tinplate. The revolution is still going on; more lately steel makers have brought out a steel foil.

In a Forum item, I made a point which has been elaborated upon since. "Wanted"—I wrote, "are Executives. The biggest shortage in the frozen foods industry is not in cabinets, salesmen, money or products. What is needed is that rarest of all species—a good executive. Unfortunately, true executives are born, not made. But too many firms put production men in sales jobs. Perhaps the best way to get a true executive is to reach out into other fields. And the rarest of all, is an executive who can *sell.*"

In July, 1960, I resumed my European trips to study frozen foods. I had let five years intervene since my last voyage, but now the boom was on in Europe. I visited eight countries and reported both in our International Edition and in QFF. But more on this later.

Loose Freezing Trend

In my 1960 west coast trips I was impressed with several developments, principally the strong trend toward loose freezing. The growth of the poly bag had of course, spurred this development and many continuous freezer belts were being installed, not only on the coast but all over the country. The trend still continues. Loose freezing lends itself to a great variety of marketing channels and in many cases, affords faster production. I was also impressed with liquid nitrogen in California. Here, diced carrots were dipped into a solution of the nitrogen for 14 seconds and merged as hard as stones. The future possbilities of such a radically fast system of freezing cannot be overlooked. The increasing use of bins for storing raw frozen vegetables was also taking over. This bulk storage of free flowing vegetables permits repacking into any size and under any label at a later date.

At this point I would like to pay tribute to Miss Laura Track, QFF home economist, whose monthly "Frozen Food Critic" has been seen for almost twenty years in QUICK FROZEN FOODS. Each month, Miss Track buys a number of new items, subjects them to several tests under conditions equivalent to those in the housewife's kitchen. QFF's testing kitchen then reports on the adequacy of the packer's cooking instructions, appearance, flavor, palatability and general consumer acceptance of the product. Hundreds of such tests have been made; the packer is never revealed and each product is given a number.

QFF greatly developed its Institutional Section, running many articles on all types of institutional buying. Stories about drive-ins, vending, in-plant feeding, etc., were covered in depth.

QFF-Life Survey

In October 1960, working with *Life* magazine, QFF published an important study on consumer attitudes. The specific purpose was to determine the consumer's image of each of eight different types of frozen foods. The findings, the results of over 1000 personal interviews, showed that the

An early QFF-sponsored salute to the advertised brands in the frozen foods industry at the Advertising Club of New York. E. Williams is chairman.

public image was favorable, and that most people regarded frozen foods as "faster" and "easier to prepare." Major complaints centered around packaging and "too small portions," which confirmed QFF's editorial policy for bigger packages. A "long thawing time" bothered many respondents; in this connection I have recently learned that some large micro-wave manufacturers are working on a relatively inexpensive household unit. The study was a good deal more comprehensive than the few points I have mentioned. In the same issue, QFF brought out a specific 100 market sales study on dinners and pot pies.

I am rather proud of the fact that about this time we ran the first frozen food study ever made of the Safeway Stores. We obtained the personal permission of Mr. R. A. Magowan, president, and the complete operation was made available to us. No other publication has before or since written the Safeway frozen foods story. In the last decade, Safeway frozen food sales had increased five times. Mr. Allan Young furnished considerable information; he is manager of Safeway's frozen food department.

Coca-Cola Enters Field

In November of 1960 important news broke—Coca-Cola had bought Minute Maid. We ran an article headed, "From Rags to Riches" and

By 1960, frozen food conventions had grown to tremendous size—a far cry from the few hundred which attended a decade before. Cocktail parties, as shown, sometimes ran over 2,000.

said: "Almost on the rocks two years ago, Minute Maid today presents a future replete with promise and opportunity. For, under the wing of the giant, Coca-Cola, MM's financial worries are over. Much credit for the company's new prosperity, of which the new juice was the corner-stone, must go to London born, 54-year-old John Fox, who had been president since the firm's inception. The company had ups and downs which might have unnerved many another executive. Beset by debt, deeply involved in an ill-advised venture into frozen vegetables and the Snow Crop purchase, plus a heavy inventory, its stocks at an all-time low, MM was faced with a loss of over $2½ million in 1957. A sudden Florida freeze turned the tables, boomed concentrate prices and transformed an expensive inventory into a profit of several million dollars. This was the turning point in MM's fortunes for the following year the company made a profit of $4.5 Million." At that time Coca-Cola's sales were $342 million and Minute Maid's about $130 million. QFF estimated that Coca-Cola has paid between $56-59 million for Minute Maid stock. Mr. Ooehlert, a Coca-Cola official became president of MM and the sales staff has remained pretty well intact with Joe Thurman and Al Muntkelt as sales managers. Mr. Fox has since left the organization and is presently board chairman of United Fruit Co. Howard Dick, former sales manager, has also departed. Following Coca-Cola's great success abroad, MM is now beginning to take advantage of Europe's fast growing frozen foods industry and already, under Jerry Bartrum, its export manager, has some European distribution. Juice is also concentrated in its plants in South Africa and in Mexico, as well as in Florida.

Fast Warehouse Expansion

Meanwhile, warehouse expansion was going ahead fast. Merchants Refrigerating Company, under the dynamic leadership of Arthur Otis, bought warehouses in all parts of the country, modernized them and made them pay. Lately, Merchants has built an immense complex in Secaucus, N.J. Another enterprising warehouseman is Ken Stepleton, president of Continental Freezers in Chicago. His warehouse has lately been redesigned and enlarged. Alford, Atlantic, U.S. Cold Storage, Commercial, York Storage, Standard Ice, Manhattan Ref. Co., under the guidance of Jack Adams, well known to the industry; National Terminals, Big Four, Plantation, Distribution Terminal, Hartford Freezer, Glassboro, Roanoke Ice, Beare Co., Quaker City, Quincy Market, Tampa Cold Storage, Terminal Ice, Pioneer Valley, American Express and others have all contributed to the frozen foods industry.

Canadian Gains

By 1960 Canadian frozen food sales had reached the $120 million mark. About half of the frozen foods sold in Canada were imported from the U.S. Frozen produce sales aggregated about 112 million pounds and frozen food sales amounted to about 4% of Canadian food store business.

In December, 1960, QFF ran an unusual article by Milan Smith, a freezer and canner, now president of the National Canners Association. Mr. Smith had once been undersecretary of agriculture and was one of the U.S. industry research team which visited Russia. He made an extensive trip, penetrating the agricultural areas and he took thousands of feet of film, some of which were confiscated by Russian authorities, only to be returned later because of his diplomatic immunity. Mr. Smith visited frozen food plants, told of harvesting peas by hand. 1% of the Russian people, Smith reported, had refrigerators; about 10,000 tons of frozen foods were being produced. But in fish freezing, Russia was way ahead; by 1965, Mr. Smith wrote, the goal is 900,000 tons of fish on factory ships alone. The article was written exclusively for QFF.

Mobile Units Grow

The mobile display unit or spot merchandiser began to get popular. The unit gave the retailer the opportunity to highlight specials, encourage impulse buying and also gave his frozen food department mobility. Merchandising brokers were using them for spot displays and the unit lent itself to displays. In Europe also, the spot merchandiser is very popular.

The "out of stock" condition was becoming a problem. We showed figures where retailers throughout the country were losing millions of dollars a year in sales by not keeping cases full.

Commissary Idea

By now the central commissary idea for restaurants and mass-feeding establishments was becoming important. One of the first, Dine-Eze Corp. in Minneapolis, a catering establishment, was using meals and entrees in boilable bags and supplying restaurants and motels. Another organization in Philadelphia, Sunny Hunny Shops was a franchise operation for restaurants; all foods used were prepared and frozen in a central commissary.

We began a campaign to make the industry more conscious of mass-feeding opportunities, increased our circulation among large institutional buyers, running many articles. We reported that 100 vending machines were now serving meals and entrees and that the Military Subsistence Supply Agency bought almost 250 million pounds of various frozen foods. Hospital purchases in the U.S. were around 18% of hospital food tonnage and was expected to go to 26% in two years.

Many Facets

The trouble was that this vast mass feeding market had many facets and it was hard to lay a finger on all of them. In the restaurant field chains were growing; some 75,000 chains purchased 60% of all foods consumed in restaurants. Besides this, there are hotels, in-feeding plants, drive-ins, meals served on planes, ships and trains, motels, quick lunch counters, old age homes, schools, etc. Of course, the appeal to this vast market all comes under the common denominator of labor saving and convenience. We predicted that a big revolution was coming in the whole field of mass feeding and that the prima donna would be frozen foods. QFF's aim was to keep this expanding industry, in all its variations, constantly before the trade, and this we are doing today.

The Federal Trade Commission reported in early 1961 that the 10 largest frozen food packers made 54% of sales and there was a record number of mergers in 1959. The report also stated that the ten largest chains bought 23% of frozen production and most importantly, that 57% of the sales of these ten largest chains was in *private label*. I think the percentage today is higher.

Armour tested its new "Continental Cuisine" gourmet dinners, consisting of more than 20 quality entrees packed in boilable bags. The idea was that now, almost any restaurant could serve a continental meal without the necessity of having a foreign cook.

I must now recount an editorial which QFF ran in October, 1960, right before the presidential election. As a trade publication, we never mix in politics, except national elections, about which we have our say. QFF then wrote: Regardless of the section of the country in which you live, or party affiliation, we fail to see how any frozen food man, from a business standpoint, can fail to support the Republican party. Every business man should want a sound dollar. This we are more liable to get under the Republicans than the Democrats." We received several protests at the time; one advertiser cancelled his ad, but this same advertiser, not too long after, reinstated his advertising and wrote QFF a letter in which he said, "you were absolutely right."

Promoting Vegetables

QFF embarked on a campaign to increase vegetable consumption. "Only a half pound more per capita, per year would change over-production to under-production" we said. Frozen pea consumption, we pointed out, was only about 1.61 pounds per capita. Two pounds per person would solve all foreseeable problems. If lima bean consumption only jumped three ounces per person the market would be hard to supply. Another four ounce increase in corn would make everybody happy. But how was this to be accomplished? Properly wielded, promotion and advertising were the tools. Too many families suffer from malnutrition, too many children and teenagers eat too many hamburgers and hot dogs, too many malteds and too few vegetables. Restaurants were serving too limited a variety of vegetables. The American mother, we pointed out, must be made to understand that she is not serving her family enough luscious and nutritious vegetables for a healthy, balanced diet. If the story were properly told, we felt, increased consumption would result. But so far, vegetable packers have not been able to get together.

About Freeze Drying

About this time we were getting many inquiries about freeze drying. Would it replace frozen foods? In an article by Sam Martin, editor of

QFF, he said: "Few industries have been so damaged by favorable and misleading publicity as freeze drying. Rarely had so much been written by so many who knew so little. Freeze drying was represented as a process which would produce better quality foods of every variety which could be kept on the shelf unrefrigerated indefinitely. This was untrue. Many companies were putting money into the process but few of these foods could be preserved cheaper or better than by quick freezing, with the exception of instant coffee and some soups. Shrimp, fruit in cereals and f.d. dinners had been failures." QFF also had this to say: "To start with, the process is expensive. Before drying, the products must first be frozen, so a processor must have freezing equipment as well—or buy frozen products. Expensive, vapor-proof packaging must be used and there is no saving in space in freeze drying, only in weight. The method too, has distinct limitations, most prepared foods could not be handled. The most obvious use would be by the army, for emergencies or for use in the remanufacture of finished foods such as stews, soups, etc. Nor does a freeze dried product have the appearance, taste or flavor of the frozen article. Dehydro-freezing on the other hand, does not cost more than freezing and is particularly useful in preserving cheap products, though this method too, has its distinct limitations. However, dehydro-freezing, which products must be kept frozen, does offer savings both in space and weight and is notably important for export." But why, we wondered, would any *consumer* want to buy freeze dried foods when frozen, canned and fresh were available?

We also noted that irradiated foods had been dropped from government experiments. So far, there had been no solution to off-flavors which the process seemed to develop.

We ran a story about Ocean Products, a company started only 13 years ago by Leo Levinson, a successful Chicago druggist who, with his sons, had come to Florida to ge into the shrimp business. A plant was built and the company has been eminently successful ever since.

About this time, Salada took a shrimp operation in Tampa, Shoreline Freezers. The company is now well run by Day Wood.

Packaging Industry—$300 Million

In 1961 we reported that over *$300 million* were being spent a year by frozen food packers for packaging. Rigid plastic containers were moving into the field. Poly bags were still growing and aluminum had a good grip on the prepared food field. Foil laminated paper-board was being tried for juices, plastic lined paper bags offered color protection. Tear-string attachments of all types were being introduced and better printing was apparent on board containers.

Mergers Continue

That year saw the continuations of mergers and acquisitions. Besides the purchase of Minute Maid by Coca-Cola, Ward Baking Co. bought Farm House, a packer of pies. Speigl Farms of California, a vegetable packer, was bought by the Commercial Investment Co., and stock was issued. Taterstate, a Maine potato packer, took over Dorann Foods. Sacramento Freezers acquired the Ruso plant in Watsonville, Calif., Gorton's continued its merger route by obtaining Fishery Products of Cleveland, an institutional house, and Pillsbury bought a broiler plant.

August, 1961 saw the retirement of a pioneer, Joseph Guinane, who worked with Clarence Birdseye and later, for 35 years worked for General Foods. He is the dean of American frozen food production men.

At the same time, Edward W. Kelley was made general manager of Birds Eye. Mr. Kelley had been director of distributor-sales services and in 1960, after only four years with General Foods, was made treasurer. His first step was to introduce a new distribution system; he then expanded distributorships to make Birds Eye products available in a maximum number of outlets. Mr. Kelley introduced eight vegetable combinations which have been highly successful.

More Baked Goods

More baked goods came upon the market. Southern Bakeries, in an ambitious attempt to rival Sara Lee, came out with a similar line under the direction of the late Sonny Greenburg, well known Atlanta broker. (He died prematurely.) Downyflake introduced a line of muffins in disposable aluminum plates. Chef Boy-Ar-Dee put out a number of pizzas; apple pies were marketed by Horn and Hardart, Mrs. Smith's Pies began to make cheese cake and Pet Milk introduced Viennese rolls.

The Carnation seafood label began to emerge. This is an interesting story. The name, obtained from Carnation Milk Co., which still gets a royalty for its use on seafoods, was first thought to be an unlikely nomenclature for fish. But just the opposite proved to be the case. Started by Jack Hice several years ago as a licensee deal, the plan had almost collapsed until it was scooped up by enterprising Bill Durney of Los Angeles. Today, the company packs a complete line under this label, has licensee producers and distributors in many foreign countries as well, and claims it does over $10 million. Murry Berger who takes care of sales east of the Rocky Mountains is captain of the ship.

A firm which was showing perhaps the greatest growth in the U.S. is Gorton's of Gloucester. One of the first to have voluntary USDI inspection, Gordon's is the first seafood company to have become a household word. In the hands of a good management team, headed by E. R. Kinney, president, and Paul Jacobs, executive vice president and general manager, the company has done an outstanding job in merchandising fish. An example was cooperative advertising campaign with Mazola Oil. Ads showed Gorton's breaded shrimp being cooked in Mazola oil.

Green Giant now entered the market with a line of vegetables in butter sauce packed in boil-in-bags. The line has since become national.

P. Jacobs

R. E. Rich

President John F. Kennedy's "E-for-Export" award was presented to E. W. Williams at the National Frozen Food Convention. in Chicago, in 1962, for the services of QFF and QUICK FROZEN FOODS INTERNATIONAL in increasing the sale of American frozen foods abroad.

Restaurant Prices—Dinners

QFF complained about the spread that exists in the price of food per ounce, in the restaurant and in the supermarket, even allowing for the costs of restaurant service. "Buy a hamburger sandwich in a luncheonette, just about bite-size—75 cents," we said. "Buy a dinner in a medium price eating place, $2.-$2.50. Get a frozen dinner—59 cents. Order a pot pie in a restaurant, 75 cents; in a supermarket, 19-25 cents." Of course the restaurant association complained, but I still think the spread is too great. The solution of course is that eating places should use more portion controlled frozen foods.

We estimated in 1961 that frozen dinners had reached sales of $130 million, meat pies, $85 million, fruit pies, $69 million. In 1960, 214 million dinners were sold!

While there have been relatively few failures in the industry, one did take place in Los Angeles. Fradelis Frozen Foods, a packer of frozen dinners, had over-expanded and went into bankruptcy, but was taken over by Nalley's. Another who followed the same trail was Gulf Stream Quick Frozen Foods, a Miami shrimp operation which had been successfully run for years by Jack Udell. Upon his death his sons took over. They couldn't carry on in their father's footsteps.

Air Curtain Cabinets

In early 1962 the air-curtain cabinet burst upon the industry. Now, consumers could reach *in* instead of down, three-decked cabinets were at eye-level. Dual parallel jet streams provided air curtain protection at zero.

The credit for this milestone in frozen food merchandising went, not to the cabinet makers, but to the industry itself. The principle of laminar air flow in refrigeration was invented by Edward Simons in San Francisco. It came to the attention of Trans-American Refrigerated Services (TARS), a unified group of refrigerated warehouses. Ken Stapleton, head of Continental Freezers, sparked to the idea and approached the Prince Interests, connected with Armour & Co. The process was purchased and the cabinet was launched. The original installation was in a Chicago unit of the Jewel Tea Co., and the sales results were most satisfactory.

Since then, large cabinet manufacturers have brought out air-curtain cabinets; Hussmann, McCray and Tyler. I believe this is one of the most important developments to take place in the last two decades and should materially aid the sales of frozen products.

These cabinets are also causing a great deal of interest in Europe. I might add that the idea was extended to cold storage warehouses in the form of an air curtain door which operates on the same principle.

In 1961, QFF reported, refrigerated trucks did 86.6% of frozen food hauling, railroads, 13.4%. Fleets of mechanically refrigerated cars however were growing; there were in 1961 about 5,200 in operation. In that year, about 5,500 insulated and refrigerated van-type truck trailers were produced.

What must have proved a big disappointment to Birds Eye was the dropping of their frozen baby foods line at the beginning of 1962. The idea had not proven profitable; the canned baby foods were too competitive.

Special Vending Issue

In January, 1962, QFF brought out a special report on frozen food vending. It showed that vending operators wanted frozen foods dinners, sandwiches, entrees and casseroles; all eyed the in-feeding business. In Wall Street, a large brokerage house had installed vending equipment for its employees. Frozen meals were put in the machines 30 minutes before lunch hour, were then heated so that at noon they were ready. The White Tower chain put in a vending restaurant. Micro-Dine in St. Louis introduced a vending machine holding 270 frozen meals. Stouffer followed with more installations. We reported other operations throughout the country as well. There was no doubt that vending had a place, but it was only part of the vast institutional picture.

In the concentrate field in early 1962, processors were worried. A record 95-100 million gallon pack was predicted. All sorts of plans were being considered; dropping the price, advertising, an 8-oz. can, a higher density juice. But, as we shall soon see, Mother Nature was to intervene— and with a vengeance!

In the broiler industry a glut appeared. Federal marketing curbs were threatened. Over one billion pounds of production was involved and prices plummeted.

Mexican Foods Grow

In the Southwest, a new nationality food was making fast progress— Mexican items. Such frozen products as Mexican dinners, enchiladas, beef tacos, tamales, tortillas were all becoming popular, not only in Texas but elsewhere. The principal firms are Patio, Rosarita, El Chico and Moreno.

Meanwhile Rich Products had developed a liquid, non-dairy product for use in coffee and cooking called Coffee Rich. It proved an immediate success. Stokely was particularly successful with the introduction of a polybag line of prepared stew vegetables; others have since appeared upon the market.

More was to appear on the AFDOUS Code, which some states have since made into law. We now published the official code as promulgated by the Association of Food & Drug Officials of the U.S., which was to become a model. Among other things, it directed that all frozen food shall be held at an air temperature of zero degrees or lower.

More and more shellfish were being imported. Enterprising seafood companies like Empress Fisheries, Continental Seafood, Leo Young, Bob Stix, Ocean Products, Rubenstein Foods, Crest Importing, Carnation, Tupman Thurlow, Seven Seas, Arista and others were going to foreign lands to get shrimp and lobster tails. The virgin waters along the coasts of Central and South America were tapped, the facilities of India, Australia, in fact almost every corner of the globe, were invaded in an effort to get shellfish. As a result, imports grew.

Nitrogen For Transport

Liquid nitrogen as a refrigerant began to make new advances. A nitrogen refrigeration system was introduced for insulated rail car reefers by Air Reduction Sales. A delivery truck was exhibited, showing how liquid nitrogen could be employed both for short and long haul transportation. An important factor is the Linde Co., Division of Union Carbide, which has done much to promote the use of liquid nitrogen for small and large size trucks. Each year the cost goes down. Liquid Carbonic also introduced its cryotransfer freezing method.

I think a future use of liquid nitrogen will be for ship transportation and this may well revolutionize international trade. Theoretically, if the gas were cheap enough, it could be pumped into any insulated container storing frozen foods, which container could be put into the hold of any ship, obviating the necessity for refrigerating machinery. This would greatly facilitate the transportation of frozen foods to all quarters of the globe.

Fish Future—A Prediction

In 1962 I predicted that frozen seafoods, especially shellfish, were going to be one of the best and most profitable categories of this industry for the next ten years, and I stick to that forecast. In the U.S., for the first time, seafood consumption has advanced, about half a pound. If this continues and I am sure it will, this means an increasing demand for over 100 million pounds each year. In Europe more fish of all forms are being eaten than ever, due to quick freezing. As here, breaded fillets, fish sticks and portions are taking over. All over the world, fish is being merchandised in the modern manner and this in turn, causes an increase in per capita consumption.

In addition, a world wide fish shortage is shaping up, at least in the quality varieties: sole, cod, haddock, etc. There is a mad scramble by fishing fleets to find new waters; almost every country's trawlers are frantically searching for new fishing grounds. Germany, Norway, England are all fishing in Icelandic waters, off Greenland, Nova Scotia and in each other's seas. Japanese fish off the North American coasts, Russian trawlers are everywhere. Europe's growing prosperity, too, has resulted in the payment of higher prices for seafoods. If the U.S. is to hold its position as a seafood producer it *must* develop its fishing resources. More lately however, seafood supplies are again more plentiful.

New on the west coast in 1962 was a bulk storage warehouse for free-flowing vegetables with an air tight silo. Items like peas, corn, etc., were pumped in and out again on a vacuum clean principle.

Winning the "E" Award

A landmark in our history was a telegram I received in May from Secretary of Commerce Luther H. Hodges. It read: *"I am pleased to advise you that you have been selected to receive President Kennedy's "E-for-Export" award for significant contributions to the export expansion program of the United States. Please accept my warm congratulations on your splendid effort."*

This was indeed an honor, since QFF was the only publication in the food field, and one of the few magazines in any field, ever to receive this award. I was subsequently given the award at the October frozen food convention; the plaque and "E" flag now adorn our office foyer.

I had made nine trips to Europe, in the course of which I had consistently plugged American frozen foods and equipment. A major step was taken in the publication of our *International Edition* which serves to spread the frozen food gospel in 64 countries throughout the world. The U.S. has since exported millions of pounds of frozen peas, green beans, potatoes, broccoli, corn and other items to Europe. Machinery developed for volume production is being sent regularly to countries whose domestic frozen food industries are just developing. In my trips, I urge foreign importers to try American foods and have made many connections between packers here and those abroad. Several years ago, we predicted the growth abroad of items such as broccoli, corn on cob, raspberries, asparagus, shrimp, lima beans, some southern vegetables, french fried potatoes, fish sticks and portions, dinners and prepared foods. This is now coming to pass. In England, consumers are trying "American vegetables" and liking them.

Export Possibilities

I am firmly convinced that as volume grows in Europe (and its present rate of growth is fast), the demand for many agricultural products will outstrip Europe's capacity to produce. This may not be true at the moment, but experience shows that when a frozen product becomes popular, the per capita consumption of that product *increases*. For instance, more people in England are eating more peas today than ever—simply because of their convenience in frozen form. The same is true of spinach on the continent and many other products. Sooner or later, the limited producing areas of Europe will not be able to cope with the growing demand made on many agricultural products to feed this huge 225 million consumer market. In small countries such as Holland and Denmark, both large exporters, a capacity has already been reached in such items as sprouts, carrots and peas. What most Americans do not realize also is that supermarkets or self-service stores are growing rapidly in Europe. They will increase consumption, and I look to Europe as a market which will eventually, in the next ten years, help reduce over-supplies in this country. We are in an excellent position. California and southern states have long production periods, not found in Europe. Duties as of now, are moderate, though transportation is high, though I think it will work lower in the future. We have the *mass producing facilities* for frozen vegetables found nowhere else in the world. But American packers must study the market, they cannot hope to develop it on an "opportunistic" basis. They must visit buyers abroad, find out what they want and how they want it. I believe there are possibilities in the establishment of American plants in some European countries in conjunction with foreign firms, especially in Germany, Ireland and Italy.

Developments in Europe

This History would not be complete without a corollary word on the most recent developments in Europe. On my 1963 visit (see International Edition and QFF, July), I found that the recent cold winter had greatly aided frozen foods because the high prices of fresh produce had encouraged frozen food purchases and wooed new users. Sales increased from 25-50% in one year. I visited ten countries and found expansion rife everywhere. New warehouses and plants were going up, more refrigerated vehicles, railroad cars and cabinets were seen. Over 240,000 stores throughout Europe now had frozen food cabinets of some sort, many with modern gondola type cases and in some countries air-curtain cabinets were being tried out.

In England, Birds Eye led the way, controlling close to 70% of the market. This alert company, doing in 1963 over $120 million in frozen foods, is under the direction of James R. Parratt, probably one of the most able and enterprising managers in this industry in the world. In 1962, Nestle bought Findus of Sweden, thus offering competition to Unilever, which owns Birds Eye. These two giants, both financially strong and quality minded, are now battling for the German market, both having erected factories in that country. Other factors have grown too. Ross Findus-Eskimo, etc., in England; Iglo in Holland and Germany; Findus, Migros, Frisco, Frionor, D-Dansk, Emborg, Groko, and many other fish, poultry and specialty packets. In all, I estimate there are over 300 frozen food producers in Europe, with production of over 650 million pounds. I was much impressed by the highly developed telephone order system in England. Birds Eye for instance, has some 40 depots in Britain, employing over 400 girls. Each girl is trained to handle as many as several hundred retailers on the phone; in this way the entire system contacts 80,000 stores each week to get orders. A very efficient system has been devised, whereby each girl is responsible for a certain area in which retailers are coded according to size and volume. In addition there are contact men, but their main job is not selling, but store merchandising and advice to retailers.

Up to now of course, American poultry has been our prime export, but recently, new high tariffs have greatly reduced U.S. exports of chickens to Germany and the rest of Europe. Every effort is being made to reduce these barriers, because U.S. poultry, first introduced in volume abroad about five years ago, created the *original* market and because of its quality and low price, made poultry a popular, instead of a holiday food.

J. R. Parratt   L. Anderfelt

This was the scene in many Florida groves on the morning of December 13, 1962, during the most damaging freeze to hit the state's citrus regions in this century. This was a man-made scene, since many growers resorted to overhead irrigation systems in an effort to save fruit and trees from the killing cold. The freeze cost the citrus industry 56,000,000 boxes of fruit and 4,500,000 commercial citrus trees.

One of the first five-tier cabinets built, McCray's unit was also the first multi-decker to be introduced in Europe. This unit gives a selection of products highlighted in brightly illuminated shelves.

More Acquisitions

Eventually, Lever Bros. took over a small, but successful company, Dinner Redy, which has sold turkey and meat slices with sauces in boilable bags. But size doesn't always seem to be a factor in this business; Lever has since shut the plant down. In this connection I would like to remark that not every large company that has come into the industry through the acquisition of a frozen food company, has been successful. It seems that this is a peculiar industry and methods which are successful elsewhere, don't always apply.

John H. Dulany & Son, one of the industry's pioneer firms, merged with the Premier Development Co., a large Hong Kong fisheries organization. Olney & Carpenter was sold to Glidden, Cleveland paint manufacturer. Around this time, Jack Fisher, the man who introduced the foil covered aluminum dinner to the industry, died. Coldwater Seafood Corp., large Icelandic fish exporters, appointed a new American president, T. Gislason; the company represents 60 fish plants. Iceland Products was another growing firm. O. Hammson is president.

Canada was developing rapidly, not only on the domestic scene, but as an exporter of frozen foods. McCain shipped millions of pounds of frozen potatoes to England, so did Seabrook's Canadian plant. An old timer, Art Reiling, Birds Eye's western production manager, retired after 40 years of service.

Mass Feeding in England

As mass feeding developed in the U.S., it also progressed abroad. In England, Smethurst (Birds Eye), had its "Top Tray" catering service which included some 18 meals and 10 snack items. These products were end-cooked quickly in the Swedish Electrohelios oven which operates on the forced air or convection principle, the oven being able to handle 72 meals at one time. Both Lyons and Eskimo used micro-wave ovens, the latter firm using an oven which can reheat a dinner from the frozen state in 1¾ minutes. Special meals for schools and hospitals have been particularly developed in Sweden.

At this time, *Frosted Food Field,* a tabloid in the frozen foods industry, was sold to the Olsen Publishing Co. Edward Sherby and Irene Seifert who ran the operation, had both resigned. The history of the publication was a checkered one; it had changed hands three times and its demise came shortly thereafter.

On the West Coast, the firm of D. B. Berelson was growing. Originally importers from the Far East, the company rapidly acquired a knowledge of the frozen foods industry and is successfully managing the sales of John Inglis, and several other companies.

A Trip to Washington

I was invited as one of a group of leading business publications to attend a White House conference addressed by administration leaders including Secretary of the Treasury Dillon, Walter Heller, chief economic advisor and finally, President Kennedy himself. The purpose of the meeting was to inform the nation's business publications that the administration was not anti-business. I was therefore surprised to hear the late President say that his party has "written off the business man's vote long ago."

More new firms came into the business. American Home Products and more lately, Quality Bankers of America, who are bringing out a line of frozen baked goods. American firms were also investing abroad; Consolidated Foods bought a Dutch freezer-canner and Beatrice Foods, a large Belgian dairy firm.

The industry was saddened in September, 1962, to hear of the passing of Philip J. Rizzuto, president of Southland Frozen Foods, at the age of 58. He started as a frozen food distributor in 1943 and later developed a packing operation which grew into one of the largest in the east.

Now, for the first time, freezer storage space represented more than half of the total available refrigerated capacity. In 1962, 516 million cubic feet of below zero space was available in U.S. refrigerated warehouses; 73% was public and 22% private capacity. In 1936, freezer space was less than 10% of all warehouse refrigeration. As the automobile made the modern highway, so frozen foods developed the zero warehouse.

The October National Frozen Food convention was a good one. In a panel of industry leaders, E. W. Kelley, general manager of Birds Eye, was asked to comment on a recently quoted statement by George Mortimer, chairman of General Foods, that his company would like to sell Birds Eye but "who would buy it?" Mr. Kelley said the statement had been widely misinterpreted and what Mr. Mortimer meant was that very few people would have the money to buy a company as large as Birds Eye. Kelley pointed out that BE profits were better than the average for the industry and that in the past five years, BE had spent more money on expansion and product development than in all of its prior years in business.

For long, QFF had advocated a more complete frozen meal. Now it came along in the form of Swanson's new three course dinner, one of which included soup, turkey and vegetables and apple crisp for dessert. The dinner, selling at 89 cents, has filled a popular need.

The Second Freeze Hits—Hard

I was in Florida's citrus area during both freezes, but the one which decimated half the crop and did its worst damage during the nights of December 12-13, 1962, was catastrophic. QFF was the first to report the freeze, fully and completely.

From the very first season that concentrates began, we have covered Florida, twice a year, and I was thoroughly familiar with the situation. After the freeze there were very few green leaves on the trees, most were brown brittle, withered. At first, concentrators saw a blessing in disguise in this devastating blow, a relief from the 100 million plus gallons which had been expected and the marketing of which had threatened even the financially strongest concentrators. But later events proved that in the loss of 50 million boxes, Mother Nature had gone a little too far. "A nice 20 million box freeze," said one juice man, "would have been enough."

Prices soared and those growers whose fruit had not been damaged, mostly in the southerly part of the state, benefitted. Concentrators tried to make the best of the situation. Fruit embargoes were declared. Quality control of remaining fruit for processing was rigidly enforced. At the time, QFF predicted a final pack of 55 million gallons. The end figure was around 52 million. Prices in cabinets almost doubled and the movement slowed down. Some concentrators: Minute Maid, Snively, Adams, Griffin brought out orange drinks. But orange juice went on allocation. Again, those with inventories were lucky; QFF estimated that values increased $40 million after the freeze. Salesmen, who a week before had planned busy sales trips, now cancelled them. How long was the shortage to remain? By mid-1963, Florida was importing some bulk concentrate. Experts foresaw no more than 65 million gallons in 1964; some said it would take six years before Florida groves came back to their pre-freeze strength. Meanwhile other juices pushed hard. Dole advertised its orange-pineapple juices, Welch its grape juice. Optimists thought Florida oranges should rebound by 1965. It remained with the weather.

Fluidized Freezing

With the increasing use of polybags, loose freezing systems grew in popularity. Fluidized belt freezing, a method using low temperature air at sufficient velocity and pressure to roll and mix the product during freezing began to get popular. The Lewis Refrigeration Co. of Seattle installed such systems. Another, Flo-Freeze, was developed by Frigoscandia in Sweden. Meanwhile Amerio plate freezers were widely used for package freezing.

Libby, cashing in on the swing to prepared vegetables, marketed seven varieties with sauces. Sea-Pak, now one of the largest in shrimp, had introduced a fish stick multi-pack and sponsored individually frozen peeled and deveined shrimp, which was growing. Sara Lee sponsored the annual motion picture Academy Award TV show, one of the biggest frozen food promotional undertakings up to that time. It also added a line of casseroles.

Unique Restaurant

A very unique restaurant experiment was opened by Tad's in New York. This consisted of an entirely automatic cook-it-yourself dining place on 42nd Street, near Fifth Ave. Thirty varieties of frozen meals were displayed. The customer entered, made his selection of a frozen meal—ranging from ham and eggs to goulash, fried chicken, beef stroganoff, etc.—and took it to a table. Each table was equipped with a microwave oven in which the diner placed the meal. Reheating took about two minutes, depending on the dish. When a green light appeared, the customer removed the meal steaming hot. The restaurant had 36 microwave ovens and meal prices ranged from 49-89 cents. All meals were prepared by Tad's in the kitchen below, sent up by dumbwaiter to the refrigerated bins from which the customer selected them. Up to now, the idea had been an experiment, but traffic was heavy. Later the restaurant closed.

Advice to Packers

QFF wrote in March, 1963, that what was needed to put private label packers in a better bargaining position was a concerted action to revise the present marketing agreement. We suggested the establishment of a super-national research agency to carefully study the maximum marketability of each frozen commodity six months before the pack, figures to be given each producer and their cooperation solicited on a voluntary basis. We urged the establishment of central sales agencies which could represent 100-200 million pounds instead of five or ten. Some efforts have been made in this direction.

Meanwhile, the pendulum was swinging back to advertised brands which were doing better. Those who advertised, researched new products and were bringing out items demonstrably different, seemed to be forging ahead.

We reported that 30 leading chains were doing $1 billion worth of frozen food business, that 17 packers were selling about $900 million. The five leaders in the field now were: Birds Eye, Campbell-Swanson, Minute Maid, Consolidated Foods and Seabrook, with Stokely and Libby next.

Chains such as Jewel Tea, A&P, National Tea and others were establishing frozen baked goods departments. A National Frozen Food Month was organized.

Living on $31 a Week

QFF now made a unique study. We wanted to determine how cheaply a family of four—two adults and two children, could live if they just ate frozen foods, excepting of course coffee, milk, butter and bread. We found that if only frozen foods were used for 21 meals, these items bought at regular (not special) prices at supermarkets, the bill would come to $31 weekly. We listed 21 individual meals. For instance, a typical dinner included 12 oz. of melon balls, Rock Cornish game hens, peas, candied yams and chocolate-cream pie, the total cost of this meal being $3.03.

Portions Pass Sticks

In the seafood business, for the first time, breaded portion production surpassed that of fish sticks. Production was 77.7 million pounds.

Onion rings were showing considerable growth, there now being 18 processors in the field, producing an estimated 5-6 million pounds. A

V. Kirby   N. Cummings

pioneer in proving that onion rings was a volume item was Sky Valley Foods, Chicago. They helped open the way for others who became giants in that particular field. Frying was growing. Pitman Mastermatic did a complete job on all types of food.

Mette Munk, Denmark, sold imported frozen pastries in the U.S., distributed nationally by the National Biscuit Co., Pet Milk introduced a "Quick-Bake" pie which they claimed cut baking time in half.

Libby Expands

In May QFF ran the "Libby Story." Now headed by young and aggressive Robert L. Gibson, Jr., the company had new inspiration and leadership. Libby had over 200 frozen items and was promoting a frozen drink line.

In June, 1963, QFF published one of the most interesting articles in years. It was entitled "A Financial Case History of a Medium-sized Packer." It described the costs of operation, of launching a new product and what happens when competition sets in. We also ran a series of articles by and about Donald K. Tressler, author of industry textbooks and dean of frozen food technology.

Cheaper Than Bread

In the course of an investigation, Senator Hart of Michigan, holding a cherry pie, complained that there seemed to be too few cherries in the pie. "But," said QFF, "in case anyone has doubts about the value of frozen fruit pie, we would like to point out that they are cheaper than bread. A 22-oz. pie can be purchased for from 23-33 cents while a 16-oz. loaf of bread costs around 29 cents!"

Boilable Bag Breakthrough

Developments , continued apace in packaging. In boilable bags the breakthrough seemed at hand, at long last. Green Giant claimed it had sold $10 million in prepared vegetables packed in pouches. Birds Eye was considering going to boilable bags. New thermoplastic trays were being introduced. A peel-off strip on the lid of prepared foods such as pies or dinners was described. Foil coated composite cans (paper and aluminum foil), now represented 25% of the total retail concentrate pack, it was reported. Polyethylene-coated cartons were ready for frozen food packages, eliminating over-wraps, as well as cartons with web corner construction and high gloss poly-wax combination coatings new cartons with poly-wax on the exterior and wax on the interior, locking on three sides were coming to be used; a window flap for visibility on certain types of products was becoming more evident. Tear-strip openers for more packages were making inroads and the same idea was expected to be used on juice cans soon. Paper pouches had taken hold to compete with polybags.

Practically all frozen peas were now harvested by machine. Automation was fast invading the fields; a snap-bean harvester, which could replace up to 100 handpickers was rapidly taking over bean harvesting. An electronically controlled asparagus cutter had gone through the experimental stage. This four-wheeled self-propelled machine had an electric eye on the front set six inches above the ground. When the eye's light beam was broken by a six-inch stalk, a piano wire swung down to cut off the stalk at ground level. Shorter stalks were bypassed and thus given time to ripen. We reported on experiments with hurricane machines to mechanize orange and grapefruit picking in Florida. Mounted behind a tractor, a high-powered fan created air gusts which caused tree limbs to shake, snapping off the fruit, which hopefully cut picking costs.

FTC Makes 270 Packer Survey

The Federal Trade Commission in June, 1963, released its long awaited survey of the frozen foods industry and the results coincided with what QFF had been saying all along. In studying 270 freezers of vegetable, fruit and juice operations only (not including prepared foods; poultry, meat or seafoods) the FTC found that these 270 freezers represented 96% of domestic output. Large companies were making money, but fully one-third of the smaller firms reported they were losing money. It was found that the ten larger chains purchased 69% of all frozen vegetables and fruits and 74% of juices under their own label. As a result, the *independent stores* remained the bastion of the advertised brand. The FTC report only saw an "intensification of private label activities . . . the large packer-label freezers selling in the national market may face increasingly concentrated retail outlets with the result that their sales of packer-label products are *likely to diminish* proportionately."

The report only confirmed what QFF had been editorializing about for ten years. The investigation proved that 1) private labels were growing, 2) industry profits were down, 3) packer-label brands faced a bleaker outlook and 4) retail outlets were becoming more concentrated. I have often wondered why large chains are permitted to buy others without protest, to merge at will and to intensify the concentration of food retailing power by consolidations, but if a frozen food packer would buy another related business he must first pass the stern scrutiny of the anti-trust laws.

Mergers Continue

Control of Libby, McNeill & Libby was transferred to a French-Italian group headed by Michele Sindona, an Italian industrial organization. Ocoma Products bought Hayden House, a large poultry packer. Tilghman Packing Co., processors of canned and frozen oysters, clams and crabmeat was bought by Richard Knapp. Campbell Soup purchased Pepperidge Farms at a price which almost paralleled Pepperidge's one year's sales volume. H. J. Heinz took over Star Kist and National Sea Products Corp. of Canada bought Shoreline Seafoods.

In June of 1963 after being on Wall Street for 17 years, we moved uptown, to 1776 Broadway, at 57th Street, occupying a whole floor. QFF now had 35 employees and needed the space. A beautiful wall mural adorned our lobby. It was a composite of pictures tracing the whole frozen foods industry from production, through processing, transportation and down to the final user. So far as I know, it was the only industry mural in existence. A permanent packaging display of hundreds of products in our spacious lobby was a magnet that fascinated everyone.

7

The Years
of Refinement

I call these last five years the "years of refinement" because many of the projects which had been begun a decade before were now in the refining process. The sharp edges had been smoothed out, many old problems which hitherto had almost seemed insoluble now somehow seemed to solve themselves. Both consumers and retailers were more receptive to frozen foods. Where scrimping and saving hand been the order of the day, now new capital, in the form of really big mergers and takeovers eased financing for many companies.

The period 1963-68 saw a host of more suitable frozen products, more intelligently marketed than ever before. Pricing policies were somewhat more stable, though competition continued keen. Frozen food commodities, especially produce, firmed up considerably. The pendulum, slowly but discernably, was swinging to a sellers' market.

But there were other changes. Many of the old faces in the industry had disappeared. A wave of new managerial talent swept in. Bigger plants were being opened, more modern refrigerated warehouses. Many things were different—and yet many things were the same.

Women Want to be Wooed

In its November, 1963, issue, QFF editorialized: "Women want to be wooed . . . there is no consumer more adventuresome than the American housewife. In no other country are women shoppers as willing to try something new. Here in the U.S., with a glossy supermarket on every corner, we have the greatest showcase for foods ever seen. Why then isn't there room for better quality and more profitable frozen products?" We suggested that those chains which had kept their private label in relation to the advertised brands seemed to make the best profits. (Lower earnings for the A&P and First National Stores, heavy in private label, were way down compared to other chains.) Were chain specifications for many frozen commodities unnecessarily high?

Back in 1963, the public was spending 26¢ out of every dollar on food; in 1967 it had dropped to 18¢, but purchases were bigger. If, QFF said, consumers were spending less on food, (though FF sales had risen), then housewives must want *better foods,* and better-priced products. This proved to be true.

Since 1959, our statistical analyst, Harold Franklin, had compiled for QFF the sales in 100 leading markets by region, state and city—a first. N.Y.C. had ranked first, with sales annually at $274.6 million, Los Angeles next at $151.9 million, Chicago third with $118.5 million, then Detroit, Philadelphia and Boston.

In 1963 I was flattered to have been named "Man of the Year" by the Delaware Valley Frozen Food Association. Mr. Mel Korn of that group was kind enough to say: "E. W. Williams today ranks with only a handful of current greats among trade paper publishers and editors. There are those who function only to pass on information and those who create. He belongs among the latter; spotting trends, making predictions, serving as a guide and inspiration, fearlessly reporting the weaknesses and strengths of the industry. . . ." Needless to say I accepted this award as a reflection upon our whole staff.

New Products, New Plants

New and often revolutionary products were making their appearance. One was tomato slices, frozen with liquid nitrogen by Libby; there were 8 slices in a package, selling for 29¢. The idea was good, since fresh tomatoes are not available the year-round. However, the product had to be abandoned since the return was insufficient to cover the cost of freezing and the special varieties which had to be used.

Another new idea which made quite a splash was frozen bread dough. Several companies such as Morton's and Bridgeford went into it. Initial sales were high, but finally the "bake-your-own-bread" idea found its own plateau and leveled off. Sara Lee introduced a line of entrees including casseroles and Chicken Sara Lee.

Freeze dried fruits now made their appearance. Sliced strawberries, peaches and other fruits were placed in a foil liner along with corn flakes and other cereals, the idea being that with the addition of milk or cream they reconstituted into fruit, providing a complete dish. The experiment was not successful; perhaps the best way to sell fruit and cereals is by use of the easy-thaw variety. One idea that did sweep the country was the introduction of *Awake,* an imitation orange juice, by Birds Eye. Sales immediately reached to phenomenal heights, giving considerable concern to the Florida citrus industry which was interested in selling solids. At one time Awake was said to have over 10% of the juice market. At the same time, BE discontinued its line of frozen dinners and meat pies in favor of concentration on new products, vegetables, and its range of boil-in-pouch butter sauce vegetables.

Prepared Vegetables—Boilable Bags

Years before QFF had suggested that frozen vegetables be given a "new look." Seabrook Farms, a pioneer in the development of boilable bags, re-entered the field vigorously in 1964 with the introduction of five vegetables in butter sauce. An advertising campaign, using TV and newspapers backed up the effort which was a forerunner of the gradually increasing sale of these "new look" vegetables.

Now another company was to make the greatest success of all—Green Giant. Enthused by the future of prepared vegetables, it introduced a new line, backed by what was perhaps the cleverest and most consistent advertising of the time, featuring the "Jolly Green Giant." Sales of butter-sauce vegetables boomed; the first year Green Giant is said to have sold some $10 million worth. Birds Eye followed and captured a share of the market, peas and pearl onions emerging as the best seller. It was not long before other packers joined, including North Pacific Canners, Libby, Morton's Stokely, Spiegl, Patterson and others. Chains first moved in cautiously under their own labels, then, following the lead of the ad brands, accelerated their pace. At the time QFF questioned: "Has this line had sufficient pre-sell by the advertised brands for it to be marketed primarily on price through private label?" This is still a question, but the ad brands, at least on this product, still retain the initiative. We estimated that by 1968 the market for all boilable bags (including prepared vegetables), would total about 1½ billion units. I think this has already been surpassed.

Another new product which immediately found its niche was the boneless turkey and chicken roast which followed the already well established turkey rolls. The roasts were introduced by Shenandoah, Armour and Ocoma, and shortly thereafter given a big consumer boost by Ralston-Purina and others. The product is also proving to be an increasing export item for Europe's institutional trade.

Frozen sandwiches had long been on the market, but Kraft Foods of Chicago now entered the field with a line of frozen salads and sandwich fillings. In all, Kraft introduced 55 items including breaded seafoods, oysters, shrimp steaks and the like, also Italian and Chinese entrees. Kraft seemed to make a strong though somewhat confused effort to get into the FF business, insisting upon going direct and eschewing brokers. The attempt, however, was unsuccessful and Kraft is currently out of the frozen foods market.

One product which stuck was the frozen bagel, mostly in large cities with Jewish populations. Sales are increasing in other areas, too, the main firms being Bagel Kings, Lenders and Abels.

Rich Products, whose earlier history has already been recounted, brought out Coffee Rich, a new non-dairy whitener. It immediately gained national popularity.

Other Products—Baked Goods

Quaker Oats Co., Chicago, introduced a toaster kitchen line which included cinnamon twists and corn sticks, in addition to waffles. The kitchen toaster, as a means of quick reheating, had long been recognized by the industry and many products had been designed to make use of it. Some were successful, others, such as pancakes, not. The latest item begging to be accepted by the toaster is an instant pizza product by Buitoni.

Eggs now flashed upon the FF horizon. The idea was to freeze the egg in which the yolks and whites were not separated. The mix was flavored so that ham, cheese and other omelettes could be quickly made. One advantage was that the egg product could be used for low temperature cooking of scrambled eggs for omelettes, with particular appeal to restaurants, schools, etc. The freezing of eggs in this manner is also a means of taking advantage of surplus production during seasons when egg laying is at its peak, thus enabling the processor to offer a frozen product at a lesser price the year-round.

After having been in the industry since almost the beginning, frozen baked goods by 1963-64 really began to hit their stride. Sara Lee opened its huge $22 million plant in Deerfield, Ill., on a 52-acre site. The new plant had 500,000 square feet of space and included a giant holding freezer which was completely computer-controlled, handling 8 million cakes. Visitors from all over the world came to see it.

The chains followed suit. Kroger and Food Fair expanded their private label baked goods line. Jewel Tea, National Tea and others brought out frozen baked products. Not long thereafter, the A&P, said to be the largest baker in the world, opened a new plant, using liquid nitrogen for freezing.

Another fast-expanding company was American Foods with its Chef Boy-Ar-Dee line of Italian specialties, headed by pizza. I want to say here that credit goes to William Mundy for having promoted this line to national recognition in a few years time. With his extensive background in marketing acquired after many years at Birds Eye, he was able to make Chef Boy-Ar-Dee the main nationally distributed pizza.

About the same time the National Biscuit Co., under the name *Pastry Chef,* brought out eight new items which included imported Danish pastries. The latter item had been introduced into this country several years before under the name of Mette Munk. Ed Coale, national sales manager, with a long background of FF experience behind him, has done a good merchandising job; more recently the company has introduced Easy Bake frozen cookies and other products.

Frozen baked goods had now grown to such an extent that one of the largest fresh bakery operations in the East, Cushman's, closed down around 1964, after 109 years of operation. The company attributed the popularity of frozen bakery products as the main reason for closing.

Another developing branch of the business was the bake-in idea. Frozen raw baked goods were delivered to retail stores and then baked in store ovens and supplied fresh to customers.

Emerging Companies

Mrs. Smith's Pies was rapidly establishing a national identity. The picture of Mrs. Smith was used on national promotion which stressed

T. Pearce, Jr.

F. Otterbein

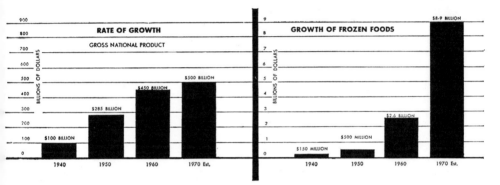

The rate of growth of frozen foods as compared to the rate of growth of the Gross National Product of the United States.

E. A. Taylor

R. W. Rutledge

the fact that her son promised he would never change her recipe excepting to make a better pie. We later ran a full section in QFF on this company which reflected the progress of a firm dedicated to quality. Mrs. Smith's now has 28 varieties of frozen cream, fruit and custard pies distributed throughout the U.S. Robert Smith, the president, was greatly aided in sales and marketing by Vince Kirby, who had a long background in frozen foods and their agency, Mel Korn in Philadelphia.

General Mills, Howard Johnson and others continued to bring out new baked goods and entree items. There were English crumpets, a hamburger "toastwich," French toast, pancake batter, etc. Chock Full O' Nuts advertised a line of chocolate cake, and Schraffts, later bought by Pet Milk, offered a fairly complete range, including an excellent meat pie at a high but fair price. Horn & Hardart promoted a line of entrees, many of which were sold in their restaurants.

In another of QFF's consumer studies, it was found that over 70% of homemakers were buying some type of frozen baked goods. About 74% are stored in home freezers of zero space. The most frequently bought item was waffles, followed by coffee cake, rolls, pound cake, cheese cake, fruit turnovers and similar products.

About this time, Gretchen Grant, founded by a creative chef, Lou Midler, was bought by Durkee Foods. Under Midler, the company had become a top producer of frozen hors d'oeuvres in the U.S. and the canape idea was growing.

A Vegetable Prediction

In August, 1964, I predicted in QFF that while, during the past 25 years there had been more years of oversupply than shortages in basic frozen commodities, such as vegetables, fruits, citrus, seafoods, poultry and meats, the situation would change. In the future I said, there would be *more years of shortages* and a few of over-supply. We made the conclusion that while U.S. population had now reached 200 million on the other hand there had been no accompanying increase in production (excepting potatos). The use, especially of frozen vegetables, was greatly increasing because of 1) population growth, 2) prepared vegetables, 3) institutional and mass feeding demand, 4) use in frozen dinners and entrees. We wrote: "We believe that in the next ten years the trend, broken occasionally by temporary gluts, will nevertheless be in the direction of gradually strengthening prices and that the pendulum, just as gradually, will swing in the direction of a seller's rather than a buyer's market. Our children may well grow up in an era of strained food supplies to meet a growing demand in a world where more and more emphasis will be placed on production rather than upon sales."

By the early part of 1964 the frozen foods industry was in better shape than it had been for a long time. Almost every commodity was either in balance or on the short side, with the exception of corn. There was a strong resurgence of the advertised brands; such firms as Green Giant, Birds Eye, Sara Lee, Minute Maid, Stouffers, Morton, Banquet,

Chun King and many localized packers were increasingly advertising and using TV and other media. In 1945 our first Processors' Directory listed less than 400 packers, while the 1964 edition contained close to 2000. This was about the highest number reached. Later directories showed fewer packers, but larger units, due to mergers. The industry also stood upon the threshold of a big revolution in mass feeding. Dining out was now a $23 billion business, with portion control taking over more and more. In early 1964 we estimated that Birds Eye was doing around $150 million, Campbell-Swanson next with $125 million, followed by Consolidated Foods at $115 million. Minute Maid was fourth with $100 million. A&P was estimated to be doing $270 million in frozen food sales, Safeway, $137 million and Kroger, $97 million.

The following year QFF reported that there were now 2,500 FF items available though the average supermarket rarely handled more than 350, and then on a rotating basis. Where would these new products find a home? We suggested that the replacement market was a big one and that enlarged cabinet space and spot merchandisers would help the exposure of many new products.

The Merger Wheel Turns

By 1964 mergers began to get into full swing. The SeaPak Corp. acquired the majority stock in Trade Winds and Tom Pearce became Chairman with H. Cofer as president of Trade Winds. Crest Importing of San Diego took over the Ocean Garden Prods. Co., large importers and sellers of Mexican shrimp.

Green Giant bought Sterling Industries, an old-line Sacramento vegetable packer. Pet Milk bought Downyflake, the originator of waffles. Pet Milk was growing in frozen foods, taking over Frosted Fruit Products in Los Angeles, run by J. Lawless, and the Angelus Frozen Foods Co. of Calif. American Bakeries acquired Dressels in Chicago.

An important acquisition at this time was made by Nat Cummings, then head of Consolidated Foods, through the purchases of Booth Fisheries, which retained all its officials. Excelsior Meat was purchased by Renaire Corp. Lamb-Weston in Oregon, a large pea packer, merged with the Snow Flake Canning in Maine. John Baxter, Jr., of this old line packer, became an official of Lamb-Weston, and E. J. Watson was named general manager.

This History would not be complete without mentioning an enterprising young man who had a checkered career. This was Charlie Stein, who started putting up fruit salad in Florida. His company grew and was sold to Kraft. Later, he was chosen to be president of Sara Lee, a post which he retained for two years until his summary resignation. Charles Lubin, the founder of Sara Lee, became chairman of the board until he too resigned.

Mr. Lubin had worked in the bakery field since the 1920's, and in 1935 raised $1,500 with his brother-in-law to buy three retail bakeries in Chicago. He developed the technique of baking cakes in an aluminum foil pan, freezing and shipping them in the same container, and thus developed Sara Lee. The company was built on a quality note. I remember going through the old company and was impressed by the fact that Lubin only used top score butter and the finest ingredients. As has been related, he sold out to Consolidated Foods in 1956.

M. Kaplan, an old associate of Lubin's, also became president, but he too has left the company and is presently said to be working on a line of entrees.

QFF Leads in Research

QFF was making about 15 research studies every year which continued to provide the industry with valuable information. Many were conducted in cooperation with the Agricultural Institute at Farmingdale, L.I., of which George Cook is the head. One study on fruit pies for instance, disclosed that 50% of consumers ate dessert pies on Sundays and that 25% of consumers interviewed bought four pies a month. About 77% preferred the standard size. All this and other data was given in detail.

Another constructive survey showed that 80% of the industry planned major equipment purchases during the next 18 months, 39% planned new plants, 46% said they would buy new packaging, and 26% said they would build new warehouse space. A warehouse boom was predicted in 1965 and while this projection was at the time criticized by one or two members of the warehouse industry it was later proven accurate. By 1967 a shortage of refrigerated warehouse space ensued. We predicted the greatest building boom in the industry.

Since 1938, QFF had made close to 400 surveys and studies. This included the highly valuable study of 100 leading markets in the U.S., showing for the first time, the actual dollar sales in all leading FF categories, both retail and institutional. This study has become a marketing standard and marketing yardstick ever since.

Another survey concerned meat pies. It was found that most meat pies were served for dinner, that the 8-oz. size was preferred, and that only 25% used one pie a week, though 42% bought pies at least once a year.

In yet another study, a team of 15 students rang nearly 1,000 doorbells to find out why consumers purchased frozen fillets, fish sticks and portions. We discovered that adults were the biggest users of fillets, portions and sticks and that teenagers and children scored a low usage. Fillets and fish sticks were bought primarily for convenience, fish portions mainly for flavor. Nevertheless, children under 12 did consume a good quantity of fish sticks. These were just a few of the many investigations into products which included meats, poultry, baked goods, juices and vegetables.

The McKinsey Report

In 1965 Birds Eye made the McKinsey study, fully reported by QFF. It proved that frozen foods were the most profitable department in the retail store. The report also showed that FF could contribute twice as much profit per dollar of volume as other store departments. The study had two main purposes; to establish the true profitability of frozen foods and to help both distributors and producers to learn more about how FF profits are affected by varying price levels, handling costs, merchandising methods and product mix. It showed that FF profitability varied considerably among various stores of the same retailer. Emphasis was laid on management of FF at the store level as the determining factor. The survey was very extensive and benefited the entire industry.

There were more changes at Birds Eye. Mag Bohm, former president of General Foods in Canada, succeeded E. W. Kelley as general manager. Kelley had left BE to accept a position with Hublein. Kelley in turn had succeeded the popular Fred Otterbein, who together with Bohm, later became important executives at General Foods. In September of 1965 Martin Gregory followed Mr. Bohm as BE manager. Trimm, one of the pioneer crew, left to join Stokley-Van Camp; he is now a broker. Joseph Harkens, probably the oldest employee in years of service, rounded out his 41st year in the FF business. Another old timer, Coe Suydam, also retired from BE. He had been there 35 years and later represented the company in Canada. Today he is a seafood consultant. Dick Steets, another long time Birds Eye man, is now comptroller of the division.

The Industry in 1964

In November 1964 we wrote that the economic health of the industry was never better. Most products were firm in price; profits were generally satisfactory, and total FF sales were over $4 billion. We also pointed out that for the first time in 25 years all branches of the industry seemed happy and contented. Nevertheless, the industry was extremely competitive and price-conscious. Per capita consumption was then 47.8 pounds, with vegetables leading at 12.2 pounds, and prepared foods at 7.6.

In 1964, QFF listed its first directory of private and controlled labels of food chains and distributors. It not only proved to be a valuable service to the industry, but it made interesting reading. It was also revealed that with the 10 largest chains who pushed their own labels, 74% of orange juice was private label and 69% of vegetables and berries. The smaller chains, independents and distributors however, purchased 84% of their requirements in advertised brands.

In June, 1964, QFF editorialized that "this business of free goods along with an initial order is getting entirely out of hand." The growing pressure brought upon many FF packers by some large retailers was practically making it impossible to introduce a new frozen product or even an old one in a new territory without exorbitant costs. It is understandable, we argued, that with the preponderance of new products seeking space in retail cabinets, there is bound to be a squeeze and perhaps the retailer deserves some allowance. If this is the case, then the way to do it might be in the form of an allowance for performing this service, say 50¢ a case for the first 30 days or for the first two orders."

But there was never a quiet moment—not in distributing. About this time Birds Eye made a decision to increase its volume of business both in its own brand and private label by establishing a rather complicated formula of freight equalization rates which was met with some consternation on the part of Western private label packers.

The Cash Discount

There was now some discussion regarding the 2% cash discount and we suggested that the points to be considered were: 1) would the packer lose a competitive advantage if he didn't have a discount? and 2) how would his cash flow be affected? Is it better to cut prices for volume customers than maintain a cash discount policy? Often customers demanded and took such discounts even though paying after the close of the period.

As a result, many large packers went on the discount basis.

Reversing a trend which had prevailed for almost two decades, some packers shifted from brokers at this time and went direct. One was Libby in the N.Y. area. Green Giant dropped its broker in Atlanta, and Morton's in a surprise move, decided to establish its own sales offices in other territories. But the move was only sporadic and did not become national.

QFF made a survey to determine which products distributors thought had the greatest potential growth. The results were in this order: French fries, baked goods, fish portions, dessert pies, meat specialties, vegetables in sauce, dinners, etc. Also, distributors were holding the line on profits with an average nationwide markup of 19.3% or 1.3% more than in 1962.

Action was being taken on cooperative advertising, too. Campbell dropped all co-op ads, so did Birds Eye. Minute Maid said it had "no formal plans."

In an article entitled "Why are frozen food prices so low?", we pointed out that in 1964 many items were actually as low or lower than they had been in 1952. This held true for peas, many vegetables, berries, orange juice, waffles and many seafood items. It still seems true today.

Changing Seafood Picture

In 1964 fish portions outproduced fish sticks for the first time, gaining 32% in six months. QFF revealed that imports of seafoods represented an all-time high; almost 50% of the supply of U.S. edible fishery products. About 166 million pounds of fish blocks were brought in for sticks and portions.

There were other changes that year. Crunchy fish sticks using batter, were introduced by Birds in England. Birds Eye in the U.S., the originators of the standard fish stick, had withdrawn from the fish business. Gorton's came out with a fish-and-chips package which carried a British flag on the label. Seafood dinners began to be popular and at the same time such pioneer exploiters as Mrs. Paul's, Blue Star, Red L, Gorton's, O'Donnel-

Advertising Club Award given to the "advertised brands responsible for the growth of frozen foods," presented by QFF every other year at a special luncheon. Award received by J. J. Dodds, president of the NAFFP.

T. B. House

L. G. Anderson

K. J. Sartori

A. N. Otis

Usen, Booth, Teddy's and others were getting strong competition from the chains. Among the chains who then launched their own seafood dinners were the A&P, Grand Union, Soprite, Bohack, First National and Safeway.

Also for the first time, shrimp became the largest dollar earner in frozen seafoods, with sales of $240 million at the retail level. In Gloucester, Mass., the Bureau of Commercial Fisheries was conducting experiments on low doses of irradiation before freezing. This, it was claimed, could triple the shelf life of fresh fish.

QFF pushed hard to get more convenient forms of frozen seafood. We said at the time: "We believe fillets should be sold in slices, strips or more easily defrosted pieces so that all does not have to be used at one time. The future lies not in the fresh frozen fillet but in its application in prepared form." At that time as now, the sale of fillets remained practically stationary. We early pushed for breaded, cut fillets, interleaved with paper and easily stripped off for cooking. The idea is now being announced as something new, though it started over ten years ago on plaice (flounder) in Denmark. We also pointed out that convenience, important though it is, never comes ahead of quality, flavor and taste. People don't mind going to a certain amount of inconvenience, as long as they know they are getting something *good* in the end.

Frozen Drinks Fade—More O.J.

By early 1964 the Florida industry had recovered somewhat from the previous year's freeze. I reported on my Florida trip that a great recovery was everywhere in evidence. At the price of 15-17¢ a can, orange drinks, introduced during the freeze, were beginning to move up. Minute Maid had three drinks, Griffin had Orange Nip, and BE pushed Awake. In 1963 frozen drinks equaled about 20% of the volume of the concentrate. The 12-oz. size, for the first time, recorded 30% of sales, but recovery from the freeze was now evident and the "drinks" began to disappear.

I would like here to comment on a controversial citrus figure, Ben Hill Griffin. Located at Frostproof, he had developed a series of excellent drinks with a high orange solids ratio. Mr. Griffin was active in politics, being a State Senator. He also ran a bank, a ranch and several other enterprises as well as his juice business, and his son is now following in his footsteps.

There were others who were helping to stabilize what had once been a wild-fire industry. Bob Rutledge, dynamic head of the Florida Citrus Mutual was widely quoted for his sound ideas, which were often followed.

Edward A. Taylor, who had previously been associated with the Nestle Co., was named general manager of the FCC to succeed Homer Hooks. Mr. Taylor has done a very fine job ever since. Charlie Der of Adams Packing was one of the newer crop of managers who helped lift the industry to a higher level. So was Ted King, now with Cypress Gardens. At Florida Citrus Canners, Marvin Walker, a former FCC commissioner, and Earl Newton, steered the ship. Bob Flippo built a huge plant,

Golden Gem, at Umatilla, assisted by Howard Sweatt. Al Snook of H. P. Hood in Dunedin, managed this complex. Herb Appel, who for many years had directed Birds Eye's Florida operations, retired and was given a big dinner. At Pasco, W. F. Edwards continued to make policy; he was an industry pioneer, and at Plymouth Citrus, Loren Mallory had been appointed to carry on the SealdSweet tradition. Harry Di Cristina had passed away and his place at Holly Hill was taken by L. W. McKnight who became vice president.

Another concentrator who had left an indelible impression upon the industry has died—Robert Mairs. He had been vice president of Winter Garden Citrus and more than ten years before had come from Baltimore, where he had been in the grocery business. He became a fiery leader in the concentrate business to which he contributed much. Mairs also had an ebullient and dynamic personality and was known for some of the unusual parties he gave at conventions, for which the most regal hotel suite was usually engaged. He had a macabre sense of humor; he once had himself brought in lying in a coffin. Mairs was succeeded by Jim Bock and "Buck" Thompson.

In early 1964, the first easy-opening cans appeared and within two years they quickly caught on. The FCC launched new advertising campaigns and the term OJ was introduced.

One of the most active persons in the juice industry at that time was Benjamin H. Oehlert, Jr., who has since become an ambassador to a South American republic. He was president of Minute Maid and one of his contentions was that citrus solids should be sold in any form which proved popular. He did much for the industry but was also the center of much discussion. At that time MM Groves Corp. controlled some 35,000 acres of citrus land in Florida.

Sugar Is Added

In 1963 concentrate, reflecting the freeze, had hit an all-time high, selling at 2 for 79¢ for ad brands and 2 for 69¢ in chain labels. Independents were getting 45¢. But this situation was not to last. The following year the price was cut radically and later, to help move juice, a $3 million coupon campaign and an incentive advertising plan were introduced. Prices dropped and consumption went up. By 1965, the industry, with a carryover of 10 million gallons, had an 85 million gallon pack to move.

Now the addition of sugar was proposed on top of the present solids in the can. A storm of protests followed; some argued that the new standards would open the way for unfair competition from outside the state. Nevertheless, the idea has since proved sound and sweetened juice is gaining ground.

I made many trips to Florida and in each one called on almost every processor in the state. Our predictions were published in our January issue and eight out of ten times estimates on the coming pack proved to be correct within 3-4%.

We furnished information which proved to be highly valuable to the entire industry, not only to the Florida group but to retailers, distributors and brokers as well. But more than that, QFF's principles were constructive and forward-looking. We advocated the 8-oz. can to replace the six-ounce size, as a means of moving more juice. "People will drink up those extra two ounces without any noticeable deletion of the units sold," we argued. We boosted multipacks, pointing out that beer and soft drinks were now all sold that way. We particularly urged price stabilization. In an editorial QFF wrote "One of the contributing factors to the boom or bust psychology which has pervaded the Florida concentrate business in the last ten years has been the erratic pricing of the 6-oz. can. We suggest a set-aside for export or school sales each year to stabilize prices." We wanted to see the "play-it-by-year" policy under which the industry operated, modified. At that time QFF pointed out that a potentially effective price-stabilizing tool such as the futures' market would help. Since then commodity futures have been introduced with a distinctly stabilizing effect. But more on this later.

In my trips to Europe I talked about orange juice in every country. There was growing interest. An article in QFF at the time said: "The Florida citrus industry must realize it is not building for today alone. It is still the greatest source of citrus in the world with 10 times the concentrating capacity of any other area." Subsequent events proved QFF right; only two years later a big export campaign was under way to the U.K. and other parts of Europe.

We're in the Time Capsule!

On October 16, 1965, Time Capsule No. 2 was buried in the grounds of the New York World's Fair for resurrection by residents of this continent thousands of years from now. The capsule contained evidences of our great civilization of which frozen foods was one. To represent the industry QFF was chosen by a select committee and our History of the Industry published in 1963 was put in microfilm form and buried in the capsule. We felt very flattered.

In 1965 Larry Martin, who had been executive secretary of the National Association of Frozen Food Packers retired after 22 years of service. He had first been engaged during the war by Ed Gibson, then president of Birds Eye, and introduced to the industry at a meeting run by QFF. He was succeeded by a very able young man, Thomas House, who had been executive vice president of the California Freezers Association since 1958.

Two industry pioneers passed away at that time. One was Charles Seabrook, at the age of 83. He was a real pioneer in both the frozen foods and farming, having expanded his father's original 78-acre farm near Bridgeton, N.J. into a multi-million dollar farming and freezing complex. Seabrook, on whom I called when I started QFF and who always showed me the greatest courtesies, has been referred to as the "Henry Ford of agriculture." He pioneered overhead irrigation, mechanized farming and several new vegetable and fruit varieties. He later gave up control of Seabrook Farms, as related earlier.

The latest development for the quick defrosting of frozen fruits is the thaw pack. Fruit in this pack is placed in hot water and thaws in a fraction of the time formerly needed. The use of the thaw pack is being slowed by the high cost of the bag forming and closure equipment, but the package does seem to be here to stay.

G. E. Thomas of Campbell Soup, representing the National Association of Frozen Food Packers, accepts plaque from E. W. Williams, publisher of QFF, awarded in 1967 "to the advertised brands responsible for increasing the consumption of frozen foods." The plaque now hangs in NAFFP's Washington, D. C., offices.

J. L. Pearson

F. N. Grigg

Another pioneer who passed away was Max Ries, at the age of 59. Ries had been associated with the industry since its inception and was instrumental in the formation of Honor Brand, one of the trade's early brands. After that he formed a brokerage company with John Antun. He subsequently traveled widely in the Far East and established seafood connections in many countries, principally India. He was later a vice president of Continental Seafoods.

In the same year, QFF lost one of its executives who had been with the magazine 15 years, Leslie G. Anderson, vice president and sales manager. His accomplishments during his tenure with QFF were truly outstanding and he had become well-known in the industry. He loved sales and advertising and he approached his job scientifically, using industry market data as his primary tools. Previously, he had been with McGraw-Hill, F. W. Dodge and Billboard magazine.

In 1965—Over $5.2 Billion

In September, 1965, we reported that the industry had enjoyed a gain of 20% over the previous year—the largest single increase in both dollars and poundage in FF history. Products were now valued at $5.2 billion and production estimated at close to 10 billion pounds. Prepared FF had made the biggest gain, the dollar value of which was $1,190 million. In that category, frozen dinners were first with an estimated $280 million in sales, followed by baked goods, nationality foods, fruit pies, meat pies and entrees.

That October, QFF brought out its largest issue—540 pages! It included two colorful production and marketing maps, sales figures for 125 markets, a 24-page almanac, sections on freezing and production techniques, marketing, seafoods, prepared foods, packaging, four consumer surveys as well as a complete refrigerated transport-warehousing section and some 100 other features and departments. The convention that year was at the Americana Hotel in N.Y.

In packaging there were new developments. QFF reported that hot-melts, a new type of heat sealable coating material, was becoming popular in frozen food packaging. Pouches, long endorsed by us, had been perfected to the point that they were practically free of defects and in this branch Scotch-Pack had taken a definite lead. Plastics were also coming into the industry but the rigid form was not yet commonly used. Sealright, however, has been a leader with their Vari-Pak container. Polybags, however, were going strong; they were soon to move one-third of the retail poundage of all frozen vegetables. In dinners a 4- and 5-compartmented tray had been introduced.

Each year in July, QFF puts out a very complete packaging review. Wrapper-less cartons had gained a strong foot-hold in the industry and were practically taking over. Aluminum was widely used, especially in the institutional field; one company had introduced a dispensable container for steam tables.

One Convention

In April we reported that after much editorializing by QFF, an announcement was finally made that the packers' and distributors' organizations would start to have *one* convention a year beginning in 1965. The past practice of two conventions a year had reduced the effectiveness of the affairs and also the attendance. Both groups are differently financed. The Packers' Association receives most of its funds through direct dues and assessments; income from exhibits and other sources are secondary. The National Frozen Foods Association, composed mostly of distributors and associated members, is to a large degree self-supporting and must raise a substantial part of its annual needs from sources other than membership dues. QFF for many years was the only magazine which urged one convention, actually working against its own interests since two convention issues a year yield more advertising revenue than one. One of the architects of the one-convention plan was Vern Gross, then President of the packers.

I was invited to address the California Freezers Association in 1964 and said that the FF industry had reached a period of consolidation and the trend was now toward size. "Financial strength and marketing ability are the keys to success in this stage of development," I said. I also delivered a talk before the Buffalo Association in which I predicated that the increasing size of home freezers would encourage the need for bigger packages.

Warehouses Have "New Look"

QFF devoted considerable space in its July, 1964, issue to the various services rendered by the refrigerated warehouses industry as an indispensable link to frozen food distribution. Two years later an entire section was devoted to the National Association of Refrigerated Warehouses. An article by Ken Sartori, president of the NARW and of the U.S. Cold Storage Corp., pointed out that cost, labor and technical problems of constructing and running a self-owned facility were considerable, when opposed to utilizing public space. "Why keep a cow," he said, "when all you need is a bucket of milk?"

During the latter half of 1967 and into 1968, the warehouse industry was bulging with food. Some warehouses had hung up a "filled up" sign. The situation had come about unexpectedly. One reason was a great increase in frozen turkeys, but another was the general expansion of frozen foods. Also railroad cars could no longer be retained for unloading for more than 48 hours and they were also larger.

Warehouses had a "new look," many old ones were discarded in favor of warehouses which were now able to offer both processing and storage facilities. Such a huge complex was built in Secaucus, New Jersey by the Merchants Refrigerator Co. Continental in Chicago expanded, as did U.S. Cold Storage plants. Harborside Terminal was carrying out a

$15 million project to convert its terminal into a container port. National Cold Storage compartmentized its plant. The Quincy warehouse added a new branch and more lately the Stouffer Co. made history when it opened an automated high-rise warehouse in Ohio with 13 levels. There were many other such changes which space does not permit me to enumerate. But more warehouses were offering inducements to packers to locate with them. Also, many warehouses had begun to diversify into distribution; others were making trucking services available. Several had bulked together less-than-truckload lots, a valuable service to packers.

I must mention here one of the industry's pioneers, David L. Feigenbaum, whose father sold frozen cherries as early as 1908. Under the name Little America, the firm began to freeze pies in 1939, then became a successful distributor in Pittsburgh, and later switched to the warehouse business. Mr. Feigenbaum is building a huge cold storage complex in Charlotte, N.C., the first phase of which will be 1¼ million cubic feet; when finished the unit will be able to store 30 million pounds of product. Refrigerated truck lines were on the move. QFF was the only publication which ran a complete directory of truck lines in which they were listed both alphabetically and geographically, thus making it easy for the shipper to find the line he wanted. In a survey recently, QFF showed that 60% of the nation's lines hauled more frozen foods than ever before and that 57% of them increased their fleets to accommodate added volume.

Not to be outdone, railroads introduced new incentive rates by offering FF shippers better volume rates. After that railroads began to recover some of the freight losses which had gone to trucks. Such organizations as Pacific Fruit Express added 1,000 mechanical cars bringing the total of their mechanical cars up to 9,200. Piggyback trailers, expanded schedules, all aided transportation. The Fruit Growers Express and the Missouri Pacific also offered inducements to the industry.

In 1966 QFF featured its Equipment Survey in which it was found that never before had the FF industry indulged in such a buying spree for construction, freezer space and processing plants. The boom has continued ever since.

QFF Story Sections

For some 20 years QFF has been running special story sections about various growing companies in the industry. We discovered that our readers found them to be highly interesting because they gave facts about a company not generally known.

Among some of these run in the last five years was the Rich Products story and discussed how this fledgling Buffalo concern which started in 1945, doing $28,000 worth of business, had grown to $25 million by 1965. Another was the Blue Star story, telling of a firm which, under David J. Kaplan, had started as a small protein egg producer in Iowa. Other processing plants were purchased until the company is now producing a complete line of frozen meat and fruit pies, dinners and many other specialty items.

The Lamb-Weston story related facts about one of the oldest processors of frozen vegetables in the Northwest and as a major processor of peas and potatoes. F. G. Lamb is executive director and E. J. Watson chairman. The original company had been incorporated by Frank G. Lamb in 1932. In 1961 the firm became heavily involved in potatoes.

More recently, QFF ran the Southland story which covered its 25-year history. It gave an excellent background of this progressive and growing vegetable packer.

QFF also ran the Transmundo story. This detailed the large Argentine meat packer and shipper. The company had bought out Wilson & Co.'s plant several years ago and was now the principal exporter of frozen cooked beef to the U.S.

The Simplot story told how, starting in 1941, the packer had become one of the world's largest processors of frozen potatoes. Leon Jones, its president, was largely responsible for its success.

The Iceland Products story related the firm's origins in the cod and fish business in Iceland in 1902 under the Samba name and had grown steadily with a plant in the U.S. with distribution throughout the world.

One of the biggest story sections ever run by QFF was on Mrs. Smith's Pies. It was entitled "A Lesson in Integrity" and showed how the firm had built up national distribution on the basis of quality pies. This company is mentioned elsewhere in this history. Yet another story was about Potato Service, of which Jule Salzbank is president. The company has had a remarkable expansion since its establishment in Presque Isle in the heart of the Maine potato area.

Other Stories

The Crest San Diego story followed the expansion of this prominent importer of shellfish and seafoods of which Jack Willis is president. Another, the Idaho Frozen Foods story, related how this potato packer got started in 1955 using the Russet variety. Vern Routh is president and Harry Nebenzahl, vice president. In 1967 QFF ran an interesting story about John Antun, New York food broker, who had spent 50 years in the industry. He is one of the real pioneers and responsible for the formation of several organizations. He started with Merchants Refrigeration at the age of 14 and continues to operate his own business. He has many friends in the industry.

A very unusual feature and the first one run about a broker was the Howard Boerner story. The late Boerner started as sales manager of Minute Maid, then in 1957 began his own brokerage company in New York. He added many leading packers to his list and now has annual sales of over $75 million. He was assisted by a crack staff, notable among them Ned Maher, who has been elevated to the presidency. More recently, the firm merged with Harvey Radio.

About Men & Products

In October, 1966, George M. Perry became general manager of Birds Eye, succeeding Martin Gregory. James Ferguson is the present manager. About this time Birds Eye brought out a number of new, imaginative and very excellent products. One was Cool Whip, a non dairy whipped topping. Sales climbed immediately and so did distribution. It is doubtful whether any new product introduced in the frozen foods industry, before or since, has had such a meteoric rise. After more than two years, a plateau has yet to be reached.

In late 1965 Birds Eye came out with the idea of defrosting fruits in a boil-in-bag. We wrote at the time: "There is nothing tastier, fresher or more luscious than a properly defrosted dish of frozen fruits, but the stumbling block to greater sales had been the problem of defrosting, which the housewife was never quite able to master. Either the fruit was too icy or too soft. How a bag of peaches or strawberries or mixed fruit, packed in a waterproof pouch is immersed in warm water where it remains for the necessary exposure time, around 10 minutes. Upon removal, the fruit is just right for eating." Birds Eye had accomplished this with its new easy-thaw line. We predicted it would gradually increase fruit sales and, while the early introduction was slow, a reduction in price has spurred its movement.

BE also introduced a five-minute vegetable package which cut down cooking time, and its line of prepared butter-sauce vegetables which has been already related. But not all BE products were successful. Previously, a product called Sodaburst, a frozen ice cream soda, was marketed but it didn't go, despite excellent quality. Neither did frozen baby foods, endorsed by the American Medical Association. BE also discontinued its dinners and meat pies in favor of greater concentration on its other products, including *Awake*.

Cambell-Swanson brought out a line of dinners in a much greater variety, including both regular and three-course meals. One beef dinner included tomato soup, beef with gravy, mashed potatoes and corn and cherry crisp for dessert. A new range includes a wide variety of dinners, one of them German style beans and franks. A line of frozen lunch box sandwiches was also brought out; varieties included peanut butter and jelly, chicken salad, frankfurter, ham and cheese, pizza filling, etc. In this connection I must mention Gerald E. Thomas, who has been Campbell's marketing manager since 1959. He had worked under Crawford Pollock at Swanson's, which was later absorbed by Campbell. Thomas is well known to the industry and has done a sound marketing job. He has also been active in industry matters in connection with the Consumer Information Program of the Packer's Association. He is slated to be president of that Association next November.

Mergers Accelerate

As we had predicted five years before, an avalanche of mergers has shaken up the industry. Dulany Foods, which had been sold in 1962 to Green Giant, was again sold to United Foods. Ralph Dulany, its pioneer head, became chairman of the Maryland Economic Development Commission.

J. F. Paulucci

H. R. Branstetter

Officers of the Midwestern Frozen Food Association, 1967. Seated (left to right): Gilbert Banks, first vice president; J. E. Rooney, president; J. E. Horwath, second vice president; and J. H. Cunningham, secretary. Standing (left to right): J. F. Williams, executive secretary; Byron Nelson; Leo Pam, treasurer; and Elmer O'Malley.

On behalf of the Ontario Frozen Food Council, Toronto Mayor Donald Summerville presented E. W. Williams with a set of silver cuff links representing the maple leaf emblem of Canada at a September, 1963, meeting. Seated, from left, are: Bill Wade, Wade-Ryans Sales Co.; Gordon Mooney, Harry Class, Farm House Pies; John Foy, Toronto Telegram; and Bob Kelly, then OFFC president.

Seapak Corp. of Georgia, which had started small after the war, was bought by W. R. Grace & Co. Tom Pearce, Jr., became chairman of the board, and H. J. Cofer, president.

Other mergers vigorously followed. Banquet Canning bought Bright Foods, a producer of private label in California. The Pet Milk Company, of which Larry Umlauf is FF head, acquired Aunt Fanny's Baking Co.; it now owns Pet-Ritz, Downyflake and Milady. A year later it made a giant acquisition, Schrafft's.

From time to time efforts have been made to purchase Seabrook Farms. The most recent negotiations were with Winter Garden in Bells, Tenn. It is understood that these have been broken off, but additional financing, possibly in the shape of bonds, is expected. In 1966 Jerre Pearson, who had previously done a fine job as president of Southern Frozen Foods, was named president of Seabrook. The company is now definitely on an upward path.

Gorton's of Gloucester, was expanding. It owned Red L, added Freeborn Farms, a manufacturer of hors d'oeuvres, and Bayou Foods, a processor of specialty seafoods. An attempt was made in 1967 by Great Western United Corp. to take over Gorton's, but the deal never went through. A merger now seems imminent with General Mills. The staff, including Paul Jacobs and Bob Kinney, will remain, should the merger go through.

H. J. Heinz acquired Star Kist Foods of Calif. to supplement its purchase of Ore-Ida several years ago. It is still seeking other acquisitions. Snowflake Canning of Maine, an old company in the field, was taken over by Taterstate Frozen Foods, which in turn had been purchased by Agway, Inc.

Consolidated Foods bought Idaho Frozen Foods, a leading potato processor in Idaho. The Goren Packing Co. in Boston, processors of portion control meats, was bought by the Norris Grain Co. of Chicago. Polarized Meat went to the Glidden Paint Co. The Tilghman Packing Co., south shore seafood firm, was bought by Duffy-Mott Co., and Henderson's Portion Pak, an important Florida-based meat packer, developed over the years by Jim Henderson and Jack Young, was sold for a good sum to Borden's.

An expanding firm was Beatrice Foods, which had bought Lambrecht Foods and added Rosarita Mexican Foods, Beatrice also bought Temple Frozen Foods, the second largest frozen Chinese food packer. In addition, Beatrice bought a number of cold storage warehouses, including Quincy Market C. S. in Boston, Tampa Cold Storage, Inland Underground Facilities in Kansas City.

More recently, Litton Industries, a large conglomerate, acquired Stouffer Foods Corp., which included its frozen food operations. James Biggar remained as general manager. Vernon Stouffer, who had founded the company, became a Litton director and continued as head. The firm reported sales of over $79 million in 1966, and has done better since as a leading producer of frozen entrees.

Chun King, Other Sales

At the end of 1966, the R. J. Reynolds Tobacco Co. purchased Chun King for $63 million from Jeno Paulucci, who it is understood, owned 100% of the corporation. Paulucci had been a salesman for a Minnesota grocery wholesaler and in 1947 borrowed $2,000 to get into the business of growing bean sprouts for sale to retailers and canners. He then began canning his own products and brought out a line of Chinese and Italian frozen and canned goods. Through clever advertising, he built up the largest company in his field. Since the sale, Paulucci is repeating the process with Jeno's (a smaller company which he retained).

Another growing giant is Ward Foods of which Charles W. Call, Jr., is president. Previously the Johnston Pie Co. and the Farm House label had been acquired. Venturing into seafoods, Ward took over Continental Seafoods of which Irving Farber is president. Farber, who started the company in 1948, had built up an enviable business with current sales of around $12 million. He had traveled widely and was the first importer to obtain approval from the U.S. State Department to bring in Russian seafoods. With this acquisition, a whole new area was opened up for Ward, still further enlarged by the subsequent purchase of Wakefield.

At the same time Mrs. Smith's Pies acquired Bradley's Frozen Foods in Oregon, an established producer of pies. United Foods of Houston, Texas, of which Irvin Kaplan is president is another acquisition-minded packer. It had bought plants in Texas, Watsonville, Calif., Louisiana and Michigan, and now packed a wide range of frozen products. Recently, United acquired California Consumers and then added Dulany and Othello Foods in Washington. Green Giant bought Snider Farms in Gresham, Ore., old line berry packers.

Distributor Changes

There were changes in the distribution field too. The two largest independent retail FF distributors in the East, Global Frozen Foods and Snow-Kist, merged in 1966, and Herb Irving became board chairman. Jack Karger, a former Birds Eye salesman who had built up Snow-Kist, later resigned and became a consultant.

Brokers were merging also. Gay Pryor in Philadelphia bought another broker, so did Brown-Massie in California. It appears the merger trend among *food brokers,* retaining management however, is only starting.

Less Fish on Friday

At the end of 1966 a Vatican decree allowed Catholics to eat meat on Friday. This was a blow to the seafood industry and there were particular problems in areas with large concentrations of Catholic families. But the industry wasn't too worried. As it turned out, sales snapped back, but for at least a year fillets, fish sticks and portions were particularly affected, though shellfish products were hardly affected.

In 1967 breaded shrimp processors were being continually harassed by the Food & Drug Administration, which was seizing shrimp in various plants based on bacterial count. However, the FDA admitted that it had no bacteria standards on which its seizures were based. QFF strongly protested against this policy and as a result, the FDA eased its stand a considerable degree. Frank W. Holas, Sr., president of Booth, had, along with L. H. Frohman, Paul Jacobs and Bob Erkins, etc., rendered invaluable aid to the seafood industry.

There were other seafood developments. The huge Mexican frozen shrimp industry had originally been founded by Lucian K. Small, who was president of Marine Products in San Diego for many years until he sold out to Wilbur-Ellis. He had formed a close association with Abelardo Rodriguez in Mexico before World War II and brought the first shrimp into the U.S. later, Crest Importing was started in 1953 by J. W. Willis, who created an international company. Frozen seafoods were obtained from all parts of the world. A sister company, Ocean Garden Products, is now headed by Henry Branstetter, who decided to enter the FF business in 1946 after studying a complete file of QFF issues in the San Francisco library. As a result, he joined John Inglis and later introduced frozen foods to Wilbur-Ellis, where he remained ten years, before joining Crest. Gordon Murphy, a well-known New York broker, handles eastern sales.

Leon Rubin of Atlanta Trading had built up a $100 million business and a large organization. He traveled widely and first brought shrimp from India into the U.S. in 1951 as well as Brazilian lobster tails. In the trout business, a fast growing company is Snake River Trout of Idaho. Operated by Robert Erkins, this company harvests close to two million pounds of trout a year. In the shrimp field already mentioned was Ocean Products of Florida, Rubenstein in Texas and others. Notable is that the Singleton Packing Co. of Tampa in 1965 opened the first shrimp plant designed for liquid nitrogen freezing; the system was installed by Air Products Corp. In Denmark, the Danish Trout Farmers, under the brand name Danepride is selling its trout widely in the U.S. Acadia Fisheries in Canada opened a new plant.

Heath Industries, Gloucester, Mass., developed a low-priced liquid nitrogen machine to freeze its whole New England lobsters, and prospered at both.

A growing seafood merchandiser is Marty Kolen, head of Empress Fisheries. Kolen first brought in Cuban lobster tails which the embargo stopped, and more recently had developed a large and well-packaged line of Empress products, both retail and institutional, including shrimp, trout, swordfish, lobster tails, fillets and frog legs.

FCOJ Commodity Market

In January, 1967, the Florida citrus industry was bowled over by the highest product estimate yet—142 million boxes. Fortunately, the carry-over was small, nevertheless the industry was faced with a big crop and prices went down. FCC planned to spend $17 million for national promotion; the school market was opened up and coupon campaigns appeared in leading magazines. We urged the sale of multipacks in 4, 6 and 8 can units as well as the 8-oz. can to replace the 6. At the same time the state produced a new 45 brix juice which was a considerable improvement in quality over the previous 42 brix. The new juice eliminated pulp washing and offered higher concentration. The success of sweetened orange juice was evident. The Kroger chain reported one-third greater sales for OJ in stores handling both the sweetened and unsweetened, against those handling the straight juice only. As QFF had predicted ten years before, more premium juices would be coming on the market. Birds Eye introduced one in an 8-oz. can, so did Holly Hill and Minute Maid, offering a premium Valencia.

By June that year, Florida concentrate was producing the cheapest juice in the world, competing with Mexico, Brazil, Chile, Israel, Spain and North Africa. As a result, new outlets were opened in Europe. In England, Birds Eye had made an arrangement to import juice from Pasco and Winter Garden, which they introduced under the BE (Unilever) label, backed by a big advertising campaign which the FCC and the Department of Agriculture pays two-thirds. Consumption in England is rapidly increasing.

At Minute Maid a major change in operations occurred when that company became a division of Coca-Cola and moved its sales and marketing personnel to Houston, Texas. The board chairman of the new Foods Division is Charles Duncan, and Don Keough is marketing vice president of MM and SC. The following year, MM, after a lapse of 20 years, again brought Bing Crosby to the fore. Current ads read: "Bing Crosby first helped us introduce Minute Maid orange juice . . . now Bing is back." About 1947 Bing Crosby had bought a large number of MM shares for around 10 a share which he later sold for an undisclosed amount.

The commodity futures market was now introduced into the citrus industry with stabilizing effect. It became part of the marketing mechanism of Florida citrus and at the end of the first ten months of operation over 9,000 trades had taken place.

This trading was considered a hedge so that the grower, often faced with a questionable future crop, could hedge and sell to a buyer at an agreed price. Many sold future contracts which were equal to the expected crop. A leader in the move was Merrill Lynch, Pierce, Fenner & Smith. The contracts merely required that the seller deliver a set quantity of concentrate during some stated month in the future and the buyer was obligated to pay the agreed price at the time. As far as the processor is concerned, when orange prices appear relatively low he can buy future contracts in anticipation of his needs. These contracts serve as a protection against price increases and also work in reverse.

FF Abroad

Since QFF publishes the International Edition quarterly, which relates in full the progress of frozen foods in Europe and throughout the world, I will not go into much detail on foreign operations. Suffice to say that

Western Europe is the biggest potential area after the U.S., then Australia, South Africa, New Zealand, Japan and the eastern countries for frozen foods. In 1966 I estimated that Unilever's Birds Eye in England, headed by James Parratt and a fine group of directors, is now the largest FF company in the world in terms of sales, over $190 million. No single American packer does that much business, though there are several in the $100 million class. BE in England is in the enviable position of being an integrated processor and dominates the growing retail home market to the extent of almost 70% of total sales. I made yearly visits to Europe, usually covering some nine countries, all fully reported in QFF. About a recent trip, I wrote: "Europe's frozen foods industry is fully equal to the U.S. in respect to techniques, freezing, modern production, packaging and distribution. But in the area of consumer acceptance it lags by about 15 years." But the gap is closing, though faster in some countries than in others. When I last visited London I was awarded a silver cup membership in the Silver Tankard Club of Birds Eye. I read: "For Distinguished Salesmanship in the Interest of the World-Wide Development of the FF Industry."

Findus International, owned by Nestle, is the second largest organization in Europe, distributing in many countries and headquartered in Switzerland. Mr. Lars Anderfelt, its managing director, has adhered to the quality idea and his plants produce a large amount of new products. Sweden has the highest per capita consumption in frozen foods but Italy, for instance, is rapidly emerging in the production of such items as green beans, broccoli, asparagus, etc. Germany is a tremendous potential market, though the German housewife is less venturesome in trying frozen products than some other countries.

Recently the Findus branch in England merged with Eskimo, creating an important second force in that country. The Ross Group, which has important fishing interests, is third. (For complete details on frozen food growth in all European countries, see detailed report, July 1968, QFF International Edition.)

In Mexico, Findus started a company to produce and market FF for the "5% to 7% of Mexican people who have decided to be adventurous in their eating habits." Sales seem to be progressing in leading cities— Mexico City, Vera Cruz and Guadalajara. Very excellent frozen products come from Mexico now; I have tasted them. They include peas, Brussels sprouts, small green asparagus, and broccoli. Incidentally several American firms have built or leased plants in Mexico. Faced with increased labor costs in California, attributed to the discontinuation by the U.S. of the bracero program, some firms have been investing in operations south of the border where labor is more plentiful.

In Canada, I was invited to attend the first Harvest of Frozen Foods in Toronto, where I gave a talk to the local association, run by Robert W. Kelley. The late Mayor Summerville of Toronto presented me with a set of silver Maple Leaf design cuff links for my help in promoting the campaign. The Toronto group did an outstanding job and included Joe Astle of Loblaw, Bert Cooper of Dominion Stores, Harry Class, Bill Wadem, Gordon Mooney and G. Cronin.

L. Wakefield   M. Ielmini

Other Emerging Companies

One of the biggest success stories in the industry during the past five years has been the advance of frozen meats. There were now at least a half dozen companies which, six years ago, were doing around $1-2 million a year and who were now selling close to $20 million annually. The profit structure was good. The greatest growth had been in institutional products, but many new retail lines, mostly in cheaper cuts, and meat slices in gravy were sold.

A fast expanding company was Freezer Queen, which was started by Paul Snyder in Buffalo in 1957. Using sliced beef and gravy as a leader and extending into a line of convenience meat products, he attained sales of over $20 million. A pioneer portion control meat packer is Colonial Beef, which recently opened a new plant in Philadelphia. Genial Louis Waxman, president, now packs 20 million pounds of quality products a year. In New Jersey, Ten-Da Brand has been in the institutional meat business 25 years and produces a fine line of pre-cooked entrees, and other products in aluminum disposable pans. King Packing, St. Paul, had a fleet of trailers delivering meat to the entire country from one location.

A number of other names stand out, Grand Duchess, Jiffy Steak, Hendersons, already mentioned, Gol-Pak, Silver Skillet, Purdy Steak, Portno, On-Cor and others mentioned in previous chapters. While Armour & Swift have been active in some phases of frozen meats, the emphasis has so far been with the *smaller* companies.

Companies were enlarging rapidly. Space doesn't permit mentioning all, but many in the West such as National Fruit Canning, Lamb-Weston and others built large additions. Mrs. Smith's added a fully automated pie freezing system to produce 6,000 eight-inch pies an hour. Green Giant had announced a major investment of $10 million in capital expenditures for 1968; it now had 21 processing plants in the U.S. and Canada. Booth

Fisheries opened a new plant in Portsmouth, N.Y., with 142,000-square-feet of floor space. Gorton's, Coldwater Seafoods, Frionor all build new factories. The entire industry was on the move.

About this time Nathan Cummings, who had forged Consolidated Foods into a billion dollar corporation in less than 30 years, stepped down as chairman and chief executive officer in 1967. He was succeeded by William Howlett.

We published a story section about Modern Maid, which had grown up with the industry and had been a supplier of breading since 1933. The company occupied 160,000 square feet of space in two strategically located plants and was headed by Jack Silverman.

On the West Coast, Naturipe Berry Growers celebrated its 50th anniversary last year. Under the direction of Tad Tomita the firm had made rapid progress as a strawberry packer. More mechanization was apparent on the West Coast. For instance, Porter-Way had produced a machine which could harvest a ton of sprouts in 15 minutes. The big demand was for automated equipment of all types. A new freezer-cooker was developed by the University of Maryland and promoted by Robert Spence, food service director. The unit would both hold frozen foods and reheat them for service when wanted.

A Host of New Products

And still the avalanche continued, in the period 1965-68 many other new products, besides those mentioned heretofore, contended for the consumer's nod. Among them were: pancake batter, seven new 10″ pies priced at 89 to $1 by Morton's; strawberries with 50% *fewer* calories by Birds Eye; a frozen concentrated vegetable milk; a line of diet dinners by Weight Watchers, and many more.

Two commodities I have long advocated as "underprivileged" items were becoming popular. One was corn on the cob which I had always felt deserved more popularity because most people like it and it is hard to get fresh, even in areas where it is grown. The only difficulty was the users had a tendency to overcook it and restaurant prices were too high. Nevertheless, the vegetable has spurted in recent years: in 1967 production was 400% over 1963. Some 20 packers now sell cob corn in poly bags and QFF estimates its potential production at from 150-170 million pounds.

Another underprivileged item is the freestone peach. For the first time in many years this fruit was up by 60% in sales in 1967. This increase was partly due to the easy defrost pouch, and I think freestone peaches will someday rival the canned clings.

Eastern Washington was growing as a potato-producing area. The Columbia basin began to accommodate many new plants, although the frozen potato industry had doubled its plants and increased production by 385% in the past several years. Some of the new plants included Chef Reddy, Rogers Walla Walla, Pronto, Unique FF, L-B FF, Prosser, Lamb-Weston, and Libby.

Ellis Arnall (pointing), ex-governor of Georgia and long-time counsel for the National Frozen Food Association, with Association officials.

Strawberry sales began to perk up too, especially IQF. Many companies were beginning to sell whole, unsugared berries, a throw-back to the early days of the industry. Berries were short, since in 1955 production was around 312 million pounds; in 1967 only 198 million. Baking was on a decline and many preservers packed their own. On the other hand the new easy-thaw idea may increase usage. In an excellent article in QFF written by Gary Valentine of San Antonio Trading Co., in June, 1968, he pointed out that Mexico was increasing its production of fresh strawberries and that more would be exported to the U.S. in this form. Sam Skolnick of Imperial Foods, wrote that American growers would ship more fresh and less frozen to the U.S. market in the QFF June, 1968, issue.

Passing of Some Industry Leaders

During the past five years the industry has sorrowfully lost some leaders. One pioneer who died at the age of 82 was A. F. Wentworth, former owner of the Fairmont Canning Co. In his later years he operated a shrimp plant in Florida and developed a new freezer for shrimp.

In 1966 Hy Epstein, the founder of Milady Frozen Foods died. He had also been president of the Nat'l. Prepared Frozen Food Association, in which he had been very active. Together, with a partner, he entered the FF business in 1945 and began to manufacture blintzes. Epstein did a fine job in promoting his product and later sold to Pet Milk.

Another pioneer, Fritz Brahm, well known FF broker, died in 1968 of cancer. He had been associated with the industry from its beginnings, at one time representing Birds Eye. He was active in association work, not only with frozen food groups but with brokers as well.

Frank Blum, a Pittsburgh distributor, who began selling FF in 1937, died, as did another pioneer, Harvey Osborn, a food broker. Only recently, the industry saw the passing of Carl Seabergh who, in 1954 opened the first and one of the few FF stores still operating. He created and had packed to his own order many new foods and ran imaginative ads which read like news items. B. J. Eldridge, a pioneer production executive, for many years with Birds Eye and later with Snow Crop, died also. Still another frozen food broker, one of the very first, passed on in 1966, Edward J. Hayes, head of the firm which bears his name. He was responsible for the first cross-country shipments of frozen fruits in bulk and was instrumental in bringing the first peas to the Midwest. Joseph Carpel, president of Carpel Food Distributors, died in Washington; he was a pioneer too and a past director of the Natl. Frozen Food Ass'n. In the seafood industry, a colorful old-timer John R. O'Donnell, chairman of the board of O'Donnell-Usen, died at 73. He started in the fishing industry as an office boy and eventually rose to a top position, founding the firm which bore his name and later merging with Irving Usen. I knew all of these men well.

Twenty Years

Dean of our staff is Leonard Natter, QFF's production manager, now rounding out his 20th year of service. He handles the printing of three QFF magazines, two directories and all promotional material with great skill.

In 1968, QFF installed a special INSTITUTIONAL SECTION, covering portion control, in each issue. This carries more information on frozen foods in the mass feeding market than any other magazine.

The institutional section continues to run stories about the use of frozen foods by hospitals, schools, airlines, restaurants, drive-ins, etc. and proves a very important medium for those wishing to expand in this field. QFF also enlarged its coverage of leading mass feeding chains, covering all angles.

For instance, one story was about a New Jersey hospital where 650 patients were being fed twice a day by a unique frozen meal program using a small kitchen staff which could only handle 300 patients under a regular bulk feeding operation. We also published at this time the leading 100 FF institutional markets which gave the industry a yardstick of actual institutional sales of leading products. This was the first time anything of this type was available.

Frosty Acres—Brokers

The Frosty Acre label was started for a group of distributors who wanted something of their own. Today, 75 major wholesalers handle the brand which covers a complete line of retail and institutional foods and includes practically every popular item produced. Much of the organization's success goes to Dick Page, one of its prime movers and Mel Winton, its broker.

Considerable credit must also go to Watson Rogers, president of the National Food Brokers' Association, who was responsible for continuing a code of ethics, developing broker programs and running an excellent convention each year. The association now numbers some 1,400 members.

The NAFFP issued a code of ethics also, which was widely circulated. The trade practices were directed at manufacturers of frozen foods, distributors and retailers. Incidentally, Jerry Webster is a strong right hand at the NAFFP to Tom House. His ability in public relations has given the association a strong image.

This history must also give credit to Harry Schauffler and Gordon Griffith, coordinators in the now national "Buy-Time" promotions, usually held in the fall of the year. The movement became widely supported by local FF groups and individuals, chains and other media. September has been officially sanctioned by the USDA as frozen food month.

In early 1968 the Midwest Frozen Food Association held its first frozen food buffet in Chicago, with an attendance of over 1,000 and 37 exhibitors. QFF and its midwestern representatives aided the association of which Gil Banks was president. The idea, which I first used many years ago with the Eastern Frosted Foods association, was to permit packers to sample new products which served as a buffet and could be eaten by buyers in the area.

In 1968 QFF carried a history of the Southern Frozen Foods Association and the Southwestern group. Both groups have done much to further FF activities in these areas.

Our Ad Club Meetings

Every two years, QFF runs an outstanding event at the Advertising Club of N.Y. The last affair, which took place in April, 1967, was most impressive, and QFF played host to the greatest array of FF executives ever to sit at one table. This was in the form of a salute to the advertised brands; I was chairman, and presented a plaque to the ad brands to be hung up in the headquarters of the NAFFP in Washington. On the dais were: Nathan Cummings, chairman of Consolidated Foods, John A. McGlinn, Jr., senior vice president, Campbell Soup; C. W. Cook, chairman, General Foods Corp.; William May, chairman, American Can Co., Vernon Stouffer, Stouffer Foods, Minute Maid; the late H. M. Shattuck, president, Schrafft's; E. A. Taylor, manager of the Florida Citrus Commission; George Vail, president, Mortons; John Bittner, president

Pet, Inc., FF Division; Paul Jacobs, vice president, Gorton's; Vincent J. Kirby, vice president, Mrs. Smith's; Gaylord LaMond, president Chock Full O'Nuts; Leo Levinson, president, Ocean Products; Tom Pearce, chairman, SeaPak, and Norman Cahners, chairman, Cahners Publishing Co.

More than 300 were in the audience and a complete frozen meal was served. We applauded the advertised brands producers in the FF industry who, "through their creative effort, original research, vigorous advertising and promotion, have *alone* developed all the fine products being offered the consumer today."

QFF Joins Cahners

In March, 1966, I decided to merge with the Cahners Publishing Company of Boston. This fine organization now has 36 trade publications and is second only to McGraw Hill in the trade publication field. Norman L. Cahners, board chairman, founded his group in 1946 with Modern Materials Handling and now publishes publications in design, electronics, metal working, construction, factory, plastics, appliance manufacturing, purchasing, volume feeding, transport, public utilities and other fields. Through this new association, QFF was better than ever able to render the highest type of service to the growing frozen foods industry. There were no changes whatsoever in management, I continued as publisher and our staff has remained intact.

In November, 1968, in cooperation with Du Pont, QFF for the first time published a computer estimate of frozen food growth involving pounds, dollars and per capita consumption. These estimates were arrived at using growth, normal experience in the introduction of frozen products, and other yardsticks. These were fed into computers with very interesting results. The estimates did not allow for the developments of new product categories, and assumed that products already existing would continue to grow according to a pattern established from 1949 through 1966. The figures which emerged were therefore on the conservative side.

Prepared Foods First

The computer estimate, published in November, 1967, showed that in the next 10 years, prepared frozen foods would grow from $1.5 billion to $6.8 billion by 1966. Frozen meats were expected to increase by 184% to $1.8 million. Frozen seafoods came next, with an increase of 154%. Vegetables were slated to advance by 85% from a production of around 3 billion pounds to 6.30 billion by 1966. Orange juice was expected to go up 45%, frozen poultry about 22%, and frozen fruits with only an 8½% gain. The publication of these computer estimates was most enthusiastically received by the industry and today constitute an economic yardstick. Another QFF first! We also pointed out that in the past 10 years the growth rate of the FF industry had proceeded *3.6 times as fast* as the U.S. growth.

C. W. Cook

G. R. Vail

W. P. McCaffray

J. A. Schlindwein

E. J. Piszek

Never before had there been so many personnel changes, due mainly to the great number of mergers. We wrote at the time that the FF industry was beginning to resemble Madison Avenue's advertising business. We estimated that over 3,000 leading FF packers, distributors and brokers had experienced over 10% important management changes; more than 30% underwent replacements in junior officers and 50% in sales help.

The future of frozen potatoes also went through the computers and in December, 1967, we made our first such projection. It was estimated that by 1976, frozen potato sales would amount to $870 million, an increase of of 270% over 1966. It was also estimated that there would then be a total poundage of 3.9 billion, compared with around 1.5 billion now.

In April, 1967, QFF ran a special section on Buffalo. The Frozen Food Association of Western N.Y., headed by Burt Flickinger, covers an area doing an annual business of over $80 million. Similar sections have appeared on Miami, the Midwest, Dallas and other areas. In the Florida market there are several good brokers. One is Budd Mayer. He first distributed Minute Maid in Baltimore in 1947, and had mobile frozen food stores. Others are A. A. Green, C. G. Trigg, formerly of Minute Maid, Columbia Brokerage, Weil Bros., West Coast, Bonacker & Leigh and many more.

We Make Consumer Surveys

QFF continued to make many consumer FF surveys, something done by no other publication. Some of these were through the mails, from which we received prompt and excellent industry reports. Others were made by the N.Y. State University Agricultural College in Farmingdale, L.I., whose 16-man team interviewed housewives, either at their homes or at the FF departments of supermarkets.

One such survey was on poultry; we found that frozen turkey, chicken and duck were the most popular; only 8% of those interviewed bought frozen parts. About 46% of frozen turkeys were bought only on holidays. More imagination in presenting poultry is now being used. For instance, Jesse Jewell offers a complete chicken line—diced chicken for salads, drumettes for children, precooked and breaded frying chicken, rolls for sandwiches, boned chicken meat, etc.

In a cream pie survey, the most popular proved to be chocolate cream, then banana, neopolitan, lemon and strawberry.

One of our most interesting consumer surveys was on nationality foods. It was learned that the largest percentage of distribution was Italian, followed by Chinese. In the Italian category, pizza was first, ravioli next, followed by manicotti and lasagna. Among Chinese dishes, dinners came first, then egg rolls, chop suey, chow mein, etc. In Mexican foods, dinners were also first, then enchiladas and tacos. In Jewish foods bagels topped the list, followed by Jewish Rye, kosher dinners, blinzes and potato pancakes. Italian food sales were estimated at $100 million annually, Chinese foods, $30 million, and Mexican products, $25 million. All frozen, of course.

Last Round-Up

This history concludes with the July, 1968, issue. I was, at that time, proud to have received an award for meritorious service from the Midwestern Frozen Food Association.

Our most recent contribution to the industry is perhaps our *SAMI* reports. These studies, supplied to QFF by the Selling Areas-Marketing, Inc., an influential research organization, gives our readers each month frozen food retail ratios for all major categories in seven prime marketing areas. This service is continuous and when kept and read over a period of time, it provides movement information unobtainable through any other publication.

Our RETAILING magazine has been improved and its circulation is now over 42,000—the only mass-circulated medium devoted to FF retailing. In November, 1967, we issued one of our finest numbers, 406 pages, containing complete sections on every facet of the industry.

QFF's Annual Directory of Processors, which had grown from pocket size in 1945, last listed 2,084 processors throughout the world, of which 1,450 were in the U.S. as well as warehouses and refrigerated trucklines.

Since starting QUICK FROZEN FOODS in 1938, I have lived and dreamed frozen foods. It has always been my feeling that a trade magazine must go far beyond merely reporting news. A new industry needs guidance, it needs inspiration, leadership, ideas, enthusiasm, criticism and direction. All this, QFF has attempted to supply over the years and will continue to offer in the future, mirroring and predicting key events.

—THE END—

Appendix

Selected "Forum Items"
from *Quick Frozen Foods*

What follows is a compilation of the best, the most provocative and inspirational Forum Items which appeared in QUICK FROZEN FOODS during the period 1955-1969.

They Did It

Imagination is the one inspirational quality that put the frozen foods industry where it is today. It was present at the industry's inception and has been constant all down the line. Such advances as the industry has made have been accomplished by people who were told it couldn't be done. *Yet they did it.*

No one would buy frozen products, it was confidently predicted 15 or 20 years ago but proponents of the freezing idea went ahead and sold them. You couldn't make a self-service cabinet that remained open was the general opinion, yet manufacturers have made them. A complete cooked frozen meal would never be practical it was said, yet an equipment manufacturer developed it.

These are but a few of the many things which have been and are being developed by those who don't believe it can't be done. And very often the impossible is being achieved by non-technical men, perhaps because they don't know the rules, only the *exceptions* to the rules.

The future of frozen foods lies in the hands of the men who just don't believe in the so-called impossible.

Don't Die, Just Fade

When I was a boy of twelve I read Scott's Ivanhoe. It was considerably over my head and I didn't enjoy it. In later years I read it again and found it engrossing. *Maturity* made the difference.

In frozen foods, some items that failed when the industry was young might succeed now. I was never fully convinced that frozen applesauce was the "loser" it was said to be just because it was overproduced at a time when the industry went through a depression. Then, many items took the "rap" because they were big in inventory at a time when the industry was vulnerable. Frozen applesauce, well packed, can be superior to the canned product and certainly saves time.

Now I don't mean to say that *all* past failures should be resurrected. Frozen baked beans were consigned to the dust bin and belong there. But precooked meals are by no means through; they await proper development and marketing at realistic prices. In 15 years from now many housewives may be eating catered meals. Many old frozen food items never die; they only fade away—*and they often make a comeback.*

Mentality of an Industry

Outsiders sometimes find it hard to "understand" the frozen food industry and those who go to make it up. This is quite natural. Those who constitute this industry, packers, distributors and often brokers, may be termed, "industrial pioneers." They walk untrodden paths, they cut their own way through an unexplored wood. They blaze a new trail.

This makes the frozen foods industry different from older established businesses, such as canning, ice cream etc. where the road ahead has been well marked and laid out.

In every fresh turn of its progress, the frozen foods industry finds a new situation looming in the form of an unexpected, and often unsolved problem. That is why its members must be tough and rugged, ready for the unexpected, wary, quick acting and hard hitting if necessary.

But the pioneer who runs the dangers and risks of the unexplored also has his compensations. For he is the builder of a new industry and no matter how rugged the road he also very often, has the advantage of making the "first strike."

Don't Refreeze

Certainly, no one appreciates the necessity of warning a housewife not to refreeze after defrosting any more than the writer, but it isn't necessary to scare her to death to do so.

The principal reason for not refreezing is the *impairment of flavor* which follows, but in 99% of the cases, there is no real danger in it.

How much more tactful to merely say, "It is suggested that the contents of this package, when once thawed, are not refrozen, since impairment of flavor follows."

Complete Line?

There used to be a theory that you had to have a complete line to get into the retail cabinet. I have never really believed in this theory; on the contrary, sometimes too big a line is a hinderance rather than a help. A quality reputation built on just a few items, *merchandised to the hilt,* is often far better than a farflung line, much of which may be packed un-economically, including many "fringe" items.

Wanted—Executives

The biggest shortage in the frozen foods industry is not in cabinets, equipment or any products, nor is it in production men or salesmen. What is needed more than anything else is that rarest of all species—*good executives!* Unfortunately, true executives are born, not made, although training helps. Many frozen food firms are run by production men or salesmen but when a company reaches any size at all, it needs a trained executive. Many firms have found it to be to their advantage to reach out into other fields and hire proven executives, even though they have no experience in frozen foods.

Fish Future

Every effort is being made to increase per capita consumption of fish in which effort QFF heartily joins. But the more I think of it, the more convinced I am that one of the main spurs to greater fish sales lies in a *good sauce.* Whether the fish is broiled or fried, a good sauce helps and very few housewives either have the ability or time to make such a sauce. Why not freeze a ready-made sauce in an envelope and enclose it with each fillet sold? Then, at least, the fish would have a head start when it reaches the kitchen.

How They Buy

What makes women stop and buy food packages? One meat packer contends that the average woman handles eight packages of bacon before she selects. The "average" American housewife is often unpredictable. One packaging firm sums her up as follows: "She's a woman with 20 minutes $20, a second child waiting in the car and a third in escrow. Her shopping list is incomplete at best and many of her buying decisions are made in the seven or eight seconds it takes her to pass the counter where the items are displayed." Some call it *impulse buying.* Frozen food packers are well aware of the importance of designing; QFF estimates that more than $8 million is being spent yearly by frozen food companies on package designs. Nothing pays like a well-designed package—providing, of course, the quality inside is consistent.

Eating

Back in 1908 the USDA made a survey on per capita consumption of food—all foods. It was then shown that the average American consumed about 600 pounds of food per year. Another survey was made a couple of years ago. What did it show—800, 900 or 1,200 pounds? Not at all—just about the same, *600 pounds.* All of which indicates that the human stomach can hold just so much food. But times do change and people may eat the same amount but they eat *different* foods. For instance, they eat more frozen foods, less fresh produce, more meat, less fish (except frozen), less hearty breakfasts, etc. But the important thing is that today there is more competition for space in that stomach (which still only holds 600 pounds of food a year,) *than ever before*. The foods that people *want* are the ones which will always be welcome in the cabinets.

Short or Long?

If common sense and the infallible law of supply and demand teach us anything, it certainly teaches that it's better to be *short* than long on merchandise. Suppliers are rarely satisfied—either there is a big inventory or else there isn't enough to go around. But whichever way you look at it, if a choice must be made of both extremes, the short position is better. Best of all, of course, is a *good middle position* wherein a frozen food inventory is geared to the market, so that it is neither too big nor too small to place itself off balance. A balanced production, adequately related to what the market is estimated to be able to absorb is the *ideal* position to be in. This year, we hope that frozen food producers will work toward this goal.

The law forbids any concerted group action to restrict or regulate production, but it doesn't forbid the use of *judgment* by an individual packer who profits by information obtained through a central source. Each item should be analyzed methodically three or four months before the pack is scheduled, drawing on the previous season's experience, the experience of others and the probable number of new customers. This is the only known way to achieve the ideal of a "balanced inventory position" which, in turn, assures a fair return and a fair profit.

The Magic "9"

One chain buyer brings up an interesting point. "Experience has taught us," he says, "that prices ending in nine either for individual packages or for a multiple number of packages are attractive to consumers." Thus 19¢ 29¢, 39¢ etc. are all considered to be prices with appeal providing, of course, the items so priced have good consumer value. Likewise, 2-for-29¢, 2-for-39¢ or 3-for-69¢ also seem to have consumer attraction. This buyer urges that packers keep this buying psychology in mind when pricing their products. "For example", he says, "it might be better to put nine ounces of a product into a package and get a 39¢ retail price, than to put up an eight-ounce package which would sell for 35¢." He urges that packers first determine the consumer price at which an item is offered before setting the selling price. Seems as if this makes good sense.

Meat's Future

I believe that the future of frozen meat, by no means as yet decided, rests with the *chain stores* who today hold the balance of power in the food industry. Whether eventually, the bulk of red meats will be sold in fresh or frozen form is a decision which no longer remains that of the packer, but of the large retailer. If the multiple store operator can be convinced that in the end, the economics of frozen meat products will yield him a better profit and quicker turnover than unfrozen meats, accompanied by its expensive fresh meat cutting department remains to be seen. Theoretically at least, a variety of frozen meat cuts, emanating from central plants, with their accompanying saving in uniformity, packaging, weight, bone elimination, etc. must eventually triumph over the present archaic methods of meat merchandising. But the big retailer will have to be convinced.

Seasoning FF

I may be sticking my neck out (nothing new to QFF) when I say I believe many sales in some prepared foods are being lost due to *under-seasoning* rather than overseasoning. The general custom among American food packers has been to produce a bland product, allowing the consumer to season at will. But in frozen foods the situation is a little different. Here, the consumer expects to buy a "ready made" product, stream-lined for convenience and with the minimum amount of preparation necessary. Today consumers are more educated to flavoring in their foods than twenty years ago, more sophisticated if you wish. At any rate, too bland a taste in some prepared food doesn't make an impression, and the average Mrs. Housewife isn't "seasoning minded" enough to take the trouble to give the product the necessary taste. The proper seasoning (not overdone of course) gives a product "character" and if 70% of the buyers like it and 30% don't it is still a success. But if it lacks this "character" 60% of the buyers may not bother to try it again. It may pay to *sacrifice the minority in favor of the majority.*

Out of Stock

One of the most serious problems facing the industry today is the "out of stock" condition which prevails in many retail stores. Often a market will run out of merchandise on a Thursday with no delivery in sight until the following week. Profitable week-end business is consequently lost. This may be an opportunity for the distributor who has the advantage of personalized service. It is certainly an argument for *backroom storage* which is a necessity today for any supermarket doing a sizeable volume.

Corn

I have written before about corn-on-the-cob and why I think it is the most under-rated and under-privileged item in the vegetable line. Sales are nowhere near what they could or should be. Cob corn has all the inherent advantages of a naturally big seller because 1) the fresh season is very short, 2) most people like it. Why then has cob corn not equaled many other vegetables? In the first place many packers consider it a hard item to process. But most important, cooking directions have been generally wrong for which reason corn has not cooked out as well as it should. In my house we eat frozen corn-on-the-cob all year round and it is always fresh and crisp. Here is how we treat it. The frozen ears are never boiled; boiling cooks out the juices leaving the grains flabby and waxy. We put the ears in sauce-pan which is placed under a hot-water tap (which must be very hot). The water is allowed to run over the corn for about 5 minutes, after which the corn is left sitting in the sauce-pan of hot water for about five minutes more until ready to serve; the whole procedure should begin about ten minutes before serving. I will guarantee you the finest ear of corn you ever ate. I hope that some packers will make this experiment and urge restaurants and institutions to follow this procedure. It is simple and effective. Once restaurants begin to feature corn on their menus at a reasonable price, sales will boom and diners will have a very welcome and interesting change from the usual vegetable routine.

Testing New Products

There is a great deal of "hit-or-miss" in the testing or marketing of a new product. Very often a so called "typical market is selected, generally a small city upon whose consumers hinge the failure or success of a new product. In the first place, it is doubtful whether one market is *enough* to test a product, and it would seem that the fairest way is to include a suburban area, a big city and several small ones at the same time. If only one market is used, certain *local conditions* may prevail which might mitigate against the success of the item, whereas if several markets were tried a better average might be arrived at. We find, too, that many packers limit testing the merits of a new frozen product, or its method of packaging or re-heating, to their own organizations or their own brokers. In the first place, no man's word should be accepted as the final criterion about the desirability of a new product—it is *the woman* who must decide. Processors would do better to test a new product on their wives, or their wives' friends, because these are the consumers who will eventually make the final judgment. Far better to take the advice of the first ten women who pass the processor's office, than the word of the most knowledgeable frozen foodster in the business.

Gullibility

It is sometimes amazing how far the word "consultant" will go with otherwise hard-headed and realistic business men. A consultant is generally someone who has had more or less experience in an industry, and who sets himself up in an advisory capacity with no more investment than an office and a telephone listing. He then gives out glibly and with an expert fluency that is impressive, on the most intricate business problems, the solutions for which are generally very expensive. Some business men will heed such consultants with breathless awe, though the consultant in question may have one-tenth of the experience of those he would advise. A recent survey of consultants in general brought out many facts. One case was cited where a firm of consultants, upon first ascertaining how much a company had in the till, tailored their work to finally milk the company dry and put in into bankruptcy. We don't mean to imply that there are not many good, reliable consulting firms with fine records. But there are also many fly-by-nights; the answer, of course, is to check the background of a consultant carefully before hiring him.

How Frozen Is Frozen?

Quick frozen or just plain frozen foods, it's all the same today. Very recently the editors of QFF received a call from a distraught woman who said she was having an extremely difficult time finding food items in the refrigerated cabinets marked "quick frozen." All she could find was just plain frozen, and she had been told that only "quick frozen" foods are good. This was not the first such calls this magazine has received. Promoting our industry's products to non-frozen food eaters is tough enough without losing potentially big repeat buyers solely through misconceptions. We are reminded of the woman who said she threw $18 worth of frozen foods out because her refrigerator-freezer went off for a few hours and some of the products were beginning to thaw, and she thought they might be harmful. You can bet that this woman won't buy ahead and get stuck again. It's extremely important that good consumer and handling information be disseminated for the benefit of the consumer as well as the industry. There are untold millions lost each year because housewives do not know enough about frozen foods.

Who Makes the Sale?

Who really sells Mrs. Housewife when she takes a package out of the frozen food cabinet? Is it consumer advertising, is it the retailer, is it the price—or a combination of all three? Consumer advertising does a great deal to help, of course, but I think that much could be negated by the retailer himself. In reality, it is the *atmosphere* which the retailer creates for a given product or group of products in the retail cabinet that has a tremendous influence on what the buyer picks up. It is the *attitude* of the retailer which indirectly influences the sale . . . the way he displays a given brand, price-marks it, the position he gives it in the cabinet, how near it is to a lower priced competitor, the amount of facings it has. What is most important is *how a retailer feels about a product,* the company behind it and how far he is willing to go with it. Therefore, the creation of a proper *image* in the retailer's mind is of prime importance, and here is where a good trade publication comes in. Survey after survey shows indisputably that the constant switching of brands hurts the retailer, for customers resent not finding their favorite brand in the cabinet and they go elsewhere. Consumer advertising is great—but it can never be *fully effective* unless backed up by the right retailer education.

Peaches

Anyone in the food business knows the tremendous quantity of canned cling peaches sold each year and I have long believed that a portion of this business should go to frozen *freestone peaches*. The freestone peach, when properly frozen, is a better product, a brighter yellower fruit and tastier, when correctly defrosted. Anyone who has ever eaten a freestone peach, cool and fresh, will prefer it to the canned clings. What then has held back frozen retail peaches, and apricots as well? Obviously two factors: packaging and the uncertainty of defrosting at maximum desirability. Now however, comes something new—the poly bag, which not only gives sliced peaches visibility, but may overcome the handling problem as well. The poly bag can be held under a cold water tap to defrost and thus, by both sight and touch, the user can tell when the peaches are properly defrosted and edible—not too soft nor too hard, but just right. The use of poly bags for peach or apricot slices may well be the answer to a twenty-year old industry problem—and may yet lift these fruits from the underprivileged to the volume class.

What Is Timing?

After observing this industry for well over twenty-five years, timing I think is of utmost importance. Over and over I have seen the failure of good products just because the *timing* was wrong, though later, others who brought out the same products at the crest of the wave rode on to success. Just what is "timing"? It is an elusive element which few are smart, or intuitive enough to fathom. To time the introduction of a new item just right is often a matter of luck. When is the public ready? Dinners are an example; this product was available years before it clicked. Of course, the vigor of promotion and advertising often put over a product which had hitherto been a "sleeper." One example is frozen soups, now selling under a popular brand name, though soups have been on the market for 15 years. Today there are more and better yardsticks for measuring public acceptance than there were years ago, but timing is still the prime factor.

Home Microwave

I have often wondered why the big producers of frozen dinners, entrees, pot pies, baked goods and other convenience items have not gotten more strongly behind the manufacturers of quick heating devices to urge the production of an appliance for the home which cuts re-heating time. This is sorely needed, especially when one considers that so many of these "convenience" products are not so convenient or fast when it comes to re-heating. Considering the time it takes to heat up an oven first, few dinners turnovers, etc. are ready to heat in less than 35-40 minutes. Still a pretty long time. A micro-wave oven will do the job in anywhere from 2-4 minutes, depending on the kilowatt power. Is there a mass-market for home kitchen micro-wave ovens? I think so, at around $150 to $200. I have been assured that in volume, they can be produced at this figure. But what a boom such an appliance would be to frozen dinners and similar items! Now consumers would have a real reason for buying the quick heaters— and more—much more of the frozen products besides. I would say that what the modern store cabinet has meant to the expansion of frozen foods—so the development of *quick heating devices* will mean to the expansion of frozen prepared foods.

Chains' Specs Too High?

Are private label retailer chain specifications too high? They well may be, or at least, unnecessarily high, since most consumers still regard chain labels as being below the standard of the advertised brands. And if this is so, since chain brands are cheaper, why demand such high specs? For one thing, chain brands only have a following in their own areas. This was proven recently when a large Philadelphia chain opened stores in suburban New York areas. The chain's own frozen food brand was unsuccessful because New York consumers didn't recognize the label. In California, a state which has a high influx of families from other states, chain labels are least effective, while the nationally advertised brands are known from back home. If chains were to lower their specifications in line with their current prices, they would increase profits and a fairer line of demarcation between the retail label and the packer brand could be established.

Potato Specs

The "uniformity" fetish on the part of frozen french fried potato buyers is beginning to act as a boomerang. Also, it goes against common eating sense. The idea that potato cuts must be of uniform or near uniform size is not really what consumers, (either retail or institutional) want. If an invisible spectator could stand behind the chair of everyone who eats french fries, he might be surprised to note that the diner will generally pick out the small pieces first. Why? Because they are crisp, nice and brown and generally more palatable. I don't mean that the specifications should allow slivers, but certainly, they should be *broadened* to permit a much larger percentage of small pieces mixed in. After all, it isn't looks that count, but taste and of course, repeat business.

Known Names

I have often wondered why large companies, with well known consumer brand names, don't put these names on the products of companies they buy. Ever so often a national company will take over a smaller firm, but instead of giving it a shove in the right direction by bestowing its well known brand on the label, it keeps the old brand. If the company thought enough of its new division to buy it in the first place, why not give it *its name* and thus cash in on the accepted consumer franchise? Often, after several years, companies do finally extend their trade mark, as in the case of Stokely, which ran the Honor Brand label for many years until it was finally decided to discard Honor Brand and put the more famous Stokely brand on the package instead.

Exposure

No matter how large a company may be in this frozen foods business, the most successful have always been those whose executives mingle with the trade. Why this should be, I can't say excepting that perhaps the frozen food industry is a close knit trade where the buyer wants to see the seller's top man occasionally, especially at meetings and conventions. Or perhaps frozen food buyers don't like the idea of dealing with a cold, aloof organization which suffers from the lack of warmth which comes through personal contact. Food buyers like to be conscious of someone they know —or know of, in the company with whom they do business.

400 Million Dinners

Sounds like an incredible number of frozen dinners, but this is what the airline industry says it will be serving aloft in 1970. By then, distances, in time, will be shorter and planes larger and faster. There will be little space to heat up dinners for 200-250 people so it is now estimated that these will have to be frozen, cooked by micro-wave or by other means on the ground and kept warm on the planes, ready for instant servings. I believe also that in the next few years, with the average flight being about one hour or less, more and more of the meals will be served *cold*. This would include chicken, turkey, cold roast beef, cold cuts and other types of plates, garnished with potato salad, chips, etc. Plants producing these meals will be located in airport areas. I saw a plant in Denmark recently. It produced a cold plate of fried chicken, the parts were placed on a conveyor which ran thru a long micro-wave oven, taking about 4½ minutes to cook. The parts then, went into a fryer and breader and in another five minutes were placed on trays which were put in a refrigerator and kept until ready to be served as cold lunches.

Cob Corn—Bait?

In my recent trip to frozen food people in Europe, I came across an interesting sidelight. In some of the big supermarkets in Milan, Italy, it was noted that frozen corn on cob, not ordinarily an important seller, was bought in good quantities on Saturday mornings by men. On further checking it was found that these gentlemen were anglers, fishermen. It seems they bought the corn to take with them on their fishing expeditions over the weekend. Now the fishing waters in Italy are rather muddy, which makes it hard for the fish to see the worms and other bait, but fishermen have found that the kernels of the frozen corn make excellent bait. So the anglers sit on the bank, break off the kernels and bait them on the hook. The fish are attracted to these bright shiny corn kernels and the catches of Italian fishermen have been considerably increased.

Pioneering

Does it pay to be a pioneer? Many, in the frozen foods industry at least, don't seem to think so. Companies and individuals who pioneered new products, new ideas, new systems of freezing, packaging and processing haven't always remained on top, and were often superseded, sometimes years later, by much more successful operations which captured the market originally started by the innovator. Why should this be so? Isn't the inventor or originator entitled to the fruits of his efforts? Perhaps, but it's all a matter of *timing*. It isn't sufficient to bring out something new—the world has to be *ready* for it too. Often the originator of an idea may spend years developing it and finally gives up, only to see his idea profitably perfected later by someone else. Also, those who come later have the advantage of *benefiting* by the pioneer's mistakes which makes their job a lot easier. No, pioneering is not all it's cracked up to be, excepting, of course, if you *never* give up pioneering—like QFF.

Snacks

If I were a ff packer interested in developing new institutional outlets, I would study the snack field because I think the next ten years are going to open up some considerable possibilities for frozen snacks. Consider the airline of the future, only five years hence. We will have the big super-jets carrying from 240 to 400 people with an average flight duration of about an hour. This is too short a time for a hot meal, but a snack will do. With large food holding and reconstituting facilities on these new planes (up to five galleys) there will be adequate space to handle frozen dishes. Except for coffee, service will have to be cold on a short journey, and frozen snacks would include open sandwiches, cold chicken, turkey, roast beef, etc. horsd'oeuvres of all kinds; for desserts, puddings, fruit salads and mixed fruits, all baked goods, rolls, pies, tarts, puff pastry, etc. Yes, if I were a processor, I'd get a recipe book about snacks.

Freezing Best

As QFF has pointed out for the past three decades, the quick freezing system of food preservation is the best method of keeping foods nearest the fresh condition that has ever been devised. This contention is once again brought into focus by a recent report by the Food & Drug Administration, to the effect that irradiated foods now look to be quite hazardous, and some meats exposed to radiation may be unsafe for human consumption. It was shown that irradiated bacon and pork, fed to rats and dogs resulted in the victims developing cancer and cataracts. Furthermore, reproduction of the rats and dogs was severely affected, the officials said, with a marked increase in still births and a drop in fecundity. The Food & Drug agency has actually reversed its stand on irradiated foods, which system it approved several years ago. An official, Dr. Barnes, says: "Science changes. We now feel that high-dose irradiation of bacon does not produce a product that can be deemed safe." If true for bacon and pork, very probably the same holds true for many other foods which have been irradiated. Quick freezing, which does not cook, dry them or bombard the foods with rays, is the *only* method which does not chemically change the nature of a food product. This is why QFF believes in the long range durability of this industry.

Comeback of Independents

The independent supermarket category of the retail food business, estimated to be doing about 40-50% of total food volume, is having an impressive comeback. Of course, it is difficult to define an "independent supermarket" today, but for purposes of simplicity, we would include stores doing an annual volume of at least half a million dollars and up, and small chains. Many "independents" are in some was affiliated with voluntary or cooperative groups; nevertheless, they do retain a *certain independence* in management, buying and merchandising. In many parts of the country, independents are putting up strong sales resistance against the large corporate chains and in a surprising number of marketing areas are outselling the chains. This is especially true of frozen foods, notably by those smaller chains and independents who are going along with the advertised brands, cooperating with promotions and giving unstinted exposure to name brands. Even in stores where the prices may be a little higher, the superior service generally makes up for the difference. (QFF's Retail Edition is concentrating on this area of growing importance.)

TV Shrimp?

In Scandinavian countries there is a popular eating custom. An iced bowl, which is filled with cold, shell-on shrimp is placed before the diner. The shell is peeled off, the shrimp is eaten (with fork or finger) accompanied by a glass of beer, aquavit of wine, whatever the preference may be. This is generally an hors d'oeuvre, but, when a sufficient quantity of shrimp is served, it can constitute a meal. Sometimes, and I assume with greater frequency, this dish is consumed in front of TV. In the U.S., where shrimp is becoming more popular each year, especially in the area of the peeled and deveined, could not shell-on-shrimp be made into a popular TV delicacy? Just about everything else is eaten as a TV snack; dinners, popcorn, hamburgers, franks, fish sticks and meat pies. Or just as a conversation piece. Many would say that the best way to capture the flavor of shrimp is to eat it right out of the shell, and if it goes over in Scandinavia, why not here?

A Real Squeeze?

The PATS, "Price Time of Shipment", under which policy most private label packers have operated for several years, is bringing increasing hardships because of tight money. In the past there was some margin for carrying merchandise when money was cheaper to borrow, but today the situation has altered radically. Under the present system the packer not only does the financing, but *guarantees* the buyer that he will not pay more than the market. Even if every packer produced only the quantities represented by reservation commitments from buyers, the collective production would possibly exceed the demand. Fortunately, the past season has been good, with higher levels prevailing and most frozen vegetables in good balance. But what will future seasons bring?

Brokers Merge

The urge to merge has not left the brokerage field untouched—in fact the present activity in that field is at its height. In almost every large area we are seeing mergers and take-overs between food brokers, and we will see a lot more. Some really old time frozen food brokers are being amalgamated into large grocery broker companies which is perhaps, the best way of getting into the frozen food business. Straight institutional food brokers are at a premium; the need to get into that end of the business is pressing. As the institutional field grows, many brokers who have done well with retail accounts are going to be offered the institutional line as well. If they don't have the organization to cope with it, their retail connections may be jeopardized. It isn't easy to get good institutional salesmen. Possibly the only source is the local institution itself—but who wants to steal men from customers?

Imitation Milk

Recently, QFF ran an editorial forecasting that if the fresh milk industry did not convert to concentrated frozen, they would receive increasing competition from vegetable creams and lose a share of their market. At that time it appeared that the dairy industry had at least several years' grace before being confronted by any hard decisions. Apparently they are not going to have that much lead time. Already, across the country, imitation milk made from vegetable creams is appearing in refrigerated form. Several big companies are involved and it is receiving good promotion. However, the present approach is wrong for that product to make maximum inroads. In order to do that it must be concentrated and frozen. That will make possible national brand distribution, eliminate three quarters of its weight and a similar percentage of bulk, make it possible to distribute through conventional channels, take up only a quarter of the refrigerated space, eliminate all leakers and spoilage and permit the consumer to keep an unlimited supply on hand at all times.

The economics of this combination will make it a formidable seller. The only thing that could forestall it would be if regular milk went that route first.

On Mergers

As QFF accurately predicted five years ago, we have run into the era of big mergers, now coming hot and heavy. But how many of these mergers will turn out to be an *improvement* is another question. Past history in this industry will show that not all mergers have blossomed into unqualified successes. In some cases, where large national firms have taken over smaller frozen foods companies and integrated them into their own operations, the loss or impairment of original management frequently results in loss of leadership in the field. It does not always follow that because a large national company has been successful in its own field, the same conditions, policies and marketing procedures which brought forth this success will hold good in the frozen foods industry. Sometimes the very company being taken over reached its dominating position because of its own policies and personnel. Successful management is a delicate thing. If tampered with the result can often be lost sales and rapidly declining prestige. Industry records show that the most successful mergers have been those where the acquired company has been allowed to continue to operate under its own management, but under the financial security of the bigger company.

Is Cooking Right?

Do the cooking directions which have appeared on frozen vegetable packages for the past generation yield the best results to the consumer? Generally such directions read: "Drop vegetables into half a cup of salted boiling water, cover, bring to boil again . . ." There are many flaws to this method. First, the vegetable must be watched constantly so that it does not over-cook. Most of the nutrients, and some of the flavor is boiled away in the water, which is usually thrown out. It is also a bit messy. The *boil-in-bag* is a distinct improvement, since the vegetables are not so easy to over-cook and the flavors remain in the bag. Steaming is also a better method. I do know one thing, and that is that the greater use of corn-on-the-cob is being retarded by just such directions. If followed, the corn is usually without flavor and, having been already once blanched, is now over-done. The industry would do well to research its vegetable cooking directions in the interests of increased consumption.

Multi Everything?

I believe in multi-selling and that goes for most of the cheap and moderate priced items in the frozen food line. Selling more than one frozen package at a time is no merchandising gimmick—it is an *economic necessity*. First, more and more customers want to buy this way;

zero space is constantly increasing in the home. Most people buy at least two cans of orange juice anyway—why not a standard four or six pack? The bogey of price stands in the way—at least in the mind of the retailer but this again is a misconception. The best way to get rid of the "how much" psychology is to take a leaf from the book of the soft drink or beer people. Years ago soft drinks were bought singly or in doubles. No more. They are brought by the carton and hardly anyone *ever asks the price*. And this is the way other frozen products should be sold, especially vegetables, waffles, pot pies and maybe dinners. The day of loose, single item selling is drawing to an end. How much neater the cabinet would look if it contained more multipacks!

Teenagers

The biggest population growth of the future will be in the 10-19 year old groups, the teenagers. This group will constitute 58% of the population; young people eat more and they also take more readily to frozen foods than did their parents. Any frozen food company seeking a consumer franchise, which is looking ahead to the next ten years ought to remember that teenagers are conditioned by what they *see and hear today*. Girls and boys in this age bracket are good magazine readers of media which appeals to them; they are also ardent TV fans. Advertising makes a lasting impression. Older people today remember the slogans that impressed them in their youth—"Time to Retire." "Ask the man who owns one.", etc. Today's impressions on today's youth will spell sales tomorrow.

Dinners

For fifteen years I have stressed the continued growth of frozen dinners on this page and I still believe that the present status of the dinner market (over $300 million a year) is still in its first stage. The frozen meal will really have arrived when it becomes the type of dinner you would be willing to serve to a guest. At the moment it doesn't quite fill this niche, but it will. There is a big margin for improvement—not at the present price of course, but at a price ranging from 75¢ to $1.25, still considerably below the cost of a restaurant meal. However the meal is prepared, the day will come when such dinners, re-heated in the home, can be served on the housewife's *own china to company*. The same economic principles hold true—no preparation and quick cooking, the only addition being dish washing, but this the housewife has to do anyway when she serves company dinners. I think the upgrading of the frozen dinner points to one of the most exciting possibilities in the whole frozen foods industry today.

How To Succeed

. . . "in the frozen foods business without really trying?" Go to the

Area Redevelopment Corp. and get a federal loan. Then build a plant in a depressed area, raise the prices of local agriculture, market a processed commodity which sells and *you have it made!* This has proven true in the potato industry and might work out elsewhere. The Act is far better than the old "plow-under" policy of the U.S.D.A. which was to pay farmers not to produce. The A.R.A. on the other hand, loans money to processors to build plants, it encourages farmers to produce and usually gets them a higher return. Depressed areas can become prosperous in a short time. But the big question—where to find a depressed area with a product which can be frozen and sold?

Coming?

Westinghouse is working on a revolutionary idea, though its perfection lies a long way in the future. The principle is called thermo-electricity. It works by using the atomic structure of materials, which without the use of transistors will be able to transform spaces into cold units. For instance, ovens can be utilized for both heating and freezing. Pantry shelves could be changed into freezer storage. A little closer to realization however, is the development of a container 20 feet long by 8 ft. for the transport of frozen products preserved by liquid nitrogen, 400 gallons of LN_2 would be required to refrigerate this space, but the food would hold for weeks at a cost of only a few cents per pound. The containers could be put on trucks for direct delivery and on ships they could be stored in any hold without the need of reefers. In these days, when fact is overtaking science fiction, anything is possible.

Index

1